P9-DUU-778

WITHDRAWN

Political Theory and Social Policy

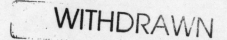

Political Theory and Social Policy

Albert Weale

Social Policy Research Unit
University of York

St. Martin's Press   New York

All rights reserved. For information, write:
St. Martin's Press, Inc., 175 Fifth Avenue, New York, NY 10010
Printed in Hong Kong
First published in the United States of America in 1983

ISBN 0–312–62553–7

Library of Congress Cataloging in Publication Data

Weale, Albert.
  Political theory and social policy.

  Bibliography: p.
  Includes index.
  1. Political science. 2. Social choice. 3. Social
policy. I. Title.
JA74.W36 1983.   361.6'14   83–42846
ISBN 0–312–62553–7

Contents

Preface

As individuals we stand in many and diverse relationships to one another. We bargain and we contract; we give or we receive orders; we are variously manager, supervisor, unionist, colleague, controller, worker, hireling, labourer, neighbour and citizen; in these roles we request, deny, cajole, entice, implore, excuse, explain or thank one another. To some other persons we stand in a special relationship like that of daughter, son, brother, sister, mother, father, friend or lover. Throughout these diverse relationships it is possible to ask one question: in what form of political community can we as individuals approach one another as free and autonomous persons?

I take this to be the central question with which the western tradition of political theory confronts us. Nor is the question merely theoretical. The political movements of liberalism and socialism have both been preoccupied with the problem of how human autonomy could develop in modern political and social conditions. For us (by which I mean those ordinary citizens of liberal democracies with only limited access to the corridors of power, who will, I suppose, constitute the bulk of those who read this book) these conditions are those of the welfare state. For us the question is: what does the welfare state contribute to the development of human autonomy?

This central problem of political evaluation has been answered in different ways. Some have seen the mechanisms of a redistributive tax-transfer scheme and the state supply of education and health services as steps down the road to serfdom. Others have seen the welfare state as providing a set of institutions through which individuals can realise the positive freedom that comes with identi-

fying individual interest and the public interest. Yet others have
seen the economic security provided by the welfare state as a necessary condition for the full enjoyment of the traditional civil and
political liberties. And again others have seen the principle of satisfying needs, on which the welfare state supposedly rests, as pre-
figuring a form of social organisation in which persons are freed
from the constraints of private property.

In what follows I have tried to offer an account of the relation
between the welfare state and individual autonomy, and to show
how the value of autonomy is connected with other values like
justice, welfare and democracy. I begin by offering an account of
normative political theory which I see as the enterprise of constructing a set of principles capable of justifying some forms of political
arrangements relative to others. I then propose an account of what
it means to say that a political arrangement is good for persons, and
in the subsequent chapter give my understanding of the place of
autonomy in the scheme of human goods. Chapter 4 explores the
institutional question of what arrangements might secure individual
autonomy; the claim I make is that a reform of income maintenance
and educational programmes, with which we are already familiar in
the welfare state, is sufficient to secure a minimally adequate level
of autonomy. However, there are welfare considerations above the
minimum, and Chapters 5 and 6 are taken up with the question of
the principles upon which that welfare should be distributed, and a
discussion of the fact that much current welfare state activity takes
the form of in-kind programmes. The next chapter provides an
account of rights that is intended to show how the concept of a right,
so extensively used in popular discussions of politics and social
policy, can be understood in a fashion consistent with the earlier
theory I developed. Chapters 8 and 9 discuss specific problems in
the functioning of resource-allocating mechanisms in the welfare
state. The final chapter proposes a set of principles by which democratic responsibility for decision-making in the welfare state can be
allocated.

Even if the argument were persuasive at each step it would not by
itself settle the question of how we should evaluate any particular
welfare state. A normative political theory provides a framework in
which we can organise our thoughts; it does not provide a battery of
instant diagnostic checks by application of which we can pass judgement on the health of the body politic and declare it fit or unfit.

What, then, is the point of constructing such a theory? Why should we try to arrange our thoughts into general and coherent principles? One reason, of course, is simply to satisfy our intellectual curiosity and to exercise our minds on problems that have vexed those with vastly more capabilities than we have. Passion for the intellectual problems that politics raises is no more to be deprecated than any other sort of passion. There is, however, a more practical answer. We have to share a political community with those with whom we have our varied social relationships. Our relationship with most of our co-citizens is mediated through the state, with its power to allocate income, wealth, status, opportunities, burdens, benefits, rights, obligations, and even life and death. Unless we can explain to others how and why we think the state's powers can be used in some ways and not in others, we do not have a reciprocal political relationship with our co-citizens. We confront them merely with the brute force of power or the haphazard contingency of circumstance. To fit our particular opinions into a broader theory is to hold a political position, such that we can explain the grounds of our actions and judgement to those of our co-citizens who choose to question us. Perhaps one can lead a happy life if one is never confronted by the test of having to justify one's political stance and one's position in the world; but it is doubtful whether it could ever be a valuable life; or, at least, so the political theorist whom I'm imagining supposes.

University of York ALBERT WEALE
December 1982

Acknowledgements

I have incurred many personal debts in writing this book which I should like to acknowledge. Its ground plan was laid during my period as visiting research fellow at the Institution for Social and Policy Studies, Yale University, in 1979. I should like to thank Charles E. Lindblom, who, as director, extended me the courtesy of this most remarkable academic establishment. I imagine that there are few places so stimulating to the political theorist. While at Yale I was privileged to participate in both the American Democratic Institutions seminar and the Legal Theory Workshop, the latter held at the Law School, and I learned much from those who took part in the discussions I shared in. I owe special thanks to Bruce Ackerman, James Fishkin, Theodore Marmor, Douglas Rae, Adina Schwartz and William White, each of whom has commented upon some particular aspect of the ideas this book contains, and from all of whom I have learned much about the relation of ideas to policy.

I continued to work on the book throughout 1980, enjoying in that year a visit to the University of Dar es Salaam, in Tanzania. Although my principal responsibilities involved teaching, I learned much about social policy in reflecting on the conditions of under-development, and I should like to thank both Patrick Masanja and Severine Rugumamu, who acted as my guides to Tanzanian social and political life. I also thank the University of Dar es Salaam for providing hospitality which enabled me to think and write against the background of the ever-changing colours of the Indian Ocean. This is also the appropriate place to thank my colleagues at York, especially Peter Rutland in Politics and David Austen-Smith in Economics, for bearing my share of the load while I was away on those occasions.

A central part of this book's argument draws upon earlier papers that I wrote with both Robert Sugden and Peter Lambert. I should like to thank them both for what I have learned from these collaborative efforts. Sally Baldwin, Tony Culyer, David Held and Raymond Plant have read and commented upon the manuscript, and I am grateful to them for their time and trouble. Ken Judge not only suggested that I write this book in the first place, but has commented in detail upon all its aspects and has unfailingly pointed to passages and arguments where I persist in error. Jonathan Bradshaw and Andrew Dunsire have given me much advice and support, and Hope Leresche extended me generous hospitality at various crucial stages. For secretarial services I thank Dorothy Daniel, Barbara Dodds, Julia Eastwood, Carole Hudson and Sue Walters. I should also like to thank Alan King for compiling the index.

The dedication on the next page records how grateful I feel towards the person whose support, encouragement and advice made the writing of this book possible.

University of York   ALBERT WEALE
December 1982

To Jane

1
Social Policy and the Scope of Political Theory

There are two striking features of the politics of liberal democracies. The first is that, with the qualified exceptions of Japan and the USA, they are all developed welfare states, within each of which there is a widespread consensus about there being a social responsibility for such contingencies as unemployment, old age, sickness, education, housing and social welfare. The second feature is that, despite this consensus, there exists within these countries significant controversy about the exact scope of social responsibility, the form it should take and its consequences for social, economic and political life more generally. This mixture of controversy and consensus presents a problem. How can we reconcile this agreement on basics with so much disagreement about specifics?

The purpose of the present work is to see what light the tools and techniques of the normative political theorist can throw upon this problem. The interpretation offered is that the mixture of consensus and controversy is just what we should expect from a rational reconstruction of the ethical foundations of the welfare state. There are good reasons why the welfare state should assume social responsibility for various contingencies and for the promotion of individual well-being, and the existence of these reasons accounts for the consensus we observe. Yet, within the limits of this consensus, there is wide scope for disagreement about the exact interpretation and implementation of the state's responsibility for social welfare. The political pluralism of liberal democracies is paralleled by an intellectual and theoretical pluralism about the scope of social policy in the welfare state. In exploring this problem we shall find ourselves treating a wide range of topics: the idea of welfare and needs; the theory of justice and of social choice; the nature of rights; the concept of efficiency; collectivism and individualism; and the problems of democracy, representation and community. The present chapter, however, will be concerned with some preliminary problems, in particular the meaning of the term 'social policy' and the nature of political theory.

Social policy and economic policy

Liberal democratic welfare states exercise their responsibility for the welfare of society in two main ways, which are conventionally distinguished as social policy and economic policy. Economic policy is concerned with specifying the conditions under which production and exchange take place and with the use of resources in creating the wealth of nations. Wealth here does not simply include tangible commodities like cars and washing machines, but also such intangibles as clean air, an attractive environment and the quality of work conditions. Economic policy defined broadly, then, is concerned with any object of human desire on which people may put a price in terms of productive effort expended or consumption of other items forgone. Since the Second World War most governments in liberal democracies have assumed that they should use macroeconomic instruments to control aggregate levels of production, saving and consumption. Such instruments have typically included taxes and public spending with their implied budgetary deficits (or more rarely surpluses) and manipulation of the central bank interest rate. The extent to which governments have used policy instruments other than macroeconomic ones has varied from country to country[1]. Some regimes, like France and periodically Britain, have tried forms of economic planning in which microeconomic as well as macroeconomic targets were important elements of policy. As well as securing certain aggregate rates of production or investment, such countries have tried to secure certain production and investment targets in particular industries. In Germany and the USA, by contrast, economic planning has not been a policy instrument, although in common with other countries there has been extensive regulation of markets for the purposes of anti-trust policy. Whatever type of policy instruments were used the policy objectives were broadly the same in all countries: growth of real economic resources; full employment; a stable level of prices; and balance of payments equilibrium. There is, of course, no reason to think that these four objectives exhaust the aims of economic policy; but, since the attainment of one tends to make the attainment of at least one other more difficult, the intellectual effort of policy-makers has virtually been exhausted in trying to achieve an acceptable economic performance in relation to just these four criteria.

Although the problem of distribution has received attention in economic policies, most notably in the incomes policies pursued by various governments, there is a tendency for both economists and social administrators to regard the tax-transfer system as the proper instrument for achieving distributional objectives and, therefore, assigning a concern with distribution to social policy. The identification of social policy with that area of public policy concerned with the problem of distribution contains both an important truth and a significant distortion. The element of truth is that social policy is one method by which the distribution of incomes is changed from that yielded by the processes of production and exchange. Measuring the extent of such redistribution is difficult both conceptually and methodologically. Strictly speaking we should ask what the distribution of income would have been in the absence of social policy provision, and compare it with what the distribution is with such provision. But this implies an estimate of what incomes employees would receive if some of them were not doing their present jobs, and what consumption patterns would be with such a change. Such estimates present an impossible problem. Given this difficulty the technique has been to compare the pre-tax/pre-benefit distribution of income with the post-tax/post-benefit distribution of income. Such studies seem to show a small redistribution of income from rich to poor and from small households to large as a result of social policy. The redistribution would be larger were it not for the regressive impact of taxes on alcohol and tobacco.[2]

But to see the distortion involved in the identification of social policy with policies for the distribution of income, consider the definition of social policy. A conventional way to define social policy is in terms of a specific range of services either provided directly by the government or for which the government accepts certain responsibilities. These services are: income maintenance programmes, especially those that are aimed at the relief of poverty as a result of the contingencies of old age, unemployment, the arrival of children, and so on; education, particularly at elementary and secondary school level; health care, including the provision of services like hospitals as well as public health measures; housing, either in relation to subsidised dwellings or in relation to quantity supplied; and social work support given to individuals or to specific households. Governments need not supply these goods and services themselves in order to have a social policy. Typically, indeed, significant provision in these matters is left to the private or organisational initiative of citizens. For example, there are occupational pension and insurance schemes, and denominational or church schools in all welfare states. Nevertheless, even where private action substitutes or reduces the need for public action, it is a characteristic feature of welfare states that governments accept responsibility for such matters, and this is highlighted in the fact that where private initiative fails public services are often made available, for example in provision for the uninsured sick.

The difficulty, however, with defining social policy in terms of public provision or responsibility for a specific range of services is that it is prone to prevent us thinking intelligently about how best to achieve certain objectives. Specific public services are only a means to an end, and we are better thinking about social policy in terms of ends rather than means. Consider, for example, the problem of poverty. Clearly there are many schemes of income maintenance which have a role to play in the elimination of poverty. It is equally clear, however, that full employment contributes significantly to the reduction of poverty, as has been pointed out with respect to the USA during the 1960s, when economic expansion did more for the elimination of poverty than did the War on Poverty[3]. Another example is provided in the field of health care, where we are becoming increasingly aware that industrial safety, environmental regulation and a change in personal habits, for example in respect of smoking, drinking and lack of exercise, have probably more to contribute to reductions in mortality and morbidity than do improvements in conventional health-care facilities.[4] What these examples suggest is that we should define social policy not in terms of a specific range of public policies or institutions, but rather in terms of a specific set of dimensions of individual welfare, to which a varying range of policy instruments and institutions are relevant.

Thinking about social policy in this way it is possible to list the dimensions of individual well-being that are potentially relevant to social policy. In the first place there is the concern with the distribution of the command of resources, particularly in connection with the contingencies of life, the ills to which flesh is heir in the form of sickness, invalidity, involuntary unemployment and falling earning capacity in old age. Second, there are some specific dimensions of consumption to which social importance is attached, most notably health status, educational attainments and housing consumption. In addition to these elements of consumption there is also the element of individual well-being related to the individual's capacity to take part in the life of the community, sometimes in the role of rendering community care and sometimes in the role of citizen called upon to make decisions about the future life of the community. Social policy, then, is a deliberate attempt by governments to promote individual and social welfare in certain specific dimensions using any suitable policy instruments.

It should be clear from this definition that there is no clear separation between economic and social policy. Indeed in some areas of public policy it becomes impossible to distinguish what is strictly economic from what is strictly social. The distribution of income is a problem that can be investigated by those whose interest is primarily economic policy and those whose interest is primarily social policy. It is equally misleading to distinguish between the two in terms of institutional features. Sometimes, for example, the distinction is suggested between economic policy as concerned with markets, and social policy as concerned with publicly provided services. Yet, problems of economic policy can arise in traditional non-market economies, or command economies where there is an attenuated use of the price mechanism, or in public services, like defence and environmental protection, where a market for the service does not exist. Conversely, as we have noted, a one-sided emphasis upon certain public services as being the essence of social policy can prevent intelligent thinking about alternative courses of action. Nor will the distinction between egoistic economic man and altruistic social man do the trick. A sensible public policy will be aware of the limits of egoism and altruism in all their aspects, economic as well as social.[5] The distinction between economic and social policy is merely a convention. Like all conventions it should be flouted from time to time, as it will be in this book.

Social policy is important, then, because it involves decisions on what one writer has termed 'the authoritative allocation of values'[6]: that is to say, the distribution of available economic resources; the rights and duties of citizenship; and the power to control the conduct of others. In other words, who gets what, when, where and how. Granted that it is important, how important is it? One way of measuring its importance is in terms of the proportion of Gross Domestic Product (GDP) that the tax-transfer system for social insurance and other benefits, like health care and education, absorbs.

Many OECD countries spend approximately a fifth to a quarter of their GDP on programmes that fall under these headings.[7] This means that in most cases about half the government budget at a minimum goes on social policy items. Of course, if we were to take into account items that do not enter into the government accounts, but that should nevertheless be counted as social policy matters, for example tax relief on children or the economic costs of market regulation, the proportion would be higher.

In addition to taking a high proportion of GDP, however, two particular facts about social policy expenditure deserve notice. The first is that the proportion of GDP going on social policy measures is higher in those countries that have a high GDP. The second is that this proportion rises within an individual country as its GDP rises. These trends are not universal – Japan and the USA stand out as exceptions – but they are sufficiently general to have prompted the view that there is some functional prerequisite in advanced capitalist societies for the development of such policies. Moreover, these trends are not unique to capitalist societies. Industrially developed socialist societies as well display similar trends. Hence it is sometimes argued that the development of social policy is occasioned by the functional demands of industrialised societies irrespective of their political type.[8]

The implications of this functional claim are considerable. If it is true, then an examination of the political choices involved in social policy becomes, if not redundant, simply a method by which we rationalise to ourselves a fate that is, in all crucial respects, inevitable. Fortunately we need not adopt this pessimistic conclusion. There are, in the first place, general problems of method in using the idea of a function as an explanation for what happens in a social or political system. To employ the term 'function' suggests a necessary condition for a set of effects. For example, to say that the development of the welfare state serves the function of maintaining the stability of capitalism is to say that a necessary condition for that stability is the existence of welfare state activities. To use the idea of functional preconditions in an explanation reverses the obvious logic of the situation by suggesting that the effects we observe, for example the stability of a political system, somehow give rise to their own necessary conditions. For this reason it seems best to restrict the idea of a function to its being a heuristic device, which helps us become clear in our minds about what needs explaining.[9] None the less, even if there were not these problems of method with functional explanations, there would still be difficulties in employing such explanations to account for social policy expenditures. The main reason for this is that the similarity of expenditures among countries begins to break down once they are disaggregated. For example, if we look within income maintenance programmes we find considerable variation from country to country in programme-by-programme expenditure. The proportion going on child benefit programmes as distinct from sickness payments or old-age benefits varies in a way that cannot be accounted for in terms of economic development or social structure.[10] Moreover, in explaining the exceptions to the rule, which may not be significant in a statistical analysis but which are important as difficult cases, we cannot appeal to the general conditions of industrial societies. Japan and the USA combine two of the highest per capita GDP rates with the lowest rates of expenditure on social programmes. To explain these cases it looks as though we shall have to consider the distinctive political traditions and ideologies that determine their choice of policy.

Normative political theory

The absence of a successful functionalist analysis of social policy leaves room, therefore, for a consideration of political decisions and their role in social policy. Political theorists can approach these problems in one of two ways. Firstly they may be concerned with the empirical or positive question of why and how social policies have developed in the way they have. Such an approach overlaps in many respects with the concerns of historians and comparative sociologists. The hope in such investigations is to develop a set of general propositions about the conditions under which social policy emerges within modern political systems. Typically, for example, such propositions focus on the process of party competition, the experience of war, the salience to the mass electorate of issues like retirement pensions, the impact of an emerging working-class movement and the ideological legacies distinctive of different political systems.[11] This material is important in stressing the diverse ways in which different countries came to implement social welfare legislation and the often *ad hoc* or incremental nature of policy-making within individual countries.

The second approach contrasts with the first in being normative rather than empirical or positive. Instead of asking how social policy decisions have come to be made, it asks instead about how they ought to be made. In such studies the aim is to examine a set of political principles, detail their logical characteristics and explore their implications for social policy, at least in broad institutional terms. It is primarily this second type of enquiry with which we shall be concerned in the present work. The purpose of this sort of enquiry is to ascertain the justification of social policies and the values implicit within them. It aims, we may say, at a rational reconstruction of the ethical foundations of the welfare state. The normative study of social policy in this sense involves the discussion of basic questions about the value of the welfare state. The problems involved fall into three classes. There is, firstly, the problem of why the state should accept any responsibility at all for individual welfare above the minimum nightwatchman one of ensuring that individuals do not harm the interests of others when they pursue their own interests. Call this the problem of scope. Secondly, there is the question of the form of responsibility that the welfare state should undertake once it has accepted the burden of responsibility for the promotion of individual welfare. Call this the problem of form. Thirdly, there is the question of the principles governing the practices by which the state discharges its responsibility. Call this the problem of implementation. A successful normative political theory will provide solutions to each of these problems. It will, in short, provide an account of why the state should act to promote welfare, in what specific areas it should act and on what principles its actions should be based. For the purposes of this book anyone who attempts a coherent solution to these three problems will be called a political theorist, whether or not he or she works as a professional political scientist.

To be able to provide a justification for a particular way of assigning the scope, form and implementation of responsibility to the state is not to claim that a given set of principles has historically been operative in the formation of social policy. Political theorists provide potential justifications for certain forms of political life, establishing only that some political activities are ethically defensible, not that they have been defended. How far those principles have been acted on is a separate question. Nevertheless, the principle that 'ought implies can', or in other words that we cannot properly require agents to perform what they are unable to perform, suggests that normative theory should be related to an understanding of the processes that have made and now shape the welfare state. Normative theory should be a reflection on practice, not a means of ignoring it. Just as we cannot hope to improve upon our political life unless we reflect upon the principles that ought to inform our choices, so we shall not formulate adequate principles of political activity unless we examine them emerging from practical contexts.

The political theorist, then, is seeking for a set of principles that might justify the practices of social policy institutions. In order to gain a clearer conception of the task such a theorist faces, it may be useful to compare his or her role with that of the legal theorist. Clearly much of our legal system is inherited from the practice of previous generations. Its rules of evidence, the practice of trial by jury, the separation of judicial from political decisions, and so on, have developed over a long period of time, and may be accepted in an unreflective way. However, unless we accept the principle that nothing should ever be done for the first time, questions may also be raised as to whether such practices are justified or not. As soon as we raise such questions we begin to realise that the justification for such practices depends upon certain fundamental and general principles: no person should be judge in his or her own case; both sides of the case must be fairly heard; there should be no sentence without trial; there is no offence without law, and so on. The task of the legal theorist is to clarify these principles, test for their consistency and reasonableness and discuss their implications for legal practice. Political theorists may perform a similar task in the analysis of social policy, seeking to examine the political principles implicit in social policy measures, and seeking for the grounds on which social policy practices and institutions can be justified.

It may be objected that this job specification assigns an unnecessarily conservative task to the political theorist. His or her task seems to be always justifying existing practices and never criticising them. The assumption appears to be that we have a set of considered judgements about our existing practices which makes us feel that those practices must be right. The political theorist, then, performs the virtually redundant job of supplying reasons for what we believe already. Further reflection will show this objection to be mistaken, however. In order to demonstrate why, let us take again the parallel with the legal theorist. There are at least two ways in which legal theory may fail to justify existing legal practice or opinion. Firstly, a legal theory may fail to find a coherent set of principles that justify the practices of a legal institution. Perhaps the most striking example of this possibility is the difficulty that theorists have had in constructing a satisfactory theory of punishment. If any practice stands at the centre of a legal system it is the infliction of punishment upon offenders against the law, and yet the principles that have been advanced in support of the practice are seldom, if ever, convincing.[12] Secondly, a legal theory may fail to justify existing practices because the theorist is able to demonstrate (to her own conviction if to no one else's) that these practices fail to satisfy the conditions that are implied by the application of the relevant principles. Think of the way, for example, in which American legal theorists are concerned at the practice of the Attorney-General sitting in the British Cabinet in violation of the strict doctrine of the separation of powers. By analogy we may say that there is no reason why the task of the political theorist should be construed in an overly conservative way. There is no *a priori* reason why we should not have a critical theory of social policy.

Perhaps there is a reason, however, why a theory of social policy should be critical of existing institutions? There is a conservative argument, at least as old as Burke, which asserts that any attempt at a rational reconstruction of the social order will always lead to damaging criticisms that undermine that order.[13] The existing order of things is incapable of being rationally justified. Its saving grace is simply that it works, without some of the objectionable features of rationally designed political systems. (Burke had in mind the French Revolution; modern variants usually object to socialism.) Yet this objection cannot be established without begging the question. Suppose the present system were the worst in the world, save all the others there might be. That fact alone would constitute a rational justification for our existing institutions. Indeed, far from being an argument against the rational reconstruction of the social order within a political theory, the conservative argument is an instance of such a reconstruction. How plausible an argument it is for any particular case is, of course, another matter.

Components of a normative theory

A normative political theory, in the sense we have discussed above, will contain four essential components.

(1) It should provide an account of the *good*. This should stipulate what is supposed to be of value in the implementation of social policy. For example, one account of the good identifies it with simple want-satisfaction; the aim of public policy on this account would be to satisfy the existing wishes of members of the political community. Another account of the good might identify it in terms of a few key indicators of well-being, for example educational attainments or health indicators. Whatever account of the good we discuss we should examine the arguments used to establish the particular conception advanced.

(2) The second component of an adequate political theory will be an account of the *right*. This involves an account of the principles by which the good should be distributed. One account of the right may be, for example, the principle that want-satisfaction should be equally distributed; another account might be that control of economic resources should arise from one's own efforts or the voluntary transfers of other people. Whatever the particular principle or set of principles advanced the political theorist will seek to understand the reasons by which these principles are justified.

(3) The third component of a satisfactory political theory will be an account of *responsibility*. This is to say, it should stipulate who ought to bring about the specified good in line with the principles advanced. Usually in modern discussions of social policy the government of the nation state is assumed to be the agent whose task it is to advance the good according to certain principles. However, this belief stands in need of justification, and cannot simply be assumed to be correct.

(4) A fourth component is an analysis of *application rules*. We need a set of rules or criteria which enable us to know when the conditions of the foregoing elements are met. For example, how are we to know, or have good reasons for believing, that want-satisfaction

is distributed in a certain way? Many of the benefits distributed by social policy programmes, for example psychological well-being, are not amenable to direct observation. Some method must be established, therefore, by which we may correlate our specification of the good and the right with our observations of social policy outcomes and results.

In order to illustrate the role of these components of a normative theory, consider the example of cost–benefit analysis, which is a technique for the appraisal of public projects deriving from a particular political theory.[14] Cost–benefit analysis contains each of the four components that have been identified.

(1) Its theory of the good is that economic satisfactions should be the object of concern. Economic satisfactions are determined by the preferences that individual citizens have over available social alternatives, considered as differing solely in their economic dimensions, for example whether a bridge across a river should be built or not.

(2) The principle of right adopted is straightforward. A project is beneficial if it can make some people better off without making anyone else worse off, or if it is possible for the beneficiaries of the project completely to compensate the losers. The object of cost–benefit analysis is to maximise economic satisfaction by maximising the total of consumer and producer surplus arising from a specific economic activity.

(3) By and large, the central government is assumed to be the responsible agent for implementing the recommendations contained in a cost–benefit analysis of a public project. An exception to this general assumption is when local authorities might take responsibility for policy implementation.

(4) The application rule is normally specified in terms of willingness to pay. Willingness to pay may be determined by means of charges levied on the service, but where this is not practicable then willingness to pay has to be inferred by the cost–benefit analyst from other information.

So in the example of cost–benefit analysis we see all the elements for a developed theory of how public decision-makers might make an appraisal of a set of social alternatives, and in that way arrive at a social choice. It is not a complete theory since it has nothing to say about those social choices, where some persons must necessarily be made worse off in order to make others better off. Its principle of right needs, at the least, to be supplemented by a principle of distribution.

The four components of a political theory which we have set out will be necessary elements in an adequate political theory, but they will not be sufficient for such a theory. One further component is missing, namely the ability of the theory to provide justificatory force. A theory may contain each of the four elements we have so far discussed, and yet fail to provide an appropriate or rich enough range of principles and concepts adequately to justify a practice or a course of action. In order to illustrate and develop this point, let us consider the political theory of utilitarianism and the way in which it may fail to carry justificatory force.

Utilitarianism is perhaps the most complete and pervasive theory of social choice. Attempts have been made to defend it in various ways, either by appeal to presumptive truths about human psychology, and in particular the motive forces of pleasure and pain, or by appeal to the claims of reasonableness or impartiality and fair-mindedness.[15] Our interest here, however, is not in the ways that utilitarianism may be derived, but in the ways in which as a developed theory of social choice it fits, or fails to fit, a set of practices or a course of action. To see this point, let us begin by setting down the elements of a utilitarian theory.

(1) Its account of the good is stated in terms of want-satisfaction. In modern versions of utilitarianism, preferences and their attainment have come to replace the production of pleasure as the object of action. Accordingly, a person is judged to be better or worse off as he or she satisfies more preferences or more of the same preference.

(2) The principle of right is that net satisfaction should be maximised. This principle can be understood in various ways. For example, the objective might be to maximise average or total satisfaction, the distinction becoming relevant only when considering the effects of our actions on the size of the affected population. Again, we may choose to maximise the satisfaction of all human beings or of all sentient beings. Finally the question arises as to whether the maximisation principle applies to each individual action or to actions of a certain type. That is to say, we have to decide whether the principle applies to actions or to practices understood as regular recurrences of action. On each of these issues of right various positions may be taken by utilitarians.[16] For our purposes the differences are less important than the similarities. I shall propose a set of arguments which, if they are convincing, will apply against all forms of utilitarianism.

(3) The responsible agents in utilitarianism are all persons

capable of acting on utilitarian principles. The fundamental test for utilitarians as to whether private or public action should be undertaken to promote maximum satisfaction is essentially one of efficiency. That form of action is best which, all things considered, best promotes maximum satisfaction.

(4) A simple example will show what sort of application rules might be developed in utilitarianism. We might say that an increase in income for an individual or a community, other things remaining equal, increases total satisfaction, since such an increase would enable people to achieve more of what they want. A utilitarian might use such a rule to test whether or not it was possible to increase total satisfaction by increasing real income.

How then does utilitarianism fare in terms of its justificatory force? The argument that follows suggests that it would fail to justify certain courses of action or various practices that are eminently reasonable, and that it would justify courses of action or practices that are eminently unreasonable. Of course the success of this argument depends on the willingness of the reader to accept certain standards of reasonable conduct. Equally, however, it might be suggested that someone can best come to reflect upon what is reasonable or unreasonable conduct precisely in those cases where utilitarianism throws up answers that are at variance with deeply held beliefs we may have. This is not to claim that political theory should always reinforce our prejudices. It is to suggest that the strength of utilitarianism is to be judged in the light of its deficiencies and by comparison with alternative views. Indeed a fundamental argument of this book is that there are other political theories which are capable of incorporating the truth of utilitarianism without involving its weaknesses. Let us then consider an historical example where utilitarianism would fail to justify a reasonable course of action.[17]

On Sunday, 30 September 1962, a young black, James Meredith, attempted to register at the University of Mississippi, Oxford, Mississippi. He had applied, on 21 January 1961, for admission to this all-white institution. Originally rejected by the university, he filed suit. There followed a 'calculated campaign of delay, harassment and masterly inactivity' waged by the university authorities – a campaign, said the Fifth Circuit Court, that would have done credit to Quintus Fabius Maximus. In June 1962 the court ordered that Meredith be admitted forthwith, and this in turn was followed by more delay and harassment. On 10 September the US Supreme Court, Justice Hugo Black presiding, commanded no further interference with the judicial order. On 13 September, Ross Barnett, the governor of Mississippi, announced on statewide television, 'We will not surrender to the evil and illegal forces of tyranny.'

These events did not augur well for Meredith's attempts to register. By the time of registration – a Sunday had been chosen in the expectation that it would be a quiet day – angry crowds had gathered at the university determined to use any means to prevent Meredith registering. Because the state police would have been unreliable, federal marshals had been sent in to protect Meredith. However, they proved incapable of handling the crowds and the army eventually had to be called to preserve order. Two people had been killed at the beginning of the evening, and the army's troops arrived late, but just in time to prevent the crowd getting its way. In the morning Meredith was able to register.

The problem of social choice that is posed by this example is whether it was right, and if so on what grounds, to protect Meredith's interests at the expense of civil disorder. The number of deaths as a result of the attempt to register could well have been considerable, and the political repercussions harmful even to the cause of which Meredith was a part. The imposition by federal troops of a policy that a local majority of whites appear to have opposed could well have the effect of hardening attitudes. Should the federal administration then have taken the decision to support Meredith's application, with a willingness to use federal troops if necessary? The simplest point to make here is that there was no clear-cut utilitarian reason why the administration should have taken this decision. True, his successful application would be an example to other young blacks, whose well-being might improve by the opportunity of a university education. But for a utilitarian these benefits would have to be set against the disutility involved in the breakdown of public order resulting from the registration attempt. Other, less provocative, solutions were offered the administration. Governor Barnett at one time offered financial support to Meredith if he would apply to university elsewhere.[18] In utilitarian terms this would have been an attractive solution. Moreover, even if Meredith's successful application would have been an example to other young blacks, and so worthy of support on long-run utilitarian grounds, utilitarianism cannot provide any arguments as to why consideration of Meredith's interests *alone* should outweigh considerations of public order. Yet it is at least open to someone to hold that consideration of Meredith's interests alone should outweigh a concern for the interests of those intending to prevent him registering, independent of any long-term effects or benefits to others.[19]

Let us suppose that we were to make this judgement. In what precise ways would utilitarianism be incapable of justifying our decision? Three points stand out, each of which is illustrated in the example. Firstly, the judgement that Meredith's interests outweigh those of the protestors is fundamentally a distributive one, concerned with how benefits are to be weighed. Utilitarianism is an aggregative theory which presupposes that the only consideration that matters is the extent of satisfaction or dissatisfaction arising from an action. As a result, the only weight that counts for the utilitarian is weight of numbers. Consequently, any one individual's strong preference can be outweighed by the preferences of a large enough number of other people. The numerically superior preference does not even have to be strongly felt, provided there are a sufficient number of people who feel the same way. Secondly, where preferences are equally strongly felt on either side, utilitarianism is committed to weighing them equally. Yet the Meredith example suggests that an adequate political theory should distinguish among types of preference. Meredith's preference for going to university represented merely the desire to be treated on the same terms with other members of his generation. He was not trying to gain an advantage over others. The desire to prevent him going to university, by contrast, represented a preference that was intrinsically tied to maintaining a certain group of people in a privileged position, and another group in a subordinate position. Yet one reason for supporting the federal administration's decision might be quite simply that sentiments of prejudice, whether racial or otherwise, ought not to count in the same way in a social choice as the desire to secure a reasonable advantage for oneself. Utilitarianism has no way of making this distinction intrinsically important.[20] Thirdly, the uncompromising consequentialism of utilitarianism makes it blind to the manner in which consequences come about, and therefore incapable of giving an acceptable account of responsibility for those consequences. According to utilitarian logic, if Meredith himself had seen the risk of public disorder his own decision brought about, albeit unintentionally, he might even himself have had to act to prevent those consequences, say by withdrawing his application. But such logic makes individuals prey to the unscrupulous designs of others. Whereas we can attach no blame to Meredith were public disorder to result, we can attach blame to those wanting to prevent him registering. Although both parties to the dispute could have prevented the risk of public disorder, it is quite in order to hold that only one of the parties had the responsibility of doing so. This judgement cannot be sustained by a consistent utilitarianism.

Alternatives to utilitarianism

The problems that we have identified in utilitarianism concern among other things its principle of right. The principle of maximising utility is incapable of protecting some fundamental interests of individuals. Because the disadvantages to the few can be counterbalanced by benefits to the many, utilitarianism cannot justify a concern for basic individual interests. Yet it is just such a concern that is typical of political arguments within liberal democracies. The task, then, is to find a theory that is capable of justifying this concern. One preliminary point should be noted about such a theory. Although we are looking for a theory that assigns special weight to certain individual interests, we are not seeking for a principle that assigns unlimited weight. Special weight is not infinite weight.[21] Utilitarians have quite correctly taxed their critics with the objection that any theory that provides indefeasible protection to individual interests can justify allowing extensive and severe harm to large numbers of people as a consequence. This objection suggests that an alternative theory to utilitarianism must pick out certain significant or urgent preferences or interests which cannot be counterbalanced simply by aggregating the less urgent or peripheral preferences or interests of a greater number of people.[22] It does not suggest that an acceptable theory should assign unbounded importance to such considerations.

What alternatives to utilitarianism exist? Three types of political theory can be identified. They may be labelled: (1) reflexive theory; (2) contractarianism; and (3) the 'no-theory' theory. Let us consider each of them in turn.

(1) Reflexive theory is not so much a well-developed point of view

as a mode of argument to be employed. But it may be used to establish some important conclusions about political theory. In its basic and most general form, reflexive theory requires the user of a particular intellectual technique or mode of discourse to think through the preconditions of his or her being able to use that technique or speak in that way. The paradigm of this type of argument in political theory is provided by Hart's[23] argument that, if there are any natural rights, then there is the natural right of all persons to be free. Hart establishes this conclusion by means of a reflexive mode of argument. He begins by pointing out that involved in the idea of a right is the moral ability of one person to make claims upon the conduct of another person. For example, if *A* has a right to something that *B* has promised, then *A* may require of *B* that he or she act in accordance with that promise. Why should *A* need to invoke this right, however? After all, we might simply say that *A* could claim *B*'s performance irrespective of the right. But if we argued in this way we should be saying that *A* controlled *B*, and that *B* had no independent status as an agent. So invoking *A*'s right to extract from *B* performance of a certain action presupposes that *B* has a natural right to freedom which only special claims of right can override.

This mode of argument looks rather promising in the present context. If we can show that presupposed by any political theory is a certain conception of the good and the right, then we may be at least part of the way towards providing the sort of special protection to certain individual interests the absence of which was such a defective element in utilitarianism.

(2) A second alternative approach to utilitarianism is contractarianism. The contractarian political theorist invites others to take part in a thought-experiment. Principles of social choice are to be determined by imagining that all persons in society are the signatories to a social contract. The contract states the terms of association or rules to govern the social relationships of these persons. Each potential signatory is assumed to be capable of reasoning clearly, but is ignorant of his or her own future social position. They are placed behind a 'veil of ignorance'. In other words, no one knows whether they will be rich or poor, strong or weak, male or female, intelligent or dull-witted, Greek or barbarian. Within these constraints of ignorance, each person is assumed to be self-interested in the sense that he or she wishes the contract to be as advantageous

to himself or herself as possible. The intention of the theory is to use the self-interest assumption to motivate the parties to the contract, and the veil-of-ignorance condition to constrain the choice of principles to a fair conclusion. The leading exponent of this view is Rawls, although the contractarian device has been used by a number of other writers.[24] The particular principles of social choice that Rawls and others have claimed to derive from the contract device are less interesting than the claims they imply about the method of argument that should be used in political theory. Thus I shall argue later that contractarianism justifies not one particular principle but a family of principles, and I shall also seek to show the extent to which contractarianism illuminates the truth in utilitarianism.

(3) All the accounts of political principles, including utilitarianism, that have been discussed so far, have involved the attempt to devise a decision-procedure by which different principles of social choice may be given priority in certain circumstances. The third view to be discussed, the 'no-theory' theory, rejects this ambition. It sees political principles as conflicting and ultimate. For example, in the choice between protecting the significant interest of an individual and preserving public order, the no-theory theorist sees a clash of ultimate principles between which government and citizens must choose. There is no theory, no higher-order set of principles, that would enable a decision-maker to know how much weight exactly should be given to one set of considerations or the alternative set. For this reason this theory is sometimes known as pluralism, because it posits an ultimate plurality of political principles, no collection of which can be justified by a further argument. The only qualification the pluralist may allow in this respect is an appeal to consistency. To hold that significant individual interests should be protected against the claims of public order in one case ought to imply that one would make the same judgement in an exactly similar case.[25] Both reflexive and contractarian approaches hold out the possibility of devising a theory that would give sufficient weight to individual interests, without justifying a firm insistence that public order was always to be sacrificed to individual interests. It is clear that the no-theory theory does not offer the possibility of justifying this special weight, though it clearly recognises the logical possibility that someone might wish to assign such weight.

Each of these three theories may be presented as distinct and rival accounts, and they can be distinguished in many respects from utilitarianism. Is it so clear, however, that they can be ultimately separated from one another? One of the fundamental proposals of this book is that these theories should be thought of as complementary, rather than as rivals. Political choices about social policy are not all of the same type. In some cases we are concerned to determine the minimum rights and entitlements of citizenship that all persons should enjoy. At other times we may be concerned not with the stipulation of a basic set of rights but with improvements in social welfare broadly conceived. Yet again we may recognise that within the limits of rights that are to be regarded as basic, reasonable persons may disagree about what policies are to be pursued or implemented. We may then think about the political choices to be made about social policy as a multi-stage procedure. At the first stage is the determination of minimum standards of individual well-being, or the basic rights of citizenship. A reflexive theory of political principles seems most appropriate at this stage since it suggests the minimum conditions that must be met if any form of intelligible political theory is to be constructed. At a further stage we are concerned with the manner in which social welfare can be improved. Here we shall find a revised form of contractarian theory useful, with an implied modification of utilitarianism compatible with contract theory. Finally we may recognise a stage at which judgements about social welfare may quite properly differ from individual to individual. At this point pluralism will come into its own.

The complementarity between these three approaches is implicit, it may be argued, within the theories themselves. Dworkin,[26] for example, has argued that Rawls's contractarian theory contains essential presuppositions about the status of autonomous individuals. In other words, if we reflect upon the preconditions of our being able to conduct the contractarian thought-experiment we shall already find ourselves committed to certain principles of social choice, which will constrain the results that we may arrive at as a result of the thought-experiment. Similarly, if we think of the contractarian thought-experiment as resulting in not one set of principles of social choice but in a family of such principles, sharing common resemblances but differing from one another, then we shall all the more easily see an element of pluralism contained within contractarian theory.

This approach to the problem of political choice and social policy has one fortunate implication. An account of political theory that stresses its role as providing justificatory reasons for certain social practices and policies faces one important objection. Put bluntly, it is: if reasons exist for undertaking one policy rather than another, what is the need of politics? After all, politics may be said to exist because people have differing conceptions of social choice.[27] But if a set of reasons can be given for certain social policies, why should it be necessary to gain the approval of the democratic political process? Does not the very enterprise of political theory imply what Plato proposed, namely that philospher-kings are the most reasonable way of running public affairs?[28] This objection would not of course apply if we simply limited ourselves to the no-theory theory of politics, since the task of the political theorist on that view is simply to clarify the fundamental principles of politics and their implications. But a theory that offered a justification and understanding of those principles must seem suspect from this point of view. Fortunately we are able to by-pass this suspicion. Neither reflexive political theory nor its extension in contractarian thought provides results that are stronger than limiting conditions to which principles should be subject. In other words, the political theorist cannot supply a uniquely right set of principles to which all public policy should conform. Rather, he or she proposes a list of conditions that must be satisfied by principles taken seriously by the democratic process. In this way a strong doctrine of the nature of political theory is consistent with a pluralist conception of politics. If we wanted a name for such a theory we might call it 'restricted contractarian pluralism'. Although an ugly term, it describes exactly the approach that will be developed throughout this book.

2

Welfare, Needs and the Theory of the Good

In the previous chapter I argued that a satisfactory account of social policy defined it as being concerned with specific dimensions of human well-being. The object of the present chapter is to discuss the considerations that are involved in determining the nature of human well-being, for the purposes of public policy, and in understanding how conceptions of human well-being may be related to a broader structure of political argument. The reason for undertaking this enquiry is simple. Unless we can provide reasons for placing specific emphasis on certain aspects of human well-being, the practice of much social policy will remain unjustified, and to that extent politically insecure.

In the previous chapter I also suggested that an adequate political theory will have four components: a theory of the good; a theory of the right; a theory of responsibility; and a set of application rules, giving the conditions under which we can identify whether the good, the right and the correct allocation of responsibility have been achieved. Only when we have a complete theory, containing these four components, shall we be able to make judgements of the form:

1. Agent A is responsible for acting in the designated way, ϕ, in order to secure the good, G, under conditions $C_1, \ldots, C_n$.

   The variable terms in this statement (A, ϕ, G, C_1) are determined only by reference to a theory of politics. Examples of particular propositions of this form include:

2. The government is responsible for equalising the distribution of incomes in all modern market economies.

3. All citizens are responsible for respecting the freedom of others in all democratic societies.

.
.
.

N. All rational beings are responsible for meeting the needs of other rational beings in all circumstances where this is practicable.

Such propositions can only be justified by a normative theory of politics. The task of the present chapter is to see whether there are any general reasons for restricting the scope of the variable term designating the good. That is to say, the present chapter is concerned with how a theory of the good might be constructed.

In ordinary (English) language, there are two main terms for talking about the good, namely 'interests' and 'welfare'. 'Interests' tends to connote the material and social preconditions of well-being, or welfare, and typically refers to such things as income, property, legal rights, career opportunities and so on. To say that a policy is in someone's interests is normally to say that it adds to the stock of these things that person has; whereas to say that a policy promotes someone's welfare is normally to say that it produces some direct bodily or psychological benefit. But this distinction is not a hard and fast one, even in ordinary language, and in this chapter I shall use the terms interchangeably. I want to suggest, in any case, that if there is a distinction here, it is swallowed up in the far more fundamental question of the point of view from which a person's good is to be defined. More particularly, the question is whether a person's good is to be defined from the point of view of that person, or whether it is to be defined from the point of view of an impartial observer who is capable of correcting the false choices made by individuals. That is to say, should we favour a subjective or an objective theory of the good?

Subjective and objective theories of the good

Let us begin answering this question with a clearer statement of the distinction between subjective and objective theories of the good. The simplest form of subjective theory is based on the concept of wants and their satisfaction. According to this view, persons confronted with a set of outcomes from alternative courses of action will have preferences about those outcomes, based upon their wants or desires for certain states of affairs. These wants may suggest a strict preference for one outcome over another, or they may consist of indifference between the outcomes. The crucial point is that certain features of the available states of affairs will interact with a person's desires to enable him or her to rank the outcomes from most preferred to least preferred. A simple conception of a person's good, therefore, would define it in terms of attaining his or her highest-ranked outcome. The good equals maximum want-satisfaction.

If we thought of persons purely as a series of selves, each of which contained its own bundle of wants, this conception of the good would be adequate. But in a world in which the same person can change his or her wants and preferences over time, its adequacy may be questioned.[1] Given the fact of changing desires, the theory of the good as want-satisfaction has no method by which we can pick out in cases of inconsistent wants the set that is to define the good of a person. Moreover, even the long-standing wants and preferences of a person can come into conflict in contradictory ways. Smokers may want to kick their habit even when desiring their next cigarette, and those with a voracious appetite may want to be slim. Which of these two sets of wants do we decide is to count in determining what is the good for a person? One final point is relevant in breaking the simple identification of want-satisfaction and the good. By exercising their imaginations, both about themselves and their situations, persons can come to realise what it might be like to have certain desires, which they do not presently possess. By focusing on any current time-slice of wants and their satisfaction, we are cutting out the possibility of counting this process of self-development as part of a person's good.

A convenient way of overcoming some of these problems, within a subjective theory of the good, is to introduce the idea of a person's projects.[2] A project is defined by the purposes that a person pursues over time. Commitment to a project is rather like commitment to a career; indeed one's career choice can be seen as one of the most important means by which we determine our projects. In committing ourselves to a career we are committing ourselves to a set of interrelated purposes, not all of which we currently pursue, but which we can see ourselves developing. We also commit ourselves to excluding certain possibilities and purposes from our lives. In fact, the extremely complicated projects of the members of a modern community will typically include a certain reservation in our commitments, so that we can take up forgone purposes should we later choose to do so. Even so, we are selecting only a few of the range of opportunities that might be open to us. Commitment to a set of projects, albeit a form of desire and preference, is a want that we can normally only develop after reflection and deliberation. A subjective conception of a person's good, therefore, would identify it with that set of projects to which a person would be prepared to commit himself or herself after deliberation – reflection 'in our coolest hours', to use Bishop Butler's term.[3]

A project in this sense does not have to be merely egoistic. The conception of a project allows people to set themselves altruistic purposes, just as people may choose careers like nursing or social work for altruistic reasons. It should also be clear that the subjective conception of the good in this sense does not regard persons as passive beings activated by whatever wants they may happen to have. On the contrary, since this conception explicitly includes the idea that a person's good is to be identified with those projects that he or she on reflection would pursue, it gives pride of place in our conception of the person not to wants as such, but to those formative wants that result from deliberation. This conception of the good can include, then, what Mill[4] referred to as 'the permanent interests of a man as a progressive being'; that is to say, the development and maintenance of the capacity for autonomous choice. The crucial point about the subjective conception of the good is that ultimately it allows no test of a person's interests or welfare, apart from those projects that he or she would be prepared, in suitable circumstances of judgement, to affirm as his or her own.

An objective theory of the good, by contrast, posits a conception of the good that may not figure in persons' projects. This theory may be formulated in varying degrees of strength. At its weakest it asserts that there are certain purposes, or forms of self-development, that ought to figure in any person's projects, if that person is to pursue the good. And I shall consider it in this weak version, since if it cannot be maintained as a theory in that form, it will not be capable of justification in a stronger form. In order to illustrate this theory, consider the example of political participation. In classical Athens it was asserted that participation in the public affairs of one's community was a virtue, and hence an essential element in any conception of the good. As recounted by Thucydides,[5] Pericles thought himself to be expressing a general opinion of the Athenians when he asserted that a man who minds his own business, and takes no interest in public affairs, has no business in Athens at all.

Using the example of political participation, can we provide any reasons for favouring either the objective or the subjective theory of the good? Clearly the major difficulty in asserting that participation in public affairs is an essential element in a person's projects is that not all persons place the same value on political participation in their scheme of activities. Many people prefer to dig the garden or collect antique furniture to reading the serious parts of the newspaper, attending public meetings and sifting through council minutes. This does not mean, of course, that they never have an incentive to take an interest in politics. Perhaps if the government were to propose a special sales tax on garden implements or Louis XV chairs, they would be led to participate politically. But the value of such participation for them would be merely instrumental – a way of securing results that they might not otherwise achieve. They would find political participation useful, but not a good in itself. Yet, since in objective theories of the good the value of political participation is asserted as a normative proposition, the simple fact that there are divergent and non-mutually overlapping conceptions of the good does nothing to establish the case one way or the other between objectivism and subjectivism. True it poses a problem for objectivism to explain, unlike subjectivism; but perhaps there is a way that objectivism could cope with this problem.

Let us consider to begin with two points in favour of objectivism. The first is that it is quite common for people to make mistakes in the formulation of their projects. Each of us has made mistakes about such things as our careers, choice of friends, and leisure-time activities, and these mistakes can extend even to questions about what activities we find ultimately satisfying or unsatisfying. Often in such matters others may be in a better position than we are to come to a correct judgement about the choices we should make. There is, therefore, no logical error committed by objectivism when it says that some persons may mistake their own good. Secondly, we have some evidence that persons in subordinate positions in society typically have a restricted range of ambitions, desires and aspirations. Runciman,[6] for example, found among his sample in the 1960s that the comparative reference groups of persons at the bottom of the income distribution tended to be those groups of persons adjacent to them. They rarely compared their position with those about the mean in the income distribution, for example. It is also true that the sense of political competence declines with level of education.[7] Restricted reference group comparison and a low sense of political competence will not only prevent persons from pursuing their own interests, but may also mean that others are better able to identify these interests than the persons themselves.

Are either of these points sufficient to establish the plausibility of an objective theory of the good? Take the first point. To show that persons revise their conception of their projects when they acquire new and better information does nothing to show that they should revise it in a particular way, which is what would be required if the objective account were valid. All that it does is to show that people do not always immediately hit upon what they would regard from their own point of view as a satisfactory form of life. It leaves open the possibility that someone might become disenchanted with the life of politics just as much as the possibility that someone might come to discover the value of participation in public affairs. So this consideration will not help establish the truth of the objective theory.

On the second point, the existence of restricted horizons among persons occupying subordinate social positions does not of itself imply an objective conception of the good. One reason for denying the implication is that divergent conceptions of the good can occur at all levels of the social order. It is of course true that the rich participate more in public affairs than the poor; but it is equally true that among the rich there is considerable variation in the importance attached to politics. (A significant section of the English upper classes has always regarded its enjoyment of blood sports as more important than the common affairs of the nation.) Another reason why restricted comparisons do not imply an objective account of the good is that in an open society restricted conceptions of the good become very difficult to sustain. Once traditional beliefs break down under the impact of social change and intellectual criticism, it becomes increasingly difficult to restrict the outlook of the hitherto subordinate.

Arguments for the objective theory of the good fail to carry conviction, then. Are there any arguments for the subjective conception which are more compelling? The most important reason for adopting a subjective account is that it takes seriously the idea that persons are separate individuals with their correspondingly separate aims, plans and purposes. For individuals the plans to which they commit themselves may be important simply because these plans are their own. (At a trivial level consider the hours of work that people will put in to cultivating their own vegetables, although they could often buy them more cheaply in a market; at a more significant level consider the difficulties that governments have always encountered in collectivising agriculture.) Moreover, the objectivist account of the good appears to involve a breach in the principle of responsibility. If there are harmful consequences involved in the imposition of a certain project upon persons, they fall by and large on those who do not share that project. Those on whom the project is imposed have their own projects disrupted from the inside, so to speak. Since we are always in a better position to take a knowledgeable interest in ourselves than we are in other people, we cannot appreciate the full value to people of projects and plans that to us may appear to be absurd. These considerations, then, argue for a subjective interpretation of the good. For these reasons I shall work in the rest of this book with the principle that ultimately persons are the best judges of their own welfare or interests, although qualifying the bald statement of this principle with the recognition that persons are capable of mistaking on occasions their own interests, even, in the short term, to the extent of the ends they should be pursuing.

What does this conclusion mean for the study of social policy? We have seen that social policy is characterised by a specific range of concerns, for example income in various contingencies, health status and educational attainments. The subjective theory of the good makes it more difficult to justify taking this specific range of concerns as politically important. In particular, since differing individual projects may well involve differing evaluations placed on these goods, we shall not be able to assert that it is intrinsically valuable that certain levels of consumption of these goods be enjoyed by all persons. On the contrary, judgements about the value of this consumption must be evaluated in terms of the projects of those who are to consume them. So any argument that we use for the state focusing explicitly on a specified range of concerns will have to involve an instrumental and empirical argument, and not simply a normative one.

However, the subjective theory of the good does not imply that we cannot make reliable generalisations about individuals' welfare and interests. Because certain material and social conditions must necessarily hold in order for individuals to carry out a wide range of projects, we can still generalise about a theory of social responsibility for elements of individual well-being. For example, the existence of common requirements for shelter, food, clothing and heating means that we can make reliable judgements about the necessary preconditions of persons carrying through their conception of the good. Even so, questions arise about the level of supply at which these goods are necessary in order to enable persons to carry through their projects. In order to answer these questions we require a theory saying how we should identify the basic preconditions for human projects. In other words, we require a theory of needs. Such a theory, I shall argue, arises naturally out of the solution to another famous conundrum, namely the problem of making interpersonal comparisons of welfare.

Interpersonal comparisons of welfare

The problem of interpersonal comparisons of welfare is fundamental to any theory of social choice. Let us see how the problem arises. In order to be able to justify certain types of policy recommendations it appears that we ought to be able to compare the welfare of one person with the welfare of another. A simple example would be an involuntary income transfer from *A*, who is rich, to *B*, who is in poverty. Since the transfer is involuntary we cannot say that the transfer is justified because it will improve the welfare of both parties. Instead we must claim something to the effect that the advantage to *B*'s interests when the transfer is complete will outweigh the disadvantage to *A*'s interests that it involves. Suppose, to take the most favourable case, that *A* appears to be living a life of luxury and *B* one of misery. Can we, even in such circumstances, make a judgement of their comparative welfare that might support the principle of net advantage?

Note that we cannot assume that successful interpersonal welfare comparisons will justify redistribution. We may simply want to use such comparisons as a way of knowing whether we have succeeded in increasing the gap between the luxury of the rich and the misery of the poor. Nevertheless, whatever the uses to which they will be put, it seems that such judgements will play an essential role in a fully developed theory of social choice.

Following Sen,[8] we can say that there are three types of interpersonal welfare comparisons that we may want to make. Firstly, we may want level comparability. That is, we may want to know whether *A* is better off with her income than *B* is with her income, without wanting to know the value of the difference in welfare between them. Secondly, we may want to know whether a given change in income means more for *A* or for *B*, without knowing what the relative levels of welfare for *A* and *B* were. Call this unit comparability. Finally, we may want to compare changes both of level and of unit, in which case we have full comparability. It turns out, not surprisingly, that these three kinds of comparability are closely tied to the way in which we believe we can represent our measurement of comparability. Level comparisons require only ordinal measurement, whereas unit comparisons require cardinal measurement on an interval scale, and full comparisons require cardinal measurement on a scale in which the origin and the slope of welfare functions are fixed for everyone.

The theoretical problem involved in making interpersonal comparisons can be illustrated by the simplest type of comparative judgement, namely ordinal comparisons of levels of welfare. Consider the manner in which we might judge whether or not *A* was better off than *B*. If we simply made this judgement in terms of *A* and *B*'s command over resources, then we should have no theoretical problems. We might of course have accounting problems. In calculating *A*'s wealth, for example, we might have difficulty in deciding on a value for her collection of paintings, and this might cause problems in comparing *A*'s wealth with *B*'s, who may hold her assets in the form of savings bonds. Although the solution to this sort of problem will involve a certain element of stipulation of accounting conventions, these difficulties, though formidable, are pragmatic and not theoretical in nature.

However, when we are thinking of welfare comparisons, we have to take into account not merely *A* and *B*'s wealth but also the uses to which they put their wealth and the satisfactions they derive thereby. Considering this problem in an intuitively common-sense way, many people have concluded that the more wealthy a person is the smaller the value of the satisfactions any increment in his or her wealth will be compared to a less wealthy person. This is the so-called law of the 'diminishing marginal utility of income'. The more you have, the less you value any increase. Reflection on this robust common-sense conviction would lead us to be sceptical, however. As a person's wealth increases he or she may develop tastes that require a high income to satisfy. Who is to say that A's nights at the opera give her less satisfaction than B's night in front of the television? We may make reliable inferences about *intra*personal comparisons of welfare, and so we may note that A more readily gives up her season ticket to the opera than she does her television. But it is perfectly consistent with this observation to hold that it is less satisfying for A to spend her nights watching television than it is for B. Such judgements become increasingly contentious, moreover, when we think about the impact of transferring resources from A to B, which is of crucial importance since interpersonal comparisons of welfare are intended to be of use precisely in the context of the problem of distribution. Suppose we transfer some of A's wealth to B in order to make their welfare more equal. What will be the impact upon A? We may say that it will be considerable because we are disrupting a pattern of life to which she has become accustomed; on the other hand, we may say that it will be slight because at least A has the memory of all those pleasurable nights at the opera.[9] Which interpretation are we to choose?

In the light of these difficulties, many have concluded, with Robbins,[10] that interpersonal comparisons of welfare are not judgements about the social and psychological well-being of the persons about whom the judgement is made, but rather are expressions of the relative importance that the speaker attaches to the well-being of different persons, or perhaps different types of person, in society. They are not, it is claimed, judgements of fact, but expressions of value. Must we be so agnostic, however, about the empirical or descriptive content of interpersonal welfare comparisons? In answering this question we shall see that an irreducibly normative argument is needed in order to justify certain types of welfare comparisons, but that other elements, which are not themselves normative, will also enter into the process.

When discussing the difficulties of comparing the satisfactions that A derived from her night at the opera with the satisfactions that B derived from her night in front of the television, we saw that the problem arose because A and B had different tastes and that some tastes were more expensive to satisfy than others. In other words, we were led to the conclusion that the rich might justify their wealth, in welfare terms at least, by cultivating a refined sensibility and a taste for luxury. However, variations in satisfaction can arise in another way, which contrasts with variations in taste, and which may be referred to as variation in need. The argument we shall develop is that interpersonal comparisons of welfare should be based on comparisons of wealth, controlling for variations in need but not for variations in taste. In order to establish this conclusion we shall have to pay some attention to the idea of need.

Need is a slippery concept. In particular there is a tendency for it to be over-used, so that people find themselves claiming they need certain items which others would regard as mere luxuries, or frivolities. Moreover, the concept is used in a wide variety of contexts, so that in talking about needs we may sometimes have in mind the needs of which people are aware, or express – what Bradshaw[11] has termed 'felt' needs and 'expressed' needs – or we may be referring to needs of which they are unaware – which Bradshaw has termed 'normative' or 'comparative' needs. When confronted with complexity of usage in this form, the best procedure is to begin with a stipulative definition of what one means by the term, and to work out from there, making the definition more complex in order to account for the variety of usage.

The basic meaning of the term is simply that of a necessary condition for some state of affairs. 'A car *needs* fuel in order to run' simply states a necessary condition for its working. In a human context the concept does not lose this instrumental connotation: it comes to refer to a necessary condition for carrying through some purpose. 'An author *needs* a pen in order to write', means that the possession of this implement is a necessary condition for writing. In general, in such human contexts, statements about need always make implicit reference to four elements: the purpose a person has; the person who has the purpose; the conditions instrumental to the purpose; and the circumstances within which the purpose arises. When we say that an author needs a pen, we are making clear the person who is the subject of the need as well as the instrument that is the necessary condition for that subject's purposes. And, although we are not stating the point explicitly, the purpose, that of writing, can easily be inferred. What is less clear is the implicit reference to the circumstances in which the need arises. In this particular example the circumstances must be taken to rule out recourse to other writing implements like typewriters and word processors. This being understood, the reference to needs is perfectly intelligible. When some-one claims a need for a particular item it is always a good discipline to try and spell out explicitly the reference for each of these components of an intelligible need statement. Statements about needs for particular items necessary for particular purposes may be called singular need statements; they stipulate the conditions necessary for a person attaining a specific goal.

If singular need statements were the paradigm usage for the concept of need in social judgements, then we might well be better dispensing with the concept of need and focusing our attention on a comparative assessment of the normative value of the specific purposes which different persons seek to implement.[12] There is, however, a type of usage that cannot easily be assimilated to this paradigm, namely those sentences referring to that class of conditions which are instrumental to anybody in carrying through a wide range of purposes in a variety of circumstances. Thus, in a modern economy, individuals need an income to carry out their plans and projects, and in any economy they will need some control over resources. This judgement does not carry any implications about the types of purposes involved. Even those pursuing ascetic religious purposes will need some command over resources in order to keep body and soul together, despite their intentions of cultivating only the soul. Since command over resources is normally constituted by a legal status, all persons require the freedom and status bestowed by the rules in a legal system in order to carry through their plans. This may involve their having a certain amount of political efficacy, and this in turn may require their being granted a certain position in the community in terms of the prestige and social standing that the members of society accord to one another.

Among members of a society we can find the desire for a certain minimum quantity of goods that are valued not necessarily for their own sake, but because they provide the conditions necessary to a wide variety of different projects. Food, shelter, clothing and a source of warmth comprise the obvious components of this basket of instrumental wants, as we may call them. No hard and fast distinction can be made between the instrumental and the non-instrumental or final nature of the wants that attach to these goods. The sense of sitting cosily by the fire on a cold winter's evening may be valued in itself. But, apart from the difficulty of knowing how far necessity is the mother of consumption in such cases, we should still want to distinguish between goods that are valued as a means to a wide range of purposes and goods that are valued only in relation to a specific set of purposes. Thus, if two individuals are living in different climates, the one warm and the other cold, then the individual in the cold climate will have to use resources for heating just to be in the same position as the individual in the warm climate.

The distinction that is involved here is one that is widely recognised in various accounting practices. Income tax accounting, for example, typically allows persons to off-set expenses in connection with work against income received, presumably because it is recognised that persons with work expenses would not be receiving the same real income as persons with no work expenses even if their normal incomes were the same. Similarly the British Supplementary Benefits system allows work expenses to be disregarded in the calculation of part-time earnings. A more illustrative example in some ways is the difficulty in national income systems of assigning output to the categories of 'intermediate' and 'final', when there are externalities of production.[13] Suppose a new factory begins production selling its output to final customers; the value of its output should be included as income in the national accounts. However, if the factory has a smoking chimney dispensing particulate matter into the surrounding atmosphere, those living nearby will have to engage in the 'defensive' expenditure of having to paint their homes more frequently, and the question will arise as to whether the expenditure on paint should count as another final item of consumption or as intermediate input, and therefore as an off-setting cost, to the value of the factory's output. In each of the above cases, then, accounting practices are forced to make a judgement, either implicit or explicit, between instrumental and final wants, if a satisfactory comparison of conditions is to be made. There is no reason to think that similarly intelligible judgements cannot be made in respect of the general standing conditions that must obtain if persons are to formulate their own projects.

The implication of this conclusion is that when making comparisons of individual welfare we should control for variations in levels of instrumental wants. In effect this amounts to saying that the level of income at which instrumental wants are satisfied should be taken as a standard reference point for any further interpersonal comparisons. With variations in non-instrumental or final wants the case is different. Unlike variations of need, there is no empirical evidence available as to whether variations exist, and if they do how serious they might be. Moreover, a subjective theory of the good suggests that no account should be taken of variations in taste. *A*'s choice of expensive projects by comparison with *B*'s choice should have no influence upon us when trying to distinguish the welfare that persons derive from a given income. Such a theory prevents *A* from saying to *B* that her conception of the good is superior to *B*'s from some impartial point of view. No independent observer, then, has grounds by which the value of an improvement in *A*'s welfare at a given level of income can be compared with the value of an improvement in *B*'s welfare with the same level of income. This does not mean that we cannot aim to make systematic comparisons of welfare levels across different points in the distribution of income; only that, in doing so, we should not aim to control for variations in taste. The value of nights at the opera cannot be compared with the value of nights in front of the television.

Need and the concept of deprivation

The distinction between needs and tastes can only be drawn if we have a procedure for determining when the basic preconditions exist for persons being able to formulate and undertake their own projects. As an illustration of how such a procedure may be devised, I shall discuss the problem of determining the minimum material requirements of persons in a modern, industrialised society. What follows is meant to be illustrative, rather than exhaustive. But I shall claim that the procedure I define provides a definition of the concept of (absolute) deprivation.

The fundamental idea of the procedure is to formulate a principle of minimum subsistence that captures the idea, noted by various authors, that subsistence is as much a social notion as a physical notion.[14] What this means is that minimum needs are not simply satisfied by providing the physical necessities of life, for example adequate food, clothing and shelter, but require also for their satisfaction a level of provision for persons that is suitable for social agents, interacting with others in a specific society. The basic criterion of a social minimum, then, is that when it is satisfied persons should be able to meet the obligations that are conventionally expected of all persons in that society as producers, citizens, neighbours, friends and parents. That a certain minimum level of well-being is needed by producers has been recognised at least since the time of Marshall,[15] who defines as necessities those commodities whose consumption would make persons more productive. Similarly, the duties of citizenship require that persons enjoy a certain level of well-being. Persons cannot vote, serve on juries or meet their other political obligations unless they enjoy a certain level of well-being. It is not surprising, therefore, that the cause of social reform has been much advanced whenever the occasions for mass military service have made governments aware of how many potential recruits were physically unfit for service – although presumably fit enough to stay alive. Finally, as neighbours, friends and parents, persons have obligations that are not easily ignored. They must exchange gifts, provide shelter and offer protection and scope for development. These obligations involve a level of material resources that is higher than that of a bare physical minimum. Anyone who fails to meet this socially defined minimum may be said to be in need, and anyone so in need is, stipulatively, defined as deprived.[16]

An approach of this sort has the advantage that once the social minimum has been set it is then in principle possible to determine the quantities of goods that are required to meet that minimum. This procedure is essentially that used by Rowntree[17] in his study of poverty in York, with the idea of a socially determined minimum replacing that of Rowntree's physical subsistence minimum. Three characteristic difficulties may be said to beset this procedure.

The first is that there is some inevitable imprecision involved in specifying suitable minimum quantities of these commodities. Even at the level of physical subsistence nutritional needs vary from individual to individual, as does the rate at which clothes are worn through. Although a genuine problem of operationalising the concept of a minimum standard of living, this consideration can hardly be said to constitute a decisive objection to the determination of the value of needs by calculating the costs of purchasing some minimum quantity of commodities. The range of variation is within certain limits and there is no reason to think that a suitable standard of need cannot be defined within those limits, as has been recognised in studies from Rowntree onwards. This objection would only be decisive if we were convinced that, to be useful, the concept of need had to be defined with absolute precision. But there is no more reason to think that absolute precision is called for in this case than is called for in the requirement that motorists proceed along the road 'with due care and attention'. In each case a certain amount of imprecision is occasioned by the topic at hand.

The second problem is that what constitutes a suitable social minimum will vary from society to society and in the same society over time. The criterion of the social minimum may therefore seem to be circular. What persons need is determined by reference to their social obligations, but the extent of social obligations expands as persons in society become more wealthy. Although there is some circularity here, it need not in any way be vicious or unjustifiable. The concept of the social minimum defines what individuals need to have in order to meet their basic social obligations. Individuals, however, have little power to alter the prevailing pattern of expectations. And there is no evidence that social expectations rise in response to changes in the proportion of the population who live at some prescribed minimum standard of well-being, rather than in response to general changes in the community's wealth. Changing levels of the social minimum, therefore, reflect society-wide changes in wealth, and it can hardly be an objection to the idea of a social minimum that its specification in any particular instance will depend upon the circumstances of the society within which it is used.

A third objection to the use of the concept of need comes at the problem from another angle. Instead of stressing the logical difficulties involved in using the concept, it points to the political irrelevance of relying upon it in an age where the mass of incomes in liberal democracies has risen above the basic minimum needed for survival. Although the form of the argument is correct, there is some reason to doubt the truth of its premiss. Piachaud[18] has approached the problem of determining the minimum income necessary to bring up a child by adopting an approach similar to Rowntree's. Erring on the side of stringency, he found that the cost of a child, in terms of food, shelter and so on, was nearly half as much again as was allowed for in British Supplementary Benefit scale rates. So, even on a criterion of socially prescribed subsistence, available provision does not meet minimum standards. This does not show, of course, that family or household Supplementary Benefit incomes are inadequate, since it may be that the adult scale rates are more than sufficient. It does indicate, however, at the very least, that we ought not to be complacent about the extent to which adequate minimum incomes are enjoyed by all members of the liberal democratic state.

To fall below the social minimum is (by stipulative definition) to be deprived. It is to lack resources that are essential to one's performance as a social agent. The level of welfare that one experiences may be enough for the continuance of life; but it is not enough for the maintenance of social and political life.

Internal and external preferences

The subjective account of the good, on which the above account of interests and needs has been based, says that society must only value what individuals themselves value. Earlier we noted that this does not necessarily imply a restriction to egoistic projects. Persons may take an interest in one another's interests as well as in their own affairs, and the well-being that individuals experience may depend upon how they judge other people proceeding with their projects, and not simply how they assess their own situation and projects. Call the results of one's own deliberation about one's self-regarding interests 'internal preferences' and the results of deliberating about one's other-regarding interests 'external preferences'. External preferences may be further classified into two categories: those that are altruistically inclined towards others, which may be termed 'supportive' external preferences; and those that imply a restriction on the projects of others, which may be termed 'hostile' external preferences. An example of a supportive external preference would be the widespread popularity among members of the working population for the raising of retirement pensions. An example of hostile external preferences would be sentiments of racial prejudice and a consequent desire to restrict access to certain social amenities on ethnic grounds.

Two questions arise in the theory of the good in connection with the distinction between internal and external preferences.[19] The first question is whether a social decision procedure should take equal or even partial account of external preferences by comparison with the account it takes of internal preferences. The second question is, if a social decision procedure should take into account external preferences, should these include either hostile or supportive external preferences, or both. Utilitarianism is a social decision procedure that is committed to taking account of all information about individual preferences. Should utilitarianism be the paradigm for a theory of social choice in this respect, if in no other? Granted that society must only value what individuals value, should it value *all* that individuals value?

The argument for allowing both internal and external preferences to count equally in a social choice procedure is simply that interests are interests. Since we are working with a subjective conception of the good, we may say that there is no objective standard by which we can judge the standing of peoples' preferences. No importance can be attached to the sources from which individuals derive their sense of well-being, since importance can only be determined from within a set of projects, not from without. In economists' terms we are confronted with the phenomenon of interdependent utility functions, where A's utility, for example, may be regarded as responding positively or negatively to changes in B's utility as well as to changes in A's own circumstances. Typically no attention is paid to the arguments in the utility functions, since the economist is concerned to secure general utility gains, whatever their source. We may note, incidentally, that the concept of intensity of preference is irrelevant in this context. A may or may not experience a greater utility change than does B with changes in B's condition. Whether or not a person feels strongly about an issue bears no logical relationship to whether the issue concerns that person exclusively or not. This logical independence of intensity considerations and externality considerations argues in favour of counting all preferences. Unless we do count all preferences, it may be claimed, we may find ourselves ruling out all sorts of useful information about strongly held sentiments within the community.

Does the subjective conception of the good, however, imply that both hostile and supportive external preferences should count equally in matters of social choice? As we saw when discussing variations of taste and interpersonal welfare comparisons, a subjective conception of the good prevents one person from claiming that her projects are superior to those of another person. The only judgement that A is allowed to make when comparing A's projects with B's is that A's projects are better for A than are B's. But suppose now that A's hostile external preferences towards B are unreciprocated by B. To take A's external as well as internal preferences into account is to give greater weight to A's interests than to B's, which is equivalent to regarding A's projects as superior to B's. It is just this sort of superiority, however, that is denied by the subjective conception of the good.[20] So where hostile external preferences are unilaterally held, the subjective conception of the good implies that they should not be taken into account in matters of social choice, rather than that they *should* be taken into account. What about the case where hostile external preferences are reciprocated? A may be better off if B's projects are frustrated in some way, and B may be better off if A's projects are frustrated in some way. To allow such considerations to count in social choice is to create indeterminacy in social choice, and this of itself may be regarded as a reason for refusing to base public decisions on mutually hostile external preferences. It is not of course to say that the public authorities should prevent private individuals making agreements to restrict their conduct to one another's advantage. A subjective conception of the good is not rich enough on its own to prevent mutual exchange of prejudice between consenting adults in private.

Turning now to supportive external preferences we can see that the subjective conception of the good requires first in such cases that the supportive external preferences accurately reflect the internal preferences of the intended beneficiary. If A is allowed to influence the process of social choice in accordance with A's conception of B's interests, rather than B's conception, then we shall in effect be establishing the superiority of A's projects over B's, and this we are precluded from doing by the subjective theory of the good. Intrusive altruistic conceptions of this sort are not unknown in social policy, so it is important to be clear about the basis on which we are prepared to count altruistic sentiments as having weight in public decisions. If A wishes to help B further B's projects, and B agrees, then A is not claiming that her projects are superior to B 's and so is not in violation of the subjective conception of the good. There is, therefore, no reason to refuse to count altruistic or supportive external preferences in the way there is reason to refuse to count hostile external preferences. This conclusion holds whether or not the altruistic preferences are reciprocated.

Some people have objected, however, that such a procedure involves a form of double counting, and so is unfair. Suppose that A's altruistic sentiments towards B are unreciprocated by B. Then it would seem that by counting A's preference for B's interests as well as B's preference we are giving double weight to B's projects as compared with A's projects. Is this not just the sort of superiority of advantage that is ruled out by a subjective conception of the good? To see why not, consider what would be involved in refusing to count A's supportive external preference for B. We should in fact be lowering A's welfare and paying insufficient attention to A's interests. By virtue of her altruistic sentiments towards B, A's welfare depends positively upon B's welfare. We should not be giving equal weight to A's interests, then, in refusing to acknowledge the significance to A of chosen elements within her projects. Instead we should be overriding A's conception of her own good in favour of some other view of A's good; and this we are forbidden to do by the subjective theory of the good.

In conclusion, then, we may summarise by saying that the subjective conception of the good allows us to take account of certain types of external preferences. Altruistic or supportive preferences may have full weight in social choice, in the sense that the public authorities may take full consideration of such preferences when formulating social policy. When hostile external preferences are reciprocated, we have seen that there is no reason why, within a subjective theory of the good, private arrangements may not be made between the persons involved to restrict their plans and projects to mutual advantage. One-sided hostile external preferences by contrast should have no influence on public policy.

3
Autonomy, Freedom and Deprivation

The primary task for any normative theory of the welfare state is to determine the responsibilities that governments have for securing a particular form of social and economic organisation. An answer to this question will implicitly constitute both a theory of responsibility and a theory of the right in public policy. Such an answer will tell us what governments should do to secure the conditions of the good for individual citizens. There is a useful analogy here between the ascription of responsibility to governments and the ascription of responsibility to individuals. Individuals are morally responsible for acts and omissions, that is to say for those things done that ought not to have been done, and for those things not done that ought to have been done. Similarly, governments will be subject to certain constraints, policies they should not undertake, and also subject to certain imperatives, policies they ought to undertake.

The argument I shall advance in this chapter is that there is one overriding imperative to which government action ought to be subject in the field of social policy, and that is the principle that the government should secure the conditions of equal autonomy for all persons subject to its authority. This principle of autonomy asserts that all persons are entitled to respect as deliberative and purposive agents capable of formulating their own projects, and that as part of this respect there is a governmental obligation to bring into being or preserve the conditions in which this autonomy can be realised. This principle is therefore an alternative to the utilitarian principle that the primary task of governments is to secure maximum levels of satisfaction for all persons. It constitutes the fundamental principle of right, or of justice, in public policy. The principle is fundamental in the sense that its content is both feasible and of sufficient importance to make its attainment a matter of priority for public policy. The institutional form that this responsibility should take will be discussed in the next chapter.

The priority of autonomy

In order to establish the primacy of certain principles over others we need a form of argument that produces an ordering among principles. One such form of argument is the one that I have already labelled as reflexive. The example that I am taking to exemplify this form of argument is Hart's[1] argument, to the effect that if there are any natural rights, then there is at least one natural right, namely the equal right of all persons to be free. The central point of Hart's argument is that an assertion of a particular natural right on behalf of a certain set of agents must presuppose that all those other agents obliged to support the asserted natural right themselves possess the natural right to freedom. Otherwise, there would be no need for the justification contained in the assertion of the natural right.

The appeal of this form of argument in the present context is that it appears to provide a method for establishing the priority of certain principles over others. Priority here means that the attainment of the objectives contained in one principle takes precedence over the attainment of the objectives contained in the principles that presuppose the former principle. If one principle is presupposed in the specification or assertion of other principles, then we cannot imagine a situation in which we would want to satisfy the objectives contained in the asserted principles, without first having assured ourselves that we were paying due regard to the attainment of the objectives contained in the presupposed principle. Any principle presupposed in the assertion of another set of principles takes priority over those principles.

It might seem that the reasoning involved in establishing this idea of priority is questionable in terms of Hart's own argument. Suppose, for example, that among the rights in the asserted set is included the right to the protection of individuals from physical assault. Could this assertion be compatible with the priority of the principle of individual liberty? Arguably it is not, because, although persons were being protected from *harm* by the assertion of such rights, their *freedom* was not being protected, whereas the persons whose actions were restricted by the operation of the right had *their* freedom thereby restricted. A successful rights claim, therefore, so it might be argued, supposes only that there is a presumption of individual liberty which needs to be rebutted, not that there is a priority of individual liberty over other goods. In other words, to establish the priority of freedom, Hart's argument would have to show that liberty could only be restricted for the sake of a greater liberty, whereas the form of the argument only establishes that the presumption of liberty must be defeated by some countervailing consideration, which of itself need not make essential reference to liberty. Yet this interpretation of the precedence assigned to the principle of equal liberty within Hart's reflexive mode of argument would underestimate its importance, in two quite distinct ways. In the first place, although protection from physical harm may well be logically distinct from protection accorded to individual freedom, it does not infringe the freedom of the person who is thereby protected.[2] In the second place, although it is true that the freedom of the person who wishes to commit a physical assault is restricted, this restriction can arise as a result of a feature implicit in the idea of a right, namely that the protection it affords be generalisable to all persons eligible for protection under the scheme of rights adopted. The right of physical assault is not allowed because it is not a right that can be easily generalised to all persons. Indeed, the only condition under which it can be generalised to all persons is if all persons were unanimously to renounce their right to protection from physical assault in exchange for the right to assault others. Yet the existence of this condition clearly supports our contention about the priority of individual liberty. If persons may willingly renounce the right of protection from individual assault under a scheme of rights, the fundamental notion in that scheme is not protection from harm, but protection of individual liberty.

A successful reflexive argument, therefore, will involve a method not only for identifying certain principles as being of significance for public policy, but also for establishing their priority within the total set of principles that might be advanced. This form of argument is thus ideally suited to our needs at this stage. Essentially our task will be to generalise Hart's argument. Hart was concerned with a particular form of political theory, namely one in which the concept of a right figured as the central and organising principle. To generalise Hart's approach we need to ask whether there is some central and organising principle presupposed in the activity of political theory itself. Can we find a principle that will play the same role in any political theory that the principle of the equal right of all persons to be free plays in a natural rights theory? The argument I shall develop in answer to this question will bear a close resemblance to the arguments that others, most notably Finnis, Gewirth and Plant, have advanced about the general presuppositions of action-structuring discourse.[3]

To answer the question we need a definition of what we understand by a normative political theory. More specifically we need to pick out some feature of political theories that is of very general interest, and relate that feature to the specification of a central, organising principle. Alternative political theories may be proposed for many reasons, but essential to their character is the aim of supplying standards for the appraisal of alternative constitutional arrangements and for the evaluation of alternative, feasible social states. In this sense a political theory attempts to supply reasons for favouring one social alternative over another, or for legitimating one type of political constitution by comparison with other types. The activity of supplying reasons of an appropriate sort will be central, therefore, in any account of what a political theory is. But in defining political theory in terms of these features we are also committed to certain assumptions about the persons among whom this activity is conducted; that is, we are also making implicit assumptions about the citizens of the political community. For these persons a political theory will specify the legitimacy of the acts of other citizens. Yet, in order to establish such legitimacy, these citizens must be capable of understanding the reasons contained in a political theory, deliberating upon their significance and framing their own plans and actions in accordance with those reasons that they judge to be valid. The capacity for deliberating upon reasons of a general kind and altering one's own plans and conception of one's own interests in line with an intelligent perception of the significance of these reasons may be called the capacity for autonomy. Autonomous persons are capable of planning and deliberation concerning their actions and projects. Unless a political theory assumed that persons were autonomous in this sense, there would be no point in taking the trouble to construct such a theory.

We can put the same point in another way by saying that the construction of a political theory points towards an important political ideal, namely the search for a form of political community in which persons are related to one another in terms of their reasoned commitment to a set of principles capable of regulating their common affairs. Clearly any realistic theory should recognise that citizens have other capacities besides the capacity for autonomy, including their capacity for habitual and unreflective obedience. Yet the construction of a political theory is an attempt to provide a common set of principles that autonomous agents freely accept, and that provide the basis for regulating public affairs, allocating communal resources and directing collective enterprise. As such, a political theory will presuppose the autonomy of persons.

The claim that the capacity for autonomy is generally presupposed in the activity of political theory has been contested by Habermas,[4] who distinguishes between political theories that presuppose the idea of autonomy and political theories that presuppose that persons are merely mechanical contrivances, to be manipulated by those who hold political power. One way of investigating whether Habermas's distinction is valid is by means of a test case. Rather than attempt an exhaustive (and exhausting) catalogue of political theories, the test-case strategy relies on considering an instance where one might expect the presupposition of autonomy to be invalidated. If it is not invalidated, then we have some grounds for holding that our original characterisation was correct, and that the activity of political theory does generally presuppose the idea of autonomy. In order to pursue this test-case strategy, consider an example that Habermas offers of a theory that does not presuppose the idea of autonomy, namely Hobbes's theory of political obligation.[5]

In order to support his interpretation of Hobbes, Habermas points out, correctly, that Hobbes offered an account of politics in which members of the political community were seen as the product of material forces. The laws of motion governing the social and political realm had the same status for Hobbes, and relied upon the same conceptual apparatus, as natural laws governing the physical realm. For Hobbes, then, political theory is deducible, with the aid of a set of assumptions concerning initial conditions, from physical theory. Although Habermas's account of Hobbes's theory is correct, the crucial question concerns the implications of his characterisation. It does not follow, as Habermas suggests, that such a theory can dispense with the presupposition of autonomy. Indeed it does not even follow that it is correct to maintain that Hobbes would interpret his own theory in such a way that political obligation is merely the product of processes governed unreflectively by natural laws. After all, the point of Hobbes's theory is to provide persons with an intelligible rationale for civil and political authority. His argument does not simply assert that it is prudent to obey a ruler for fear of the penalties of not doing so. Rather, the argument rests on the assumption that an appreciation of how Leviathan is constructed will supply the citizen of a community with an intelligent disposition to obey the political authorities. To be sure, appreciating the reasons for obedience, in Hobbes's view, involves persons appreciating that they are material objects moved by natural impulses. Yet, even if this reflective awareness is itself motion in the material mode, as Hobbes's own assumptions require it to be, this does not mean that political theory has somehow succeeded in bypassing the deliberative rationality of autonomous persons. It means simply that any account of that rationality will require compatibility between an explanatory materialist account, on the one hand, and a reflective, phenomenal account given by agents themselves on the other. Compatibility of this sort requires that reasons be causes; but it does not require that one should therefore eliminate reason-giving activity from accounts of intelligent human interaction.[6]

The particular case of Hobbes, therefore, does not provide an instance of the claim that there is a general distinction to be made between two types of political theory, one type presupposing the autonomy of deliberative rationality and another type not making this assumption. Moreover, in so far as this example can be taken as a test case, or an element in a more general account of intellectual history as it is in Habermas's account, then the conclusion we have reached increases the plausibility of claiming that a political theory will necessarily presuppose the principle of autonomy. Presumptively, then, we can rely upon the following argument. The principle of autonomy will occupy a central role within any political theory because it is a value presupposed in the activity of political theory itself. Unless political theorists presuppose that members of the political community to which their arguments apply are autonomous persons, there can be no point in their attempt to supply reasons favouring one set of constitutional arrangements over others, or one set of social states over others.

Some qualifications

There are a number of qualifications that need to be noted in respect of the above argument. The first and most obvious point is that the argument is hypothetical in form. The argument does not establish that one should necessarily be committed to the priority of autonomy. Instead it asserts that if one is committed to the enterprise of constructing a political theory, then reflection upon the presuppositions of that enterprise will involve giving pre-eminence to the value of autonomy. In some ways, then, the argument is extremely weak, since a person might reject the principle of autonomy by rejecting the enterprise of constructing a political theory. However, such a rejection rests upon insecure foundations if persons expect themselves to be treated as citizens entitled to a justification of the prevailing system of power, status and resources. Any reason that may be offered in justification of a state of affairs must be general in character. That is to say, justificatory reasons, as distinct from prudential reasons, cannot be reasons simply for particular persons. They must be reasons that apply to all persons in appropriate circumstances. This is a logical truth that follows from the universalisable characteristic of ethical principles. So, if anybody expects to receive a justification for some state of affairs, it follows that the content of that justification will be stated in the form of reasons that only autonomous persons could be expected to deliberate upon.

A further qualification to the present argument concerns the degree of autonomy that we ascribe to persons. In particular, is it correct to suppose that persons should be respected as *equal* autonomous agents? Consider an analogy. Each of your relatives is equally a relative, but not all your relatives are equally close.[7] Similarly, you may recognise the autonomy of your fellow citizens, but you may not think them all equally autonomous. A categorical distinction between autonomous and non-autonomous beings does not imply that there is no difference of degree among the members of the former set. So the question is whether the categorical criterion is going to govern our decision as to whether to treat all deliberatively competent persons as being entitled to equal autonomy, or whether our decision is to be governed by the criterion of degree. Since the principle of equal autonomy is an ethical one, involving a claim about the way in which persons are to be treated, the relevant criterion would appear to be the categorical one, since that covers the issue of whether persons are capable of acting on reasons of principle in framing their own projects. Moreover, any method for distinguishing among persons in terms of their capacity for autonomy would need to specify what would be relevant differentiating features among persons, and the stipulation of those features would take place within a political theory, rather than be presupposed by such a theory.[8]

Yet the distinction between category and degree does point to an important third qualification to the present argument. To say that a particular theory presupposes the autonomy of persons is not to say we should simply assume that the preconditions for the realisation of that autonomy are present in every society. A prevailing set of social, economic, legal and political conditions may well be inconsistent with the equal autonomy presupposition, for that is an assumption about the ethical status of persons, and so concerns the treatment to which persons are entitled, not the conditions that prevail at any time. Yet the priority that is accorded to the principle of equal autonomy, by virtue of its being the conclusion of a reflexive argument, suggests that establishing conditions in which the equal autonomy of persons can be realised should be the item of highest priority on the agenda of a political community. Why? After all, equal respect of itself seems not to imply an obligation to ensure a minimum capacity to enjoy that respect. And yet, if the concept of respect is grounded in the ideal of a community of autonomous persons being united by virtue of a reasoned commitment to a set of principles, then the obligation to ensure the minimum capacity for autonomy does follow. Unless all the partners to that commitment have the capacity to find their own way to the commitment, the ideal will not be capable of realisation. To understand the significance of this conclusion we need now to turn to a discussion of the meaning of autonomy and the closely related concept of individual liberty.

Autonomy and freedom

There are two components in the idea of autonomy that have been identified so far. These are, firstly, that autonomous persons are capable of regulating their conduct in accordance with a public set of principles, and secondly, that, within the limits provided by these public principles, persons are capable of formulating their own projects, appraising their circumstances to see what actions are appropriate to the attainment of the goals contained within these projects, and evaluating their past actions in judging the success or otherwise in achieving their goals. In order for citizens to be autonomous in this sense, however, the conditions within which they act and deliberate must be suitable. In particular, the political, economic and social constraints within which people act must allow scope for deliberation. Autonomous action is action that is the outcome of deliberation about one's plans and resources within the constraints facing an agent. Autonomous action is under-determined relative to a set of constraints. Autonomous choices are not those that are the product of the constraints facing an agent, but are instead the product of the deliberation an agent exercises over the options available within these constraints. In this sense autonomy requires conditions of individual liberty.

We can begin the process of specifying the conditions of individual liberty by examining the analysis of the concept of liberty proposed by MacCullum.[9] According to this analysis the concept of liberty has a triadic form. There are three elements that are necessarily involved in any statement about liberty: reference to the *agent* who is free; reference to the *range of actions* that agent is free to perform; and reference to the *constraints* from which that agent is free. To say that everyone is free to dine at the Ritz Hotel, for example, is to say of a certain group of people, let us suppose the adult population of London, that they are able to eat a meal in the specified location without their being constrained to do otherwise. The statement will be true if all three of its constituent conditions are satisfied, but false if at least one of them is not satisfied. A merit of MacCullum's analysis is that it forces one to be explicit about the elements of a person's situation that constitute that person being free. For example, persons may be legally free to dine at the Ritz Hotel if there are no special laws forbidding certain persons from dining there, but they may not be financially free to do so if their budgets do not stretch as far as they need to. Making the assertion about liberty explicit in triadic form helps to clarify the conditions that must hold if the assertion is to be true. So, it is true that people are free from legal constraints to dine at the Ritz; but it is false that people are free from financial constraints. Different conceptions of freedom will have different truth conditions; the sentences that must be true in order for an assertion about freedom to be true will, therefore, depend upon the particular range of persons, actions and constraints that are implied in the assertion itself.

A striking feature of MacCullum's analysis is that it does not in fact offer us a definition of liberty or freedom, but simply a specification of the form of sentences about freedom with which an adequate definition should be consistent. That freedom is a triadic relation gives us no information as to what exactly the relation consists in. The relation enters as an undefined term into the construction. It is as if we were told that the relation 'taller than' were to be analysed in terms of it being a transitive, non-reflexive relation holding between two persons or objects. Although the analysis would be correct, it would fail to distinguish this particular relation from all the other binary relations sharing similar properties, for example 'wider than'.

In defining freedom, therefore, we need to specify a particular relation between agents, actions and constraints. One type of freedom that persons may enjoy is simply the physical ability to undertake any one from a number of possible courses of action. Freedom here consists of a relation obtaining between agent, action and constraints, such that there is no natural law by virtue of which the agent's actions will be determined. The paradigm of unfreedom on this definition is provided by cases where agents are physically prevented from performing an action. A person in free-fall cannot reverse the direction of his or her journey, and no two persons can occupy just the same place in physical space.[10]

For agents capable of autonomous action, however, there is an additional test of freedom. It consists of being able to perform an action such that no consequence attaches to it by virtue of which the agent foreseeably suffers deprivation. Freedom in this sense involves both the ability to perform an action and the absence of foreseen deprivation consequent upon performing that action. The standard case of unfreedom in this sense arises when one person is able to threaten another person with a penalty serious enough to induce the threatened person to agree with the threatener's wishes. The legal penalties prescribed by governments as consequences of certain actions offer an example of unfreedom in this sense. In the normal course of events, they render certain actions, for example not paying taxes, less eligible for individual citizens, and, when the threat of imposing a penalty severe enough to deprive a person of some valuable good is credible, they can be said to deprive persons of freedom of action.

There is a perfectly proper sense in which instances of unfreedom so defined are compatible with agents retaining their own will. If I alter my conduct to avoid a threatened deprivation there is a sense in which I have made that choice. I might have chosen to have incurred the threatened deprivation. However, although an agent's own will is still operative in these circumstances, the notion of freedom must make essential reference to standards of reasonable choice in the appraisal of potential deprivations. The idea that free choice must be rational threatens to become what Berlin[11] has termed the 'retreat to the inner citadel'. Yet if restrictions upon freedom involve more than simply physical constraints, essential reference must be made to standards of reasonable judgement in deciding whether or not persons are free to perform a given range of actions. It is possible that some persons prefer death to dishonour, but their value commitments cannot be taken as the prevailing standards in a community in which that pattern of preferences is not widespread. Instead we must count as restrictions upon freedom those consequences that would deprive persons of central portions of their good.[12]

If lack of freedom of action can arise because there is only one way by which a person can avoid deprivation, then one consequence follows. A person who is poor, because he or she falls below some social minimum standard of living, will be deprived. So poverty in prospect can create constraints that render a person unfree. If I am faced with the prospect of unemployed poverty or taking a job that would lift me out of poverty, then I cannot be said to take the job freely, for the only way to avoid deprivation is to take the job. If I move from a job where I am not deprived, to another job on the same or even lower pay, then I have made a free choice. I have exercised my capacity for autonomy within a set of constraints that do not determine my actions. It follows from this case that to be unfree is not always to be made unfree by someone else. Someone can take advantage of the poor prospects facing another without making that person unfree. However, in taking advantage of those poor prospects, it still remains true that the person to whom the offer is made is still not free to refuse it. To be located in an economic structure that constrains one's prospects to those involving deprivation is to be unfree. (Indeed on this account an agent will be unfree when constrained by natural circumstances. Suppose the only way for a person to avoid a fatal infective disease is to drink a glass of salt water every day. Then that person is unfree not to drink the salt water. Such an example is perfectly consistent with standard linguistic usage.)

The definition of freedom that I am proposing is stronger than that found in the familiar 'negative' concept of freedom, by which freedom is defined in terms of deliberately imposed deprivations.[13] In particular, by including the location of someone in a social or economic structure that imposes deprivations, we can count as limitations upon freedom constraints that are not deliberately imposed by other persons. However, the question arises as to whether in going beyond the concept of negative liberty we are necessarily involved in defining liberty in 'positive' terms, that is as the provision of opportunities, or of powers to take up one's opportunities. To this question there is no unambiguous answer. In order to see why not, consider the following example. A person who is not free to accept a particular job, given otherwise poor prospects may be thought to have his or her freedom increased by obtaining the prospect of other work in conditions at least as favourable as the first job. In general it might seem that if employment opportunities are increased, provided they do not involve deprivations, persons will no longer face an unfree choice between no employment and employment at low wages. However, this result only follows if we define free choice in terms of the prospect-tokens that face persons, rather than the prospect-types. More available jobs may simply be more of the available types of job currently on offer. If lack of freedom of choice is construed as being faced with the prospect of poverty or *wage employment*, rather than a particular job, then an increase in the number of opportunities need not be construed as an increase in freedom. Consequently, positive freedom can only be construed as the counterpart of negative freedom provided that the increase in opportunities is appropriately identified.

What, then, is the relation between autonomy and freedom? It is simply that the sphere of free choice is the sphere within which autonomous development can take place. This is not to say that persons can be freed from the fact of finite economic resources. But it is to say that persons cannot plan autonomously if they are subject to economic deprivations. There are two ways in which this lack of autonomy can arise. In the first place it can arise as a direct effect. The circumstances of deprivation can also give rise to lack of autonomy. Economic deprivations can not only structure the prospects facing a person, so as to constrain the person's available set of alternative actions, it can also weaken the will towards autonomy directly. Thus, in his studies of the effect of poverty on individual families, the overall picture presented by Professor Townsend[14] is one of persons having to live from hand to mouth, being dependent on unreliable sources of income and unable, for example, to move house in order to avoid adverse environmental conditions. In such circumstances the basis is lacking among persons for their being able to plan their lives autonomously at all.

However, the connection between deprivation and autonomy can sometimes be in the form of an indirect effect. Deprivation may involve lack of freedom, and this lack of freedom may inhibit the development of autonomous projects because persons are forced into accepting the offers that others make to them. To be subject to economic power in this way is to be prevented from developing autonomously.

One important property of economic power is its relative nature. The amount of economic control I can exercise in a society depends not simply on the resources that I have available, but also on the resources that others have available. Wealth of £1,000 in a society where everyone else owns £100 bestows more control than it would in a society where everyone owns £1,000 or £10,000. The reason for the relative nature of economic power is that it is relatively greater ownership of resources that enables a person to control the consumption and employment opportunities of others, and it thus enables that person to structure the choices that face other persons in that society. This point has implications for understanding the place of economic equalisation in an economically free society. Clearly the analysis of economic coercion that we have developed does not imply that the economic circumstances of persons be made equal in order to eliminate economic coercion. Persons may make offers to one another from positions of unequal economic advantage, but may still not be taking advantage of a coercively structured environment. For each person to enjoy economic freedom does not require that all persons be equal in respect of economic advantages. However, given the relative nature of economic power, there is often a good case to be made for a public policy that eliminates large inequalities of wealth. Such a policy reduces the danger that one person will use his or her power in order to coerce somebody else.

A policy of limiting inequalities of power can be justified in terms of our concern with the ideal of autonomy. A political community in which the relationships among persons are regulated by a reasoned commitment to a common set of principles is one in which the principle of autonomy is respected. If some persons are subject to the economic control of others, then they cannot give their free consent to such a set of principles. For a political community to realise the ideal of autonomy among its members, it is therefore necessary to ensure the conditions of freedom for those persons. Since the state is charged with determining the fundamental conditions of the social order, it follows that it is the responsibility of the state to ensure the conditions of autonomy, and consequently to protect individual liberty, including economic liberty.

If policies are adopted to limit the power that one person can exercise over another, then freedom will be enjoyed more equally among members of the political community. If the protection of individual liberty takes the form of granting individuals legal rights and protection for their independent status, then it will be misleading to say that freedom is thereby increased (or decreased) across a whole society. To see why, consider what is involved if A is made free from B's control by being granted legal protection. Formerly, B was able to coerce A by threatening a severe deprivation unless A acted in accordance with B's wishes. The legal protection afforded to A consists in the legal threat of a severe deprivation imposed upon B, if she seeks to coerce A. When slaves are emancipated, former slave-holders not only lose rights of control which they previously enjoyed, but they will also incur legal penalties if they seek to enslave other members of their society. The legal protection of individual freedom, within the liberal tradition, therefore, has been concerned with securing the conditions in which all persons can enjoy equal liberty, and not with securing conditions in which liberty is maximised. A similar conclusion also applies to the protection of economic freedom, even though there may be no legal penalty directed at attempts of persons to exercise economic power. If, by means of a more equal distribution of wealth or an increase in employment opportunities, people have alternatives to a set of prospects each of which involves deprivation, then their liberty is protected. The liberty of the formerly economically powerful is restricted, not always by threat of legal penalty, but simply by their being unable to bring about the circumstances in which their power can be exercised. This restriction on the use of wealth represents the economic equivalent of the liberal principle that each person should enjoy a set of rights equal to every other. Again, what is important is not that liberty should be maximised, but that it should be equally distributed.

It is in fact doubtful whether the idea of maximising liberty is a desirable aim in any case.[15] Consider a straightforward case. One obvious criterion for an increase in freedom is that more persons are made free than hitherto. If there are more slaves than slave-holders, then emancipation would be considered an increase in freedom by this criterion. Suppose the numbers were reversed, however. Instead of many slaves being owned by a few masters, we can imagine a few slaves being owned by many masters. Emancipation would now lead to a decrease in liberty. To make the maximisation of liberty the goal of the political system implies a reversal of some of the priorities that are conventionally associated with placing a high value on liberty. Instead of opposing slavery, the proponent of maximising liberty may well find himself supporting it as an institution.

Quite often what theorists seem to have in mind when referring to the minimisation of coercion or the maximisation of freedom is the reduction of *government* intervention and control in the economy and society to the minimum level possible. However, there is in general no reason to believe that *laissez-faire* will always secure freedom for all persons. There may well exist private sources of power capable of threatening individuals.[16] Moreover, if accumulations of economic advantages are allowed to develop unchecked, then some people will find themselves in a position where they can take advantage of the weak position of others. Even if people are free from government power, they may not be free from private power. The government regulation and control of private power may well preserve and protect individual liberty. The only way in which we could uphold the view that the protection of individual freedom implied *laissez-faire* would be to restrict the meaning of loss of liberty simply to the control of citizens' conduct by government. This restriction is implied by some political theories, including that of Hobbes who regarded the state of nature as a state of liberty, though one infected with mutual fear. But this construal of loss of liberty has been correctly dismissed by Sidgwick:[17]

> it seems absurd to say that it is contrary to liberty to be restrained by dread of the magistrate, and not contrary to liberty to be similarly or more painfully restrained by dread of the lawless violence of a neighbour.

The accumulation of resources in private hands, which may be used for controlling the conduct of others, in principle poses as great a threat to individual liberty as government power. For this reason there is no general inference to be drawn to the effect that the protection of individual liberty requires *laissez-faire*.

Recognising this conceptual truth enables us to dissolve what would otherwise be a paradox in a tradition of political theory. There is a tradition of political theory that insists that the reason why governments should intervene in the otherwise unimpeded social and economic relations of individuals is to preserve individual freedom. For example, Eduard Bernstein concludes his defence of proposals for municipalisation and co-operative enterprise by claiming that their basic justification is the need to preserve and extend individual liberty. R. H. Tawney, arguing that freedom for the pike was death to the minnow, thought greater economic equality brought about by an interventionist government an important means of maintaining freedom. Most recently, Norman Furniss and Timothy Tilton have argued that one of the basic justifications for an interventionist welfare state is that it preserves individual liberty.[18] In each of these theories the apparent paradox of increasing government intervention as a means of preserving freedom is dissolved by recognising that government intervention is necessary in order to protect citizens from the power of other private bodies and persons. None of this is to say that one cannot imagine types of social structure in which *laissez-faire* might be an adequate, and perhaps the best, way to protect individual liberty. For example, a society suitable for Jeffersonian democracy would fall into this category. Jefferson[19] envisaged a social system in which each person, with the exception of a few necessary artisans and craftsmen, had sufficient land to support his needs and the needs of his family. In this way few people would be dependent upon 'the casualties and caprice of customers', and the independence of economic resources owned by each person would be reflected in the independent spirit of citizens. Widespread landholding was the precondition for republican virtue. If for no other reason than the growth in population since Jefferson's time, this type of social structure is no longer feasible.[20] The interdependence of persons in their social and economic relations makes the problem one of finding the modern institutional equivalent of Jefferson's plan of widespread landholding. In posing this problem we have to recognise one major difficulty. The ability of governments to prevent private accumulations of wealth and power from threatening personal freedom also grants an ability to governments themselves to make people unfree. It is possible to be pessimistic at this point and to say that the only alternatives we are confronted with involve a choice between the road to serfdom or the power elite. However, pessimism is unjustified until the possibility that other alternatives exist has been explored. In the next chapter we shall attempt this task of exploration.

4

Freedom, Income and Education

Suppose we ask the question: what institutions will best protect the autonomy of persons in a political community? An answer to this question will involve us considering those institutions that are to occupy a central place in the political, social and economic organisation of that community. The central place given to those institutions will parallel the priority of autonomy within a scheme of values. A political theory with a set of application rules, therefore, will provide us with an indication of the conditions within which its values will be realised.

In the present chapter I discuss some of these problems of application, which I treat as equivalent to problems of institutional design. This problem of design can be put as follows: given what we know about the general circumstances of human societies, what institutions must we design in order to realise individual autonomy? In the previous chapter I argued that freedom from the prospect of economic deprivation was a necessary condition for autonomous action, and so one task of this chapter will be to discuss the conditions that make for economic freedom in that sense. Yet individual liberty is only a necessary and not a sufficient condition of autonomy. To act autonomously requires persons to deliberate and plan over the choice sets available to them, within the freedom they enjoy. Since deliberative competence is developed, in part, within the formal educational system of a community, one further task of this chapter is to give an outline of the sort of educational system that is implied by taking seriously the principle of autonomy. What set of educational arrangements best promote the capacities of persons to plan their own lives, form their preferences wisely and take intelligent steps towards the attainment of their objectives?

Since individual freedom is a necessary condition of autonomous action, we can begin by considering the general circumstances within which freedom is protected, and it will be initially useful to consider other aspects of freedom apart from the economic one. Legal freedom I take to consist in the absence of the prospect of deprivations imposed by the political authorities without due process and without respect for the principles of natural justice. Political freedom consists in protection from the control of organised power, in particular organised physical force, within an extensive sphere of human activity. The institutional protection for legal and political liberties takes the form of a litany of particular recommendations. Protecting an individual's legal freedom, for example, is usually thought to involve the provision of rights on arrest, detention and trial, including habeas corpus, the right to remain silent under investigation, the presumption of innocence, the opportunity for public defence, and so on. The protection of political freedom is usually thought to include protection for free speech, the legal right to form political associations and the rights of individuals, or groups of individuals, to contest with others for political office.[1] As we shall see later, protection of these legal and political freedoms supplies not only the context, but also some of the substance, of social policy, since it is possible, for example, to raise problems about the legal status and rights of social security beneficiaries.[2] However, before discussing these problems of procedural fairness within social policy institutions, I shall bracket the concern with legal and political freedoms, to consider the problem of economic freedom.

Economic freedom involves protection from the prospect of deprivation. In this sense economic freedom requires economic security for all citizens. Yet, as we have seen, the institutional form that provision for economic security can take will vary widely from one form of social organisation to another. In principle, and leaving aside special circumstances like those of the physically handicapped, Jefferson's scheme for widespread landholding is one method by which the goal of economic security could be achieved. Indeed in those forms of social organisation in which a money economy is not highly developed, the possibility of creating economic security by widespread landholding is still open. Thus in Tanzania, it has been long-standing government policy to support the development of a self-reliant peasant agriculture, in which economic security is achieved by persons working individually and collectively on the land to supply their own subsistence needs, without help from other persons.[3] Yet there are economies in which technical developments in production and the growth of population have eliminated the possibility of meeting a public obligation to ensure economic security by a policy of self-reliant subsistence production. Where there is the production of commodities by means of commodities, then some other method is needed for achieving and maintaining economic security. In other words, some equivalent must be found within large-scale industrialised societies to Jefferson's prescription for small-scale agricultural economies.

The suggestion I shall pursue in this chapter is that the modern equivalent to the Jeffersonian scheme is to be found in nationalised systems of social security benefits financed out of the tax system. This suggestion is not original. It arose, for example, in the deliberations of the Royal Commission on the Distribution of Income and Wealth, when the Commission was faced with the problem of determining whether social security benefits, as the right to a future stream of income, should count as wealth or not.[4] For the accounting purposes of the Commission the question was important because its answer affected their estimates of prevailing inequalities of wealth. However, to view social security benefits as a form of property right also provides insight into the problem of how economic freedom can be achieved in a modern community.

It may be objected at this point that to pose the problem as one of finding the institutional equivalent of the Jeffersonian system is already to bias the form of the answer towards the establishment of a system of private or personal property rather than towards a system of collective or social property. To some extent this is true, and yet there are two independent defences of this procedure. The first is a point of principle, and derives from Hegel's argument for a system of private property.[5] Hegel points out that autonomous persons need some personal property in order to objectify themselves to themselves. I take this to mean that the mental development of persons requires their having exclusive control over some portion of the material world in order to discover what they are to make of themselves. The capacity for autonomy is not exercised unless the results of that exercise are given material effect. Any political theory that places a high value on autonomy, therefore, must be consistent with principles that secure to persons this scope for the material expression of their personalities. Such a theory may only require personal property in some means of consumption, rather than in the means of production. But in so far as this is true, it establishes the basis for a privatised system of property rights.

The second reason for inclining towards the maintenance of some measure of personal property in society is essentially political, and is concerned with the dangers to political liberty of operating a centrally planned economy in which most resources are centrally owned. In theory it is possible for central planners to provide economic security for all persons in society. Provided central planners operate the economy according to a consistent input–output schedule in which due account is taken of the limits upon production, then all workers may be guaranteed employment at a suitable minimum wage-rate and provision can be made for the contingencies of sickness, accidents and old age. The output produced may or may not be optimal according to consumer preferences, depending on how successful the planners have been in obtaining information on consumer tastes, but this is a distinct problem from that which arises in connection with providing the means of economic security. One major drawback with this scheme, however, is that no independent source of authority should be able to frustrate the attainment of planners' targets. In particular, if the provision of full employment is an objective of the planners, then it must be impossible for labour unions to negotiate wage-rates different from those proposed by the planners, or to restrict the terms on which workers can enter a particular trade. In other words, successful central planning is inconsistent with the right to the free association of labour for the purpose of collective bargaining with the state, supposedly representing the interests of the whole society including the workers themselves.[6]

Granted these two arguments, we are justified in looking for some system of personal property rights in society as the foundation for individual freedom and autonomy. The reason why social security type benefits can play the role of these personal property rights is that they are a form of economic asset which, unlike land for example, can be held by all persons in society. By their use, therefore, it is possible for all persons to enjoy the economic security that comprises their freedom. As the most important form of income maintenance in modern societies, social security provides at least the beginnings of an institutional foundation for economic freedom.

Principles of the social dividend

Programmes of income maintenance have not developed historically with the explicit intention of providing economic security for all persons in the community. So we should not expect the conglomeration of different income maintenance programmes in liberal democratic countries to exhibit clear features that indicate their role in providing economic security. However, it is possible to specify certain principles on which an income maintenance scheme should be based if it is going to achieve successfully the aim of eliminating economic insecurity. These principles, and the corresponding institutions they suggest, can then be used as a yardstick for judging the adequacy of current schemes of income maintenance. There are, in fact, at least seven principles that would describe a scheme of income maintenance adequate to eliminate economic insecurity.[7]

Firstly, the minimum level of income provided by the scheme should be equal to an income sufficient to avoid deprivation, understood as falling below a subsistence level. If this condition were not met then it would be possible for someone to benefit from a right to social security and still be in the position of being forced to accept certain economic bargains for lack of alternative opportunities. In this way the scheme would not protect economic freedom.

Secondly, the lack of alternative income should be sufficient for assistance. Even if the level of income provided by the scheme is adequate in providing a subsistence income, it will not eliminate economic insecurity unless lack of alternative income is made a sufficient condition for the receipt of benefit. Unless this principle is accepted, other conditions, apart from lack of alternative income, may be imposed for the receipt of assistance, and these other conditions will filter out those who lack an adequate income, leaving them deprived.

Thirdly, the amount of assistance should be related to the family size and the composition of an income unit. One of the ways by which an economic agent can become dependent is to have others dependent upon him or her. In order to avoid this problem it is necessary to relate the size of income maintenance payments to the composition of the income unit that is receiving income assistance. The same principle may, of course, be understood as being motivated by a concern for efficiency. It is clearly inefficient to give too much income assistance to single and childless income units and not enough to units with children and other dependents. So a concern for economic security and a concern for efficiency converge upon this principle. However, we should note that the principle itself leaves certain important matters of definition undetermined. In particular the principle does not specify how income units are to be defined. For example, it does not say whether children who have left school but are unemployed should be counted separately from their family or together with their family. None the less, in broad terms the principle is important in ensuring that income maintenance programmes are responsive to the varying needs of income units of different sizes.

Fourthly, minimum standards should be maintained nationwide, and should not be subject to local discretion. This principle follows from the desire to achieve economic freedom and security for all persons within the political community. If local authorities are given the power to determine levels of payments as is the case, for example, with Aid to Families with Dependent Children (AFDC) payments in the USA, then there may occur wide variations in payments, and some local schemes may not make adequate payments. However, since the value of money income may vary from region to region, this principle does not of itself preclude variations in levels of income assistance which are intended to take into account local variations in the cost of living. This principle is consistent, therefore, with the type of pensions' legislation adopted in Sweden in 1937, by which a nationally funded and administered pensions' scheme makes payments of varying sizes in different cost-of-living areas.[8]

Fifthly, assistance should be in the form of cash, rather than earmarked transfers designated for particular items of consumption. This principle follows from the fact that the scheme of income maintenance is intended to protect the autonomy of persons. It would in general be inconsistent with a concern for such autonomy for public officials or other citizens to be in a position where they could dictate to recipients of income maintenance how they should allocate their consumption expenditures. Once again, however, as with the principle that assistance should be related to the size and composition of the income unit, a concern for autonomy and a concern for efficiency converge upon the present principle. In general, consumers will be able to reach their highest level of satisfaction in consumption if they are free to allocate their expenditures among the various items of consumption that are available. Here again, then, two quite different motivations suggest a common principle.

Sixthly, the scheme should avoid stigma. Respect for autonomy represents, according to our argument, the basic obligation that citizens owe to one another in a political community. Since the scheme of income maintenance is the basic means by which economic freedom is to be upheld, it is important that all persons in the community have access to the scheme on equal terms. It would be inconsistent with this ideal of equal access to reduce the self-respect of some recipients by imposing stigmatising conditions upon their receipt of income assistance. However, as some writers have pointed out,[9] there is little reliable sociological evidence on what constitutes stigma and on how stigmatising conditions arise. In particular, we cannot assume that the transferring of benefits in kind, rather than in cash, will be regarded as stigmatising. (Consider the view that many potential Supplementary Benefit claims are not made for fear of stigma.) So this principle is logically separate from the previous one.

Seventhly, the scheme should have an incentive towards self-reliance. Dependence on any form of assistance carries the danger that self-reliance will be undermined by the system of public assistance itself. Many current schemes of income maintenance involve the 'poverty trap' or the 'notch', by which persons may be economically better off remaining out of employment. If the aim of a scheme of income maintenance is to uphold autonomy, then it is important to try to avoid circumstances in which persons are discouraged from earning their own livelihood.

Although all seven of these principles describe desirable features of income maintenance programmes in the light of a concern for individual autonomy and economic freedom, there may arise circumstances in which not all seven principles can be satisfied in the implementation of a particular scheme of income maintenance. Most obviously, the first three principles may clash with the last. Prevailing wage-rates in many industries may be near the subsistence consumption level, and it may be impossible to secure people a specified minimum level of income, taking family size and composition into account, without undermining the incentive to seek employment. So in appraising particular proposals for schemes of income maintenance, we may find ourselves balancing conflicting principles against one another.

Few schemes of income maintenance currently in operation can be characterised by all of these principles. One common defect is that the payment of benefit is not linked to absence of financial resources but to prior payment to a national social security fund. Moreover, when prior contributions are not required in order to benefit, persons do not automatically qualify for assistance when their income drops below subsistence level. The working poor are typically excluded from the payment of social security benefits, for example. Only certain categories of persons are able to benefit from social security payments, usually on the grounds of sickness, handicap, old age or unemployment. Current schemes of income maintenance cover certain contingencies, but not the contingency of lack of adequate income. This remains true despite the existence of schemes like Family Income Supplement in Britain. The level of benefit paid under FIS is inadequate to guarantee the lifting of recipients out of poverty, leaving aside the problems of take-up that are inherent in conventionally means-tested schemes. This is not to say of course that current schemes of income maintenance do not go a long way to providing for economic security. Since there is a large overlap between being poor and being sick, handicapped, old or unemployed, we should expect current schemes of income mainte-nance to contribute greatly to the reduction of poverty. Thus, in a recent study, Beckerman[10] has shown that social security in Britain was responsible in 1970 for reducing the number of individuals in poverty from 22.7 per cent of the population to 3.3 per cent of the population, closing the poverty gap from £5,858m. to £250m. We must acknowledge, then, that current income maintenance pro-grammes considerably reduce hardship in society. Yet this acknow-ledgement must be qualified by the recognition that categorical schemes of income maintenance have intrinsic limitations which mean that they cannot be used to reduce further some types of remaining poverty, particularly that which occurs among the work-ing poor.

The categorical basis of current schemes of income maintenance imposes certain other constraints upon the development of adequate schemes of economic security. Perhaps the most impor-tant of these constraints concerns the level of income that should be secured to persons in the event of certain contingencies. If the rationale for a scheme of income maintenance is that it protects persons from certain contingencies, then there are strong argu-ments for relating the level of payments to the standard of living enjoyed by persons before the contingency occurred.[11] The protection afforded to people includes protection of the standard of living they have come to expect as rightfully theirs before the contingency occurred. In other words, the contingency rationale for social security suggests that the schemes of benefit should be earnings' related. Yet the public transfer of resources to social security beneficiaries, in schemes that relate benefits to previous earnings, means that money is thereby pre-empted from use to support those whose income falls below the subsistence level but who do not fall into one of the appropriate categories. Thus the amount of resources transferred by the existing US social security programmes is sufficient to close the poverty gap, yet the gap remains open because the resources in question are not concentrated on the poor as beneficiaries.[12] A categorical approach to income maintenance schemes thereby defeats the objective of eliminating poverty and economic insecurity, by building in an incentive to allocate social security funds to other uses.

Are there alternative forms of income maintenance that would not run into this difficulty? One form of income maintenance that would meet this problem is a demogrant or social dividend scheme of the sort discussed by Meade.[13] The essence of a social dividend scheme is to replace wholesale nationalised insurance and social security by a system in which a flat-rate payment is made to all income units or households, the value of which varies only with their size and composition. In the particular schemes discussed by Meade the payment level in Britain would be equal to the prevailing rate of Supplementary Benefit, with an additional allowance given for housing, which is currently excluded in the calculations of the SB scale rate. All income apart from this demogrant or social dividend would be liable for income tax. At a certain point, called the 'break-even' point, the amount paid in tax by a unit would exactly equal the amount given in the demogrant. With earnings past that point an income unit would cease to be a net beneficiary from the scheme and would instead become a net contributor. The chief attraction of such a scheme in the present context is that it provides economic security for all income units whatever the circumstances under which a low income arises. By avoiding the categorical constraint it provides a universal scheme of income maintenance available to all persons on test of citizenship alone.

A scheme of this sort can be characterised by considering three of its aspects: the level of the minimum income guarantee; the level of break-even point, that is the point at which benefits received equal tax paid; and the marginal rate of taxation.[14] Considerations of economic freedom may be thought to imply a high minimum income guarantee. Considerations of efficiency suggest that the break-even point should be low, in order to concentrate resources upon those most in need. Unfortunately these two conditions together imply high marginal rates of taxation, which may well create difficulties for the seventh principle noted above, namely that there should be no incentive to lack of self-reliance. In the simplest form of social dividend scheme that Meade discusses the minimum income guarantee is set at 25 per cent of average earnings, and the corresponding marginal tax rate is 25 per cent across all income groups. If other calls on public expenditure are taken into account, this raises the marginal tax rate overall to around 50 per cent (assuming no changes in respect of expenditure and other taxes). Meade suggests a modification by which a lump-sum levy is raised on all income apart from the demogrant, thus in effect imposing a 100 per cent tax rate on the first part of income but enabling subsequent marginal tax rates to drop to around 40 per cent.

From the point of view of our design principles high marginal rates of taxation may lead to several difficulties. High marginal rates for those earning an income just above the level of the social dividend may lead them to reduce the time they spend working. In other words, the introduction of a social dividend scheme may lead those with wages that are low, but not below the poverty line, to reduce their working hours and hence lower even further their incomes. Persons in this category would in effect be choosing to take the gain in increased security in the form of an increase in leisure. Respect for the autonomy of persons implies that they should be allowed this freedom of choice, but the possibility alerts us to the point that the test of an income maintenance scheme is the success with which it raises consumption possibilities rather than simply raising income.

A further problem with high marginal rates of taxation in schemes of income maintenance is their effect upon those relatively high-income earners who are net contributors to the scheme. Here the concern is whether the high tax rates will lead to a reduction in work effort and hence to a general decline in productive output in the economy. Social dividend schemes imply high marginal rates of taxation, because a proportion of the tax payments made are returned in the form of a social dividend to those paying the tax. One way to avoid this problem is not to replace wholesale existing social security programmes, but to supplement them with a scheme that supports those not already covered. One such scheme is Tobin's[15] negative income tax proposal, in which a reverse tax payment is made to those whose income, from whatever source, falls below a specified level. The payments made would be sufficient to raise all income units above the poverty level. In conjunction with other social security programmes, the effect would be to provide economic security for all income units.

Like the Meade scheme the Tobin proposals are caught in the trap that the higher the minimum level of benefit and the greater the efficiency of the scheme, the higher must be the marginal rate of tax on low-income earners. It would be useful at this point to have some empirical evidence about the effect of such rates on work behaviour. The US Department of Health, Education and Welfare commissioned a number of controlled experiments of income-maintenance schemes, in part with the intention of discovering the effect of varying rates of taxation on the working habits of recipients. The results of these experiments are difficult to interpret, because it is hard to maintain controlled conditions (as when in the middle of one experiment New Jersey changed its AFDC laws to allow payments to be made to households in which the father was unemployed) and because experimental subjects know that they are only involved in a short-term programme. It would, however, be nice to have some evidence in an area where, to adapt C. P. Scott's dictum, opinions are plentiful but facts are expensive. The early results from the New Jersey–Pennsylvania experiments suggested only a low rate of withdrawal from the labour market for those receiving income supplements, but subsequent experiments and analysis suggest wide variations in the estimates, and in policy terms we are back to the point before the experiments were conducted.[16] At present there is no reliable estimate of the size of labour market withdrawal that could be expected if the incomes of the working poor were supplemented, or if persons received an unconditional income guarantee.

One significant point to note, in this context, particularly in connection with the Meade scheme, is that there is no work-test imposed upon recipients. Meade explicitly comments that he would be happy to see people choosing not to work if they were prepared to live at the standard of living implied by the demogrant.[17] What this attitude, in effect, implies is that persons have the right to live off (certain sorts of) unearned income. Yet there is clearly a difficulty here: not everyone can enjoy the right to live off unearned income! If an unconditional income guarantee did lead to a large reduction in work effort, then it would be necessary to impose some form of work-test upon receipt of the demogrant, either in the form of a reduced payment for those who will not voluntarily undertake work[18] or in the form of an absolute restriction upon payments to those eligible to work.

The imposition of the work-test in such circumstances would be justified by a pragmatic argument about the need to maintain resources to fund the overall scheme of income maintenance. However, it might be argued that there was a reason of principle for maintaining a work-test, namely that it is inconsistent to place a heavy emphasis upon individual autonomy and not retain such a test. The principle of autonomy might be taken to suggest that there was a social obligation to provide an adequate minimum income only when individuals faced the prospect of no employment or of employment below subsistence wages. To provide support in other circumstances, it may be argued, is to undermine the responsibility of persons to provide for themselves when they are able, and this is inconsistent with the presumption of individual autonomy.

In analysing the force of this argument, one approach would be to rely upon pragmatic arguments about the difficulties of implementing a work-test in a fair and reasonable way. Empirical evidence from various sources suggests that a work-test is difficult to enforce without some persons being compelled to do unsuitable work or others having their benefit withdrawn without good reason. In general, the burden of proof is upon benefit-recipients to show that they have genuinely sought work, rather than upon the public officials to show that they have not sought work. Leaving these pragmatic arguments to one side, however, is it possible to show that not requiring a work-test is consistent with the principle of autonomy? The effect of a demogrant or negative income tax payment is to provide recipients with an income rather like a dividend on the ownership of capital. It is a dividend on collectively owned resources. To qualify for receipt of this dividend by a work-test is to discriminate among potential recipients in terms of whether or not they own some other sort of capital. Clearly those who have other capital will be less affected by such a test than those who do not. Imposing a work-test, then, reduces the extent to which the conditions of equal autonomy are secured to all persons. Moreover, the capital endowment provided by a comprehensive scheme of income maintenance provides some independent test of whether persons are entering labour markets out of free choice or not. It creates a situation in which persons can enter employment as economically free agents concerned to improve their circumstances, rather than their being forced into the labour market through economic necessity. In other words, it creates a situation in which persons may begin to develop their own projects.

A standard objection to schemes of income maintenance is that they rest upon a false picture of the nature of economic relations.[19] In particular, this objection runs, schemes of income maintenance treat at least some portion of economic output as though it were a collective pie to be allocated in appropriate proportions to different individuals. However, economic relations are not like that. People do not produce for an aggregated collective output, but in accordance with specific contracts to particular persons. Quite right. But it does not follow from the claim that there is no collective pie that it is wrong to treat (some portion of) a community's income as though it were a pie of this sort. One reason for treating a community's income in this way is that the prevailing system of property rights receives collective support from the legal system and customary practice, so there is already a collective interest even in the most individualistic system of property rights. Moreover, a social dividend scheme lays claim only to that portion of a community's income that is necessary to avoid deprivation. Since it is not possible to allow individuals to acquire property in the Lockean way, by allowing them to mix their labour with it leaving 'enough and as good' for others, and since it is impractical to rectify all historic injustices in the acquisition and transfer of property, the obvious way of implementing the liberal aspiration towards the independence of persons is to provide each individual with sufficient social property to meet his or her minimum needs, and then allow those individuals to make of themselves what they will (subject to any further ethical constraints it would be justified to impose).

There are two important qualifications we must add to our account of the social dividend. The first is that the principles we have so far developed do not generate rules for second-best situations, in particular where the total volume of transferred resources is insufficient to close the poverty gap. Our present stock of principles does not tell us whether we should favour concentrating resources upon the poorest persons in order to raise them from poverty, or whether we should devote resources to those just below the poverty line, raising a larger number of people from poverty but leaving others a long way behind.[20] We need principles additional to those that have so far been developed in order to make this choice. It is theoretically useful to consider why we have to resort to supplementary principles at this stage. Within the present account, meeting economic needs is motivated by a general concern to secure conditions of equal autonomy. Autonomy is a categorical concept, however. Persons only enjoy the conditions of autonomy when they are free of the prospect of falling into economic need. It makes no sense within this categorical framework to say that those with lower incomes should receive priority, since those who have higher incomes, but are still poor, have a claim upon resources under the principle of autonomy. Making a judgement as to the best method for closing, rather than eliminating, the poverty gap must necessarily depend upon principles that are supplementary to those we have developed here. The second qualification stems from the fact that a social dividend will be insensitive to special needs, for example medical needs, the existence of which will threaten personal autonomy. However, this problem is part of the more general problem of how we make provision for such needs, and we shall discuss it when we consider specific egalitarianism.

Autonomy and educational opportunity

The provision of conditions of economic security is not the only implication of the principle of equal autonomy. Being autonomous also involves the possession of certain skills with which one can take advantage of the opportunities offered by conditions of economic security. This means equipping persons with the cultural resources that are necessary if they are to be autonomous citizens in the community. The major methods by which these skills are transmitted from one generation to another are the family and formal education. Public policy does not always shun the problems of regulating internal family relationships, but the prospect of manipulating these relationships in a systematic way, in order to attain certain educational goals, is so remote that we are better off concentrating exclusively on the formal educational system in achieving these goals.

If we think about the relationship between education and the principle of equal autonomy, we need to be able to define a sense for the notion of equality of educational opportunity. If the aims of the education system are to be conditioned by the goal of securing autonomy to all persons in society, then it is clear that what is at issue is the ability of the educational system to provide an equal opportunity to acquire the cultural skills and resources that are a condition for persons to exercise their autonomy. Yet the notion of equality of educational opportunity is itself obscure, and there are at least three senses in which the idea can be used. Firstly, it can refer to the principle that the formal educational resources devoted to each child should be equal, at any particular stage of schooling, thus ruling out significant variations in such matters as pupil/teacher ratios, laboratory facilities and the like. Secondly, the idea of equality of educational opportunity can refer to the principle that, for students with the same levels of ability, there should be statistical independence between their socio-economic background and their educational attainments. This second principle would license variations of resource inputs to compensate students from particular social backgrounds for disadvantages they suffer. Thirdly, the idea of equality of educational opportunity may refer to the principle that educational attainments should be equalised for students of different socio-economic background *and* ability. In this sense the aim is to eradicate variations in academic performance among children of the same generation.

Although early research on inequality of educational opportunity tended to employ the first of these three principles,[21] that is clearly an inadequate basis on which to assess the performance of the educational system if that system is intended to contribute towards the objective of promoting individual autonomy. Assessment of the educational system in terms of this objective requires us to look at output rather than input. Evidence from a number of countries[22] supports the view that parental social and economic status is an important determinant of how well a pupil does at school, although the exact mechanisms at work are difficult to detect. The stronger such evidence is, the greater the reason for moving beyond the principle of equal resource inputs for all students towards a system in which inputs are varied in order to provide a compensating environment which offsets the social disadvantages suffered by some children. Yet this still leaves us undecided between the second and third interpretations of the idea of equality of educational opportunity. How do we choose beteen these two?

The third interpretation, requiring equal educational attainments at the end of schooling, is the more stringent of the two. The goal of equalising across all abilities presents a rather daunting prospect to the policy-maker, although there are some current educational programmes that might provide a hint of what this might mean in practice. For example, special language tuition for minority ethnic groups rests upon the premiss that it is possible for students of otherwise varying linguistic ability to attain a certain standard of performance. By contrast, the second interpretation, in which unequal attainments are allowed provided they are not the product of social conditioning, appears much less stringent. So much so, in fact, that it may be derided as consisting in the equal opportunity of students to become unequal, a thought well expressed by Michael Young's satire *The Rise of the Meritocracy.*[23]

If the meritocratic view of education offers too little by way of equality, it must appear that the third interpretation offers too much. Although equalising performance may make sense for some special programmes, like special language instruction for minority groups, it does not make sense for the whole range of the curriculum. To see why this is so, we have only to consider two subjects in which some children display precocious ability, namely music and mathematics. Equalising the performance of the least able and the most able in these subjects would involve devoting considerable time and effort to raising the standards of the least able to a level that would probably not even approach that of the most able. The sacrifice of resources in this direction would involve there being fewer resources for the most able, with a subsequent failure to achieve the potential of which they were capable. The product of such a system would be mediocre musicians and mathematicians as the standards of performance were brought closer to one another for the two groups. This is hardly an inspiring policy objective!

The examples of music and mathematics are untypical in that they are fields where natural ability appears to have a powerful impact upon final standards of performance. Yet although they are untypical they highlight the more general problem of combining consideration for equality with consideration for opportunity, the twin aspects of the principle of equal educational opportunity. Now, the problem could be solved of course if ability were equally distributed. So it is perhaps not surprising to find the logic of the strong principle of equal educational opportunity driving towards the equalisation of ability. Genetic engineering on this scale is science fiction; but is it attractive fiction, or is it, to borrow the term Bernard Williams[24] uses in this context, 'dizzying'? If we take the motive of equal educational opportunity to be the principle of autonomy, then we have to reject the idea of equalising abilities by standardising persons. To respect the autonomy of persons means respecting those qualities that make for their distinctive individuality. This involves not altering their physiological make-up in order that they conform to a pre-set pattern.

An adequate account of equality of educational opportunity must therefore satisfy two conditions. On the one hand it must go beyond the meritocratic view, which accepts natural differences of ability and which attempts to counteract circumstances of a social or economic kind that prevent the full development of abilities in some persons. On the other hand, it should not seek to eradicate entirely differences in ability when this would involve an allocation of resources which prevented the development of the most able to no good purpose, or when it would involve violations of respect for the distinct identities of persons. This policy dilemma will disappear of course if we assume that in fact abilities are more equally distributed than appears to be the case at present, but this particular disappearing act only solves the problem by wildly counterfactual speculations. We need a formula that satisfies our two conditions.

The solution to the problem involves distinguishing between those cultural and intellectual skills transmitted by education which are essential to any person if he or she is to develop an independent plan of life, and those cultural and intellectual skills which are essential to the development of particular plans of life. In effect, the problem amounts to determining what should be in the common curriculum of the educational system and what should be in the specialised curriculum reserved for higher and further education, and professional training. Equality of educational opportunity, according to this conception, means securing a specified level of performance in the common curriculum which all persons should be taught to master. In other words, the principle of autonomy leads to the conclusion that abilities should be equalised, but only within a specific range of subject-matter and only up to a specific level of competence.

It is worth noting exactly how this conclusion follows from the principle of equal autonomy. As we have already noticed in connection with income maintenance programmes, autonomy should be regarded as a categorical concept. That is to say, the ability of persons to make autonomous decisions depends upon the presence or absence of certain conditions, not on the extent or degree to which certain conditions are satisfied. Just as autonomy involves the freedom from economic insecurity by means of a guaranteed minimum income, so it also involves a minimum level of educational competence securing to persons the skills of acquiring information, reasoning, computation and expression. Without a certain level of attainment in these skills the conditions that make for autonomy cannot be realised. But, since autonomy is a categorical concept, once these skill levels have been attained there is no reason, on grounds of autonomy, for ensuring equal attainment beyond that level. The policy of a guaranteed minimum income sufficient to provide economic security finds its counterpart in an educational policy that aims to secure for all pupils a specific level of attainment in a common curriculum, comprising those subjects whose mastery is necessary for an individual to plan his or her life in a rational and independent way.

In practical terms there are two problems to be faced in connection with such an educational policy. The first is to determine the range of subjects that should comprise the common curriculum. The second is to determine the level of attainment that should be expected of every student in respect of these subjects. The answer to both of these questions will depend greatly on the particular social context in which the education takes place. To give an obvious example: children who will grow up to be consumers of technically complex durable goods will need greater training in technical and scientific subjects, if they are to make informed and autonomous consumption choices, than children who will grow up in societies where there are few such consumer durables. In all societies, however, the capacity to read and write, the ability to reason, quantitatively as well as qualitatively, and an acquaintance with the basic physical and social facts about one's own society would appear to be essential. If persons are to transact freely with other members of their society, then they will need the skills provided by these disciplines.

The most obvious subjects that are not essential on this criterion are those aspects of history and literature that are intended to acquaint children with the basic cultural traditions of their society. This exclusion is not accidental. Both history and literature have appraisive as well as instrumental aspects. That is to say, they are not only concerned to equip children with skills which they can use in their adult social transactions. Rather, they provide children with an appreciation of certain cultural accomplishments. Because the basic criterion for inclusion in the common curriculum is that the subjects should provide a range of instrumental skills, it is not surprising to find history and literature excluded. This is not to say that there is no reason for including these subjects in a common curriculum, but only to point out that any justification for their inclusion will depend on considerations quite distinct from those captured within the principle of autonomy.

The level to which the common curriculum should be taught will again depend on the particular circumstances of the society in which the schools are found. The achievement of universal primary education in developing countries in which all children are taught the elements of literacy and numeracy, would contribute significantly to the ability of citizens in those countries to live autonomous lives. Where levels of economic development permit, the standard may be raised beyond the primary level to include secondary education. The historical trend has been for the school-leaving age to increase as levels of economic well-being rise. In principle there is no reason why the complexity and range of choices confronting the average citizen should not grow to the point where post-secondary education becomes a necessary condition for autonomy. However, there is clearly a conflict between increasing the level of educational competence expected of persons and enabling all persons to attain that minimum level of competence. No general principles exist, however, for saying exactly what level should be attained or aimed for within the educational system.

The structure of educational provision which emerges from the foregoing discussion of equality of educational opportunity is one in which priority is given to high-quality mass education up to the standard school-leaving age, with the aim of equipping all children with the cultural resources necessary for them to become autonomous social agents. How does this interpretation compare with the meritocratic account of equality of educational opportunity? Since the equalisation of educational performance applies only up to a specific level, it is obviously possible for educational provision to be made beyond this level with the intention of developing particular skills and talents of some individuals. Equality of opportunity at this further level will take a meritocratic form. However, it is important to note that the justification of equality of opportunity in this case will be in terms of considerations of fairness rather than autonomy. This must be so, because specialised education beyond the common curriculum cannot be justified on the instrumental grounds of securing equal autonomy. Instead it must be justified by the non-instrumental consideration that it is unfair that the development of some persons' skills and talents should be hampered by circumstances not of their own doing and beyond their control.

It may be argued, however, that there is a fundamental difficulty in hoping that a mass educational system will promote equality of educational opportunity. The reason for this difficulty is that it is possible to doubt whether it really makes sense to compare the abilities of different individuals from different socio-economic backgrounds. Children from different backgrounds may grow up in distinct cultural environments, and the abilities promoted and developed within those cultures may well vary from one culture to another. If children are full participants in the culture of their own background, then it might be argued that the appropriate standards for their abilities were relative to that culture, and not common across different cultures.[25] From this point of view, mass education up to a certain standard of performance in a common curriculum threatens to become a form of cultural exploitation.

The reply to this objection leans on the distinctive nature of intellectual skills and abilities in enabling persons to come to reflective self-awareness. Linguistic ability provides the paradigm here. Speaking a language involves speaking a particular language, and this in turn involves being unable to formulate and express certain sentiments as well as one might do in another language. And yet any language will be a medium through which persons come to self-awareness and by virtue of which they discover their identity as social agents. To train persons up to a level of intellectual skills at which they can make autonomous choices is to leave them free to affirm any particular cultural identity they choose, provided that schools are sensitive to local dialect and regional variations. Equality of educational opportunity is incompatible with unreflective participation in a particular culture; but this restriction on participation is due to the role of education in fostering personal development, and not to education being provided equally.

What are the institutional implications of the above argument? There are only three alternatives to be considered; deschooling, vouchers, and state-provided education. Deschooling must be rejected for the same reason that universal private education must be rejected. There is no reason to believe that privately financed and privately controlled education is capable of educating to the prescribed standard of a common curriculum. Between a regulated voucher scheme and state-provided education the choice is less clear. Too many unresolved empirical issues intervene for us to be able to say that equality of educational opportunity favours one scheme over the other.[26] Because the effects of educational institutions can vary widely, depending on the particular cultural context in which they operate, our discussion of the implications of the equal autonomy principle must remain at the level of institutional objectives rather than specific institutional forms.

5

Contractarian Principles of Social Choice

So far in the discussion we have restricted ourselves to problems regarding the most fundamental principles governing social and political relationships and the basic institutions of the social welfare system. The priority to be given to the principle of autonomy within a system of social choice implies the prescription of minimum standards of institutional provision, adequate to prevent persons suffering deprivations which defeat their projects by taking them below a social minimum level of well-being. Even this minimalist argument, however, carries implications for the organisation of social policy, suggesting a more comprehensive system of income support than is typically found in liberal democracies and a strong principle of equality of educational opportunity. In general, the institutional implications of the equal autonomy principle are consistent with the standards that Furniss and Tilton[1] prescribe for the 'social security' state. The question now arises as to what sort of considerations would be sufficient for taking us beyond the social security state to what Furniss and Tilton[2] call the 'welfare' state. Governments have power to make a wide range of social welfare provision above the minimum implied by the equal autonomy principle. How should they use this power? For example, we have seen that the principle of autonomy implies a social security system guaranteeing an income sufficient to eliminate poverty. But once the system has achieved that objective, how far should it go in bringing about greater equality in the distribution of income? In other words, in this chapter we shall consider the theoretical problems that bear upon issues of relative deprivation.

In theoretical terms these issues involve us in a second stage of social choice, distinct from the arguments about the basic structure of social welfare institutions. Because the principle of autonomy prescribes only minimum standards of well-being, a second stage of decision-making is needed in order to appraise what the distribution of resources should be once this minimum has been achieved. In this chapter I shall argue that the appropriate theoretical approach at this second stage is a contractarian one, in which the relevant principles of social choice are derived from a hypothetical set of decisions made by persons ignorant of their own future role in society; and I shall further suggest that this theoretical approach is reflected in the practice of liberal democratic politics.

At this second stage, governments have to be concerned about both the size and the distribution of economic satisfactions. Their programmes may have the effect of increasing those economic satisfactions, or they may have the effect of redistributing them. If both these effects result from a particular policy, then relatively few problems of choice arise. However, suppose that one policy has the effect of increasing economic satisfactions in the aggregate, and another policy has the effect merely of redistributing the existing total of satisfactions without increasing that total. If these policies are mutually exclusive of one another, then the government must choose between them. On what principles should it base its choice?

In order to fix our ideas on this question, let us consider some examples of specific policy choices that governments may have to make in which these contradictory effects are involved. Suppose, for example, that the government operates a tax-transfer scheme in which social security benefits are financed out of general taxation on a pay-as-you-go basis. The government will be able to promote greater economic equality by making higher social security payments and increasing taxes on the better off. However, such a policy may create disincentives to work both among beneficiaries, for whom the benefits of work will be lower relative to their social security income than it otherwise would have been, and among taxpayers, who may reduce their work effort in order to reduce their tax liability. Greater economic equality, therefore, may be obtainable only at the cost of smaller increases in total income, or even perhaps a decrease in total income. A similar problem can arise in connection with private schemes of occupational benefits. Here the government may influence the rate of saving either by direct regulation of the terms and conditions of occupational benefits, say by insisting on a minimum level of benefits payable, or by granting tax allowances which have the effect of providing the private scheme with an incentive to adopt a more equal pattern of benefits than it otherwise would. Here again the conflict between equality and growth may arise, because wealthier individual savers may be less willing to invest in the private scheme if the pattern of benefits is too egalitarian as a result of state control. The subsequent loss of savings may mean lower investment and a consequent lower rate of growth in productive potential. A final example along similar lines is provided by tax-funded training schemes, where the provision of facilities to enable the poor to improve their productive potential may still involve a net loss of economic satisfactions, if the increases in taxes to pay for the programme have disincentive effects on other portions of the workforce.

These examples are merely three instances of what some persons regard as one of the central dilemmas of modern political economy, namely the conflict between equality and efficiency. So the task that faces us is whether we can develop any theoretical arguments that will enable us to assign relative priority to one or other of these principles in the appropriate circumstances.

Equality, the Pareto principle and some assumptions

The principle of equality states that a more equal distribution of economic satisfactions is ethically preferable to a less equal distribution. The principle of efficiency I shall dub the 'Pareto principle', following the conventional usage of economics. The Pareto principle states that if all persons can be made better off as a result of a change in policy, then that change should be adopted. A state in which all persons are as well-off as they can be is ethically preferable to one in which persons are less well-off than they might be. The potential conflict between these two principles was instanced in the three examples I gave earlier. In order to identify this conflict more precisely, and then focus on its resolution, I shall make a number of simplifying assumptions throughout the rest of this chapter.

(1) I shall assume that both of these principles are regarded as sufficient conditions for the government to act.[3] In other words, each principle imposes at least a prima facie obligation upon governments to bring about either greater equality or economic growth.

(2) Any changes induced by policies in pursuit of these objectives are marginal, in the sense that they do not touch upon such matters as the structure within which work is organised or prevalent patterns of household formation. This assumption excludes changes in economic welfare being counterbalanced by changes in welfare brought about by broader social changes.

(3) The units by which economic satisfactions are measured are standardised at the household level for variations in the size, composition and needs of the household.

(4) The population is constant, and the pursuit of one objective does not have a special effect on the birth rate not shared by the other policy.

(5) Economic inequality is measured in such a way that uniform changes across the population in the level of economic satisfactions do not affect the measure of inequality. So, if everyone in a community has a doubling of income, the measure of inequality remains constant.

(6) The sentiments of relative deprivation to be taken into account are those in which persons feel that they personally could gain an advantage by a greater degree of economic equality in society.

Having made these assumptions, the problem is to reconcile the conflict between the principle of equality and the Pareto principle in those cases where they come into conflict. For example, economic growth may raise the economic satisfactions of everyone in society, but simultaneously increase the inequality in the distribution of those satisfactions. One, apparently attractive, way of reconciling this conflict is to adopt the following principle: the government should prefer a more equal to a less equal distribution, unless the inequality makes everyone better off. The rationale of this rule of combination follows from a principle of fairness that is sometimes assumed, namely that there is a burden of proof upon the proposer of an inequality in the distribution of satisfactions, but this burden may be discharged by showing that the inequality benefits everyone. By combining the Pareto and equality principles in this way, we never allow a social arrangement with greater inequality to be preferred to one with lesser inequality, unless the inequality in question can be shown to improve everyone's welfare. The benefits to the more advantaged are not achieved at the expense of the less advantaged.[4]

Part of the formal attractiveness of this approach is that it yields a complete system of social choice; that is to say, for any two distributions we can say which is to be preferred to the other by reference to this principle. By itself the Pareto principle is not complete, since there are often cases where, for a pair of distributions, neither produces a higher level of welfare for everyone than the other. The principle of equality by contrast can be defined so that it can be used to evaluate all possible distributions, and this feature is carried over into the rule that requires that we prefer equality except where there is a Pareto-superior alternative. Unfortunately, this property of completeness is obtained at the price of inconsistency. By applying the rule to a set of three alternatives we may find ourselves going round in a vicious circle of choices. For example: in alternative A everyone might be better off than they would be in alternative B; welfare might be more easily distributed in alternative B than in C; but it does not follow from the conjunction of these propositions that A is to be preferred to C. For the distribution of benefits in C might be more equal than in A, and it might also be the case that not everyone is better off in A than in C, and so we ought to prefer C to A. The application of the rule, therefore, will lead to a situation in which A is preferred to B, B to C, and C to A. (A parallel: everyone may be richer in the USA than in Yugoslavia; and Yugoslavia may have a more equal income distribution than Britain; but it does not thereby follow that everyone in the USA is richer than their counterparts in Britain, nor does it follow that income is more equally distributed in the USA than in Britain.)

The upshot of this inconsistency is that no satisfactory combination of the equality and Pareto principles can be attained simply by laying the burden of proof on the proposer of inequality and assuming that the burden is discharged when the proposed inequality leads to an all-round improvement in everyone's level of well-being.[5] In one way this conclusion is hardly surprising. The Pareto principle is a measure of social welfare based essentially on the test of how individuals fare in one social alternative by comparison with how *they* fare in another social alternative. Equality, by contrast, focuses on how individuals fare relative to *one another* across different alternatives. It is hardly surprising, then, that a more complicated procedure is needed to define a satisfactory relationship between these competing considerations.

The contractarian theory of social choice

In order to develop a consistent set of combination rules for the equality and Pareto principles we may turn to the device of social contract theory. The specific version of social contract theory which I shall present in this section follows closely the formulation of the theory proposed by Robert Sugden and myself in an earlier paper.[6] In that formulation an attempt was made to specify a version of social contract theory, based upon a weak set of axioms which nevertheless yielded definite conclusions about the correct requirements to be satisfied by a system of social choice.

The contractarian theory of choice attempts to base the formulation of social and political principles upon a hypothetical choice situation of imaginary individuals. In its modern version this theory begins with the idea of an 'original position', corresponding to the 'state of nature' in classical contract theory, in which all persons are equally free, rational and self-interested, and in which each is located behind a 'veil of ignorance' about his or her place in society.[7] Ideas of social choice are accordingly understood as those principles that would be agreed by persons behind the veil-of-ignorance as the principles to govern the terms of their association within society. The object of modern contract theory is to specify a set of axioms that adequately characterise the choice situation of these hypothetical individuals, and the implications of which lead to definite conclusions about the type of principles they would choose. I adopt this theory at this stage in the development of the argument for two main reasons. In the first place, the inconsistency of Paretian egalitarianism, under a simple rule for combining these principles together, requires that we have a more elaborate account of the relation in which the equality and Pareto principles stand to one another. We could of course try to reason our way directly to a more elaborate account of this relation, but we may obtain a clearer idea if we consider postulates of individual rationality, which is what social contract theory requires us to do, and then read off from those postulates corresponding principles of social choice. In the second place, social contract theory is to be tested like any other theory, in terms of its ability adequately to account for what is problematic. I shall argue that contract theory is able to provide an adequate account of the relation between the Pareto principle and the principle of equality.

In using contractarian theory I shall make one special assumption. I assume that the distributional constraint set by my previous argument about the principle of autonomy is binding, and in particular that all alternatives are excluded from the scope of contractarian social choice which involve some persons suffering a deprivation that would take them below an adequate minimum standard of living. The parties to the contract are presumed to be free and rational persons. The present assumption amounts to the claim that they each recognise one another as such, and in recognising one another as such they also acknowledge the claims that each has to the conditions for autonomy. We may say that the idea of autonomy is built into the specification of the contractarian thought-experiment, and that in turn the ethical commitments presupposed by the idea of autonomy act as constraints upon the range of allowable outcomes from that experiment. Although in general the attractiveness of contract theory is to be found in its making use of only mild ethical assumptions in order to generate reasonably strong ethical conclusions, we must include among those assumptions any implications following from the contract's being negotiated among free and equal persons. In effect these assumptions define the scope of the contractarian theory of social choice. That theory is limited in its application to those cases of social choice that are left undetermined by the principle of autonomy. It thereby restricts the application of the equality and Pareto principles to those cases of social choice in which no instance of severe deprivation occurs among the feasible set of social arrangements.[8]

We are now in a position to list a set of axioms that would characterise a contractarian thought-experiment.[9] The chief principle in the selection of such axioms is to choose only those that are the least controversial in terms of postulates of individual rationality, as we presume it to operate behind the veil-of-ignorance. Two axioms define the scope of the theory: (i) there is a set of social alternatives; (ii) there is a set of social roles in each of the alternatives. Two axioms define the nature of the preferences of those behind the veil-of-ignorance who might occupy those roles; (iii) for each role in society there is an ordering determined behind the veil-of-ignorance that is complete, reflexive and transitive; (iv) when only one person occupies a social role, the role-ordering of the decision-maker behind the veil-of-ignorance is identical with that one individual's ordering. Two axioms define the way in which sets of role-orderings are to be combined; (v) for each set of roles there is an ordering; when the set contains all roles it is equivalent to the social ordering; (vi) if two disjoint, non-empty sets of roles are combined, then, provided the members of one set thought one alternative at least as good as another and the members of the other set thought that alternative better, the combined set of persons should regard the combined set as better.

The key axiom in this set is the final one, but it is merely the contractarian version of the sure-thing principle of rational choice. The sure-thing principle states that if, under every contingency, one course of action yields just as much benefit to the decision-maker as another course of action, and under some contingencies it yields more benefit, then that course of action should be preferred. Nothing is lost by adopting that course of action, and something may be gained.[10] For a party to a hypothetical social contract the appeal of this principle of choice is obvious. If, for example, all men in society are indifferent in a choice between two social states, but women prefer one of those states to the other, then the combination of men and women should prefer what the women prefer.

If these axioms correctly characterise the contractarian thought-experiment, then it is possible to draw some conclusions about the form that judgements about social welfare should take. In particular, it is possible to show that social welfare will be a weighted sum of individual welfares, with the weights defining the amount of priority that is to be given to the poorer members of the community. The value of the weights will be determined by the assumptions one makes about how risk-averse the contracting parties would be behind the veil-of-ignorance. If we assume that they will not be prone to any risk-aversion, but will simply be risk-neutral, then social welfare will amount to the sum of equally weighted individual welfares, and our social welfare judgements will be utilitarian in character. If, on the other hand, we assume that the contracting parties will be risk-averse, so that they are prepared to forgo the prospect of some gain in order to secure for themselves a higher minimum standard of living, then social welfare will give greater weight to the gains and losses of poorer members of society and correspondingly lower weight to the gains and losses of richer members of society.[11]

The contractarian social welfare judgement has two important properties. The first of these properties is that the weight to be assigned to any role within society, and hence to the welfare of any person occupying a role within society, is always positive. This means that an overall growth in welfare will always be preferred to equality of welfare when it is impossible to transfer any of the gains from the better off to the worse off. In other words, inequality is allowed not simply when it serves to improve the position of the poor, but also when it fails to harm the position of the poor. Pareto improvements should always be taken advantage of. The second important property of this contractarian sum of welfares approach is that because it is possible to assign greater weight to the welfare of poorer members of society than to the richer members of society a contractarian decision-maker can order Pareto-equivalent distributions. In particular, the contractarian can allow what Okun[12] has termed 'leaky bucket' redistribution. A leaky-bucket redistribution is one in which there is some monetary loss to society in making a redistribution from rich to poor, just as there may be some loss of water from a leaky bucket when it is passed from person to person. Because the contractarian is prepared to allow that the value of a given sum of money is greater to a poorer person than to a richer person, it follows that the value of a smaller sum of money may be greater to a poor person than a large sum of money to a rich person. Exactly how leaky the bucket should be will depend upon the weights assigned to different social roles by the degree of risk-aversion of the contracting parties behind the veil-of-ignorance, or, more precisely, by one's estimate of that degree of risk-aversion.

What is forbidden by the contractarian approach is the imposition of losses upon better-off members of society without there being any improvement in the position of the poor. To use the leaky-bucket analogy again we may say that the contractarian approach forbids our simply throwing some water away. To use another analogy that has been suggested in this context, the contractarian approach forbids the attainment of equality simply by means of a 'burnt offering' by which the advantages of the better off are simply sacrificed to the goal of equality without there being any gain to the poor.[13] For example, a contractarian social welfare judgement sees no advantage in a tax on better-off members of society that is so expensive to collect that none of the proceeds are available to transfer resources to the poor. A strictly egalitarian theory by contrast might see an advantage in such an arrangement.

It is interesting to see why contract theory does not give intrinsic weight to the idea of equality, but only such weight as is implied by the effect of inequality upon individual welfare. The set of axioms that are suggested as characterising contract theory require the contracting parties to have preferences over social alternatives conditional upon their occupying any set of roles within society. By assumption these sets of roles may be partitioned, and so the contracting parties are forced to evaluate social alternatives independently of the overall structure of well-being within any one alternative. This does not mean that relative deprivation is excluded as such from influencing judgements about social welfare; but it does mean that the existence of relative deprivation within a community will only influence judgements of social welfare via its influence upon individuals' sense of resentment or envy. Relative deprivation may figure in the way that a social state is described, but its importance for the contractarian is related solely to the way in which it affects individual well-being, not to any intrinsic social importance that may be placed upon it. Judgements of social welfare are required to reflect conditions of individual welfare.

Contract theory, then, defines social welfare as the weighted sum of individual welfares. What does this imply about the solution to the problem of combining the Pareto and the equality principles? There are two ways of answering this question, depending on whether we think of the relevant social judgement as being synoptic in character or partial. If we think of the judgement as being synoptic in character then we are asking for a system of social choice that will order all feasible social alternatives. We can accomplish this simply by making the ordering depend upon a weighted sum of individual welfares. This approach will imply that a Pareto-superior state will always be preferred to a Pareto-inferior one, but it will not imply that Pareto-equivalent states will always be ordered simply according to the degree of inequality they contain. For it may be that a less equal distribution of welfare gives rise to a higher weighted total of social welfare even after sufficient weight has been given to the position of the poor.

In practice, judgements about social welfare are rarely synoptic in character. As citizens or as policy-makers we are not called upon to order all feasible sets of available social alternatives. Rather, we take the status quo as a starting point and we see where we can move from there. What does contract theory suggest should be the procedure for making judgements about social welfare in this case?

Because a contractarian ordering of social alternatives will always be consistent with the Pareto principle the first step in the procedure is to test for whether it is possible to make any all-round gains, or in other words to take society to its welfare frontier. For example, if the construction of a public-works project, say a bridge or a hospital, will make everyone better off, or at least some persons better off and no one worse off, then the project should be undertaken. If, however, society is already at the welfare frontier then the task is to see whether there are any feasible redistributions of income that will keep society at the welfare frontier whilst simultaneously altering the distribution of advantages. If such redistributive potential exists, then the next question to raise is whether the redistribution, if accomplished, would bring society closer to the preferred alternative of a contracting party behind the veil-of-ignorance. The answer to this question will depend on the degree of risk-aversion that one ascribes to contracting parties. If one believes that they would be highly risk-averse then redistributive moves towards greater equality in the distribution of income will be in order. If, on the other hand, one believes that the contracting parties will not be particularly risk-averse then a lower degree of equality in the distribution of income will be admissible.

In the absence of any convincing evidence or argument about how risk-averse contracting parties are likely to be, it may be thought that this result is not particularly informative. However, even at this very general level, it is possible to derive results about the specific form that such inequality judgements should take, although it is not possible to say how much inequality is implied by the process of decision-making behind the veil-of-ignorance. In a paper published by Peter Lambert and myself[14] it was shown that the income measure that corresponded to variations in attitudes to risk behind the veil-of-ignorance was that measure of income inequality known as the Gini coefficient, even when an extremely wide definition of risk-aversion was allowed for. In other words, it is possible to show that at least one conventional measure of inequality is implied by social contract theory for a specific range of comparisons.

The hypothetical compensation test

So far we have seen that a contractarian system of social choice will always be consistent with the Pareto principle, although not every Pareto-equivalent alternative will be regarded as as good as any other. Given this basic consistency with the Pareto principle, however, the next question to ask is whether a contractarian system of social choice also sanctions the use of the Kaldor–Hicks compensation test.[15] In its original form the compensation test was supposed to be an unambiguous measure of an improvement in social welfare. According to this criterion we are entitled to say that social welfare has increased not simply when no one loses by a policy change but also in that case where the increased benefits of those who gain from a policy change would be large enough to compensate the losers in such a way that no one was made worse off, *even though the compensation may not actually be paid*.

The justification for this principle runs something along the following lines. By assumption a Pareto improvement would register an increase in social welfare. If we could reach a state of affairs in which a Pareto improvement is attainable, even though we choose not to attain it, we must have achieved a change that is at least as valuable as the one we could have achieved had the compensation been paid. Since society could achieve the Pareto improvement after the change has been made, the uncompensated state of affairs must be one that is at least as good as the Pareto-superior point.

As it happens, the hypothetical compensation test is not as unambiguous as at first sight it may appear to be. There are circumstances in which it yields contradictory instructions for public policy. That is, its application at one stage of decision-making would lead one to make a policy change, which would then have to be reversed on exactly the same grounds at a later stage of decision-making.[16] However, even if we overcome that problem, by restricting the application of the compensation test only to those cases where no reversal of policy would be implied, we are still not yet out of the wood, since the compensation test takes no account of the distributive implications of any change that follows from its application. For example, suppose the losers by a policy change are relatively poor and the gainers are relatively rich. Suppose also that the gains of the rich are large enough that compensatory payments could be made to the poor, leaving them no worse off than they were before the change, but that the compensation will not in fact be paid. Can we say that this uncompensated state is as good as the compensated one? We could only say this if we were prepared to count the marginal gains and losses to rich and poor as being equal in value.[17] Yet, as we have seen, if the parties to a hypothetical contract were risk-averse, it would not be correct within the contractarian framework to equate the marginal changes in income of rich and poor in this way. The insensitivity of the hypothetical compensation test to distributive consideration is hardly surprising given the origin of the argument for the test. For the compensation test was intended to extend the partial ordering of alternatives secured by the Pareto principle on the assumption that it was not meaningful to compare the welfare changes of different persons. In the richer framework of contract theory, the contracting parties are required to have orderings over social alternatives conditional upon their occupying different roles, and so the prohibition upon interpersonal comparisons of well-being no longer applies. In the framework of contract theory, therefore, it makes sense to ask whether the overall gain to some individuals by a change is more than offset by the loss to other individuals, and to allow the answer to this question to be negative.

The conclusion of this argument suggests that distributive constraints need to be set upon any application of the hypothetical compensation test. However, this of itself does not show that the compensation test is inapplicable to a social policy concerned with income distribution. Indeed, it might be urged that a contractarian approach required a policy-maker to act in accordance with the hypothetical compensation test, provided it met the appropriate distributive conditions. The form of this argument would be as follows. Behind the veil-of-ignorance no intrinsic importance is to be attached to the roles that the contracting parties might occupy. A gain for bookmakers is of equal value to a gain for bishops. The effect of the veil-of-ignorance is to impose a condition of anonymity upon the ordering by roles. Gains and losses are not to be weighed more heavily depending upon the nature of the role being considered. Consequently a contracting party behind the veil-of-ignorance will be neutral between the role changes in the income distribution. If bookmakers swop places with bishops, so that each comes to have what the other once had, there is no reason, behind the veil-of-ignorance, for preferring one arrangement to another.

Let us suppose, then, that a policy change brought about a change in the relative position of two social groups, so that they exchanged relative positions in the income distribution, but with the gains of the gainers being slightly greater than the losses of the losers. Would it not follow from the above argument that a contracting party was required to judge the change to be desirable? The answer to this question must be positive, but the implications of this assent are not clear when we move to the real world of policy-making. In that world, the compensation test is applied to a movement from one state of affairs to another. Judgements about social alternatives from behind the veil-of-ignorance are essentially timeless comparisons of states of affairs. In other words, judgements from behind the veil-of-ignorance take no account of the disruptive effects of change. To show, therefore, that a suitably constrained hypothetical compensation test is implied by a veil-of-ignorance decision is not to show that such a test can be applied to real-world situations in which the disruptive effects of change are present and in which expectations that people have about their possessions have important welfare implications. Conversely, the time-bound nature of real-world policy choices does not show that there are never any circumstances in which the hypothetical compensation test can be applied; it shows only that its application may be more limited than the anonymity implicit in contract theory might suggest.

There is, however, one conjunction of circumstances in which the hypothetical compensation test can be unambiguously applied, namely where it marks an improvement both in the overall stock of resources available and in the distribution of those resources. If we believe that the direction of change implied by a policy represents both an increase in social welfare and an improvement in the distribution of social welfare, by reference to the principles implied by a veil-of-ignorance decision, then we may say that the hypothetical compensation test can be applied without qualification.

Are contractarian principles acceptable?

So far the argument has focused upon the clarification of the equality and Pareto principles and upon the construction of a theoretical framework within which the conflicting considerations that they represent can be reconciled with one another. It is now time to attempt some test of the results of the theory, and in particular to see whether the propositions that we have derived can be brought into what Rawls[18] terms 'reflective equilibrium' with our intuitive convictions. Just as we noticed in the case of desegregation that the utilitarian calculus cannot be made consistent with the idea that individuals have basic claims upon certain social resources, so it might be that the results we have derived from the contractarian thought-experiment cannot be made consistent with our judgements about how the social product above the minimum should be allocated. In carrying out this test I shall assume that the direction in which the contractarian results are likely to err is in not giving sufficient weight to the idea of equality. It is not uncommon to find persons professing a preference for equality, even when an equal distribution does not help the worst off and only reduces the well-being of others. Accordingly, the question we may ask is whether the results that have been derived acknowledge sufficiently the idea of equality. There are three reasons why someone might think that the results were not sufficiently egalitarian: (i) they took no account of the diminishing marginal utility of income; (ii) they ignored the fact that no one deserves more by way of economic advantage than anyone else; (iii) they failed to see the value of economic equality in promoting social and communal solidarity, which was a goal over and above the simple maximisation of individual welfares. Let us look at each of these arguments in turn.

As far as diminishing marginal utility is concerned this will only be true if it is assumed that the contracting parties will be completely risk-neutral, in the sense that any utility function representing their ordering of social alternatives is linear. If, instead, the contracting parties are risk-averse, then the priority they assign to the less well-off members of society will be the equivalent of the assumption of diminishing marginal utility in the conventional psychological interpretation of that notion. Indeed, the extra weight potentially given to poorer persons in the contractarian framework has some theoretical advantages over an argument that bases the case for equality on a contestable psychological premiss such as the claim that the intensity of a person's wants declines at successively higher levels of income. Precisely because this assumption of diminishing marginal utility is an empirical claim it is susceptible to observed counter-examples. Most obvious among such counter-examples is the fact that the intensity of wants is liable to vary, depending on personal factors, within income categories as well as between income categories, and there is no reason why this personality effect should not be greater than the variation in intensity that is induced by income levels. Moreover, it is an observed fact that persons quickly become habituated to a certain standard of living so that deprivations at higher income levels may be felt just as keenly as deprivations experienced at lower income levels. By contrast, the greater weight given to poorer persons within contractarian theory follows as a direct consequence from assumptions about risk-aversion behind the veil-of-ignorance and has its counterpart in an ethical principle of fairness, namely that greater attention should be given to the wants of the less well-off than to those of the better off.

The second reason why someone might think that the contractarian argument does not give enough weight to the idea of equality is that no one in justice deserves more by way of economic advantage than anyone else, and therefore it is unjust that some people should be allowed to have more than others. Schematically the argument may be set out as follows:

1. Everyone should receive what they deserve.
2. No one deserves more than anyone else.

Therefore,

3. No one should receive more than anyone else.

In criticising this argument it is common to focus upon the second premiss of this argument, by asserting that persons may well have achievements or characteristics by virtue of which they deserve more than others. The reply to this line of reasoning is typically that no one deserves the natural abilities by virtue of which they have certain characteristics or have achieved certain accomplishments, and so such characteristics or achievements cannot be the ground for a desert claim. The argument then turns on whether one accepts or rejects the principle that an undeserved feature or characteristic of a person can form the ground for a claim of desert. In the present context, however, it is possible to move beyond the agnosticism in which this dispute appears to leave us. For even if the second premiss of the argument is correct, the first premiss would have to be stronger in order to deliver the conclusion of the argument. In particular, it would have to require that everyone should receive *only* what they deserve (and no more). But while we can agree that people should receive at least what they deserve, this is no reason to think that they should receive *only* what they deserve. To believe in this latter principle is to believe that the claims of desert exhaust all the reasons that we might have for distributing benefits in a certain way. We can make this principle tautologically true by equating the idea of desert with what persons are justly entitled to; but, in any sense of the term 'desert' in which the notion functions as a distinct claim under the principles of justice, there is no reason for believing it to be true that persons are entitled only to what they deserve (cf. pp. 159–60). Consequently, the claim that persons should possess equal economic advantages because their deserts are equal falls.

The third reason why someone may think that a contractarian system of social choice does not give sufficient weight to the idea of equality is because equality is an essential precondition for social solidarity. Here the idea is that persons should share similar economic circumstances if they are to enjoy solidaristic social relations. This argument presupposes, of course, that solidaristic social relations are desirable, but even granted this assumption, how true is it that equality is a precondition for social solidarity and fellowship? Strikingly, those who have argued for greater economic equality on grounds of social solidarity have in fact appealed to the idea of justice. Thus R. H. Tawney[19] thought that payment according to social contribution would necessarily bring about greater economic equality (because no one could contribute to the common good in proportion to the prevailing ratio of the highest incomes to the lowest), but he did not assume that a strict economic equality would be necessarily, or even usually, implied by adhering to the principle of payment proportional to social contribution. More generally, if the right ordering of economic relations among persons is a necessary condition for social solidarity, then what is presupposed in the search for fellowship is economic justice, not simply equality. No one can therefore assert that fellowship presupposes equality without begging the question as to whether economic justice implies equality. There may, of course, be an argument for making this claim, but such an argument has to be logically independent of claims about the instrumental value of equality in promoting social solidarity. So the present argument against the contractarian theory of social choice falls, and we are left with the conclusion that the principles that that theory proposes are indeed in reflective equilibrium with our intuitions.

The final task of this chapter is to discuss the interpretation and significance of the results we have arrived at. We have seen that the contractarian theory of social choice implies that social welfare will be maximised when the weighted sum of individual welfares is maximised. The weights that are ascribed to different roles in society will depend upon the extent of risk-aversion behind the veil-of-ignorance. Two noteworthy special cases of this general principle of social welfare are utilitarianism, with its principle of maximising the equally weighted sum of individual welfares, and the Rawlsian principle of maximising the welfare of the least well-off in ascending order of priority.

The first question to ask, then, is whether the results of contract theory, in this general form, are consistent with the principles of justice. After all, as we saw in Chapter 1, a utilitarian calculus appeared liable to yield results that were contrary to intuitions about justice when applied to the case of enforcing desegregation. Can it be, therefore, that a utilitarian result is a possible social choice system, consistent with the requirements of justice? A positive answer to this question simply depends upon noticing that the scope of contractarian social choice is constrained to operate upon that set of distributions that secure to all persons the conditions of autonomy, by avoiding severe deprivations. If a utilitarian calculus is the outcome of a contractarian thought-experiment, then it cannot press someone into supporting an unjust course of action, as, for example, appeasing segregationist sentiments, simply because the distribution of the sort of fundamental opportunities involved in the Meredith case will be covered by the principle of equal autonomy. Utilitarianism, then, can be seen as a valid method of making social decisions, but only at the second stage of the social choice process. It operates after the autonomy principle has set the basic constraints both on the scope for distributing resources and opportunities and on the institutional pattern that is necessary to realise that distribution.

Granted that contractarian principles are consistent with a just principle of social choice, can we also say that they constitute a just system of social choice? The precedents for treating the results of the contractarian thought-experiment in this way are considerable. Both Rawls and those who have worked in the contractarian tradition are prone to think of contractarian principles as principles of justice. Yet there are those who doubt this interpretation. Feinberg,[20] for example, distinguishes between principles of justice and principles of the right public policy all things considered, and concludes that contract theory can provide us with an example of the latter rather than the former. The primary reason for making this distinction is the stringency of obligation that is implied by a principle being a principle of justice. A principle of justice provides minimum standards of conduct and social organisation which it is incumbent upon all persons to help secure. Above this minimum there will be a wide range of social goals which it will be desirable to achieve, but where failure to achieve them does not signify any injustice. We may distinguish, therefore, between principles of justice and principles of the socially desirable. Principles of justice prescribe the basic terms of association among persons living in a society; principles of the socially desirable, including the principle of increasing welfare, prescribe a set of end-states that it will be ethically desirable for a society to achieve. One reason for thinking that contract theory provides us with an account of the socially desirable rather than of the just lies in the indeterminacy of its results. Because there is no independent argument as to why the contracting parties should display a particular attitude to risk, we are left in contract theory with results as widely diverse as the average utility principle and the Rawlsian principle of maximising the welfare of the least well-off in ascending order of priority. An inability to settle the terms of the controversy between these principles would amount to a very substantial failing in a theory of social justice but not in a theory of the socially desirable.

One reason that someone might have for rejecting this account of the relationship between social justice and the attainment of a socially desirable goal such as an increase in welfare is that it may not seem demanding enough. It might be taken to imply that liberal democracies had already attained the minimal requirements of justice, and that the pursuit of goals above that minimum was a matter of political discretion. This would be a complacent attitude, but it would also be unjustified by our account of justice and of contractarian principles. To interpret a contractarian principle as a principle of the desirable rather than the just or the right is to give it less priority, but not thereby to make it a matter of discretion. By virtue of contract theory we can still provide reasons for favouring one policy rather than another. Moreover, we would only be complacent about liberal democracies attaining the conditions of justice if we believed that they really had satisfied the principle of equal autonomy, by guaranteeing all persons against deprivation and by securing for them all the conditions of equal educational opportunity up to an adequate level of skill. As we have already noted, there is enough evidence of poverty and educational inequality for liberal democrats not to be complacent on that score. Moreover, as we shall see later, the principle of autonomy also carries implications for the processes by which social policy goals are achieved, in particular relating to the importance of citizen participation and consumer representation, and in that area too the autonomy principle has not been satisfied. (In all this we are leaving aside problems like that of justice in the distribution of property, which if included would add another item to the justice agenda.) To say, therefore, that principles of the socially desirable are not demanding enough is to overestimate how easy it is for liberal democracies to attain the conditions of justice and to underestimate the strength of claim implied by a principle of the desirable.

The indeterminacy of contractarian principles may seem to be a drawback, but there is a way in which it can be interpreted more positively. One of the characteristic difficulties with a normative political theory that is concerned to evaluate end-states is in leaving room for politics. If contract theory is interpreted as providing the general form of principles of the socially desirable, rather than as justifying a particular principle satisfying that general form, then politics may be seen as the process by which particular principles are selected and implemented. Liberal democratic politics simply is that process. The typical problem in liberal democratic politics lies in deciding how much economic equality there is to be, and this resembles the problem facing a contracting party as to how much risk to incur and, hence, where along the welfare frontier to locate the best alternative organisation of society. The contractarian theory of choice sets limits on the scope of political discussion within liberal democracies, for example by requiring that social welfare be an additive function of individual welfare, but within those limits there is wide discretion in determining the weight that is to be given to different claims. What better metaphor could there be for the observed processes of liberal democratic politics?

6

Specific Egalitarianism

In the previous chapter we were concerned with principles governing the distribution of general purchasing power or consumption opportunities. We saw that varying degrees of inequality were possible as solutions to the problem of distribution, consistent with the requirements of justice. Let us suppose, then, that we are social planners confronted with an unequal distribution of income. Let us also suppose that we are convinced that a more equal distribution of resources would raise social welfare; in the contractarian framework we are clearly supposing that the existing degree of inequality is greater than would be justified by assumptions about risk-aversion behind the veil-of-ignorance. The question to be discussed in this chapter is: under what circumstances, if ever, would it be right for us as planners to aim for a further redistribution in respect of certain specific commodities, rather than a redistribution of general purchasing power?

The answer to this question is fundamental for any normative theory of the welfare state. The welfare state is characterised by two types of redistribution. One is a vertical redistribution of income from rich to poor. The other is a horizontal redistribution within income classes, from those without occasion to use services like health and education to those with the occasion to use these services.[1] In public expenditure terms the second type of redistribution probably predominates over the first. In other words, the welfare state is characterised by what Professor Tobin[2] has termed specific egalitarianism: the belief that some scarce commodities should be distributed less unequally than the ability to pay for them. Among these commodities are goods like housing; most aspects of medical care; food and food provision; some specialised household services like home helps; and the services of social workers, lawyers and other trained personnel whose function is to help households improve their decision-making capacities.

Governments can use various policy instruments for promoting greater equality. General egalitarianism can be promoted by the redistribution of income and property. Specific egalitarianism can be promoted: by government provision in kind; by governments paying private producers to supply commodities at below market prices; or by governments supplying vouchers to consumers tied to specific commodities which can be cashed with producers. For the purposes of this chapter I shall treat all these devices as falling into the same category. Their similarity in promoting specific consumption is more important for present purposes than their distinctiveness from one another.

There is one major preliminary objection to be overcome before discussing the rightness of specific egalitarianism. It has been argued that specific redistribution in the welfare state is counter-productive from the egalitarian point of view, and that the welfare state has not been successful in redistributing life-chances, like health, income and housing, across income classes.[3] If true, this argument suggests the conclusion that there is little merit in aiming for specific redistribution by means of state power. However, for present purposes, this rather negative conclusion has to be qualified in two ways. Firstly, the withdrawal of only some public expenditure programmes in specific fields would suffice to produce much greater equality of result than at present. Public spending on higher education, tax subsidies to owner-occupiers, the free provision of road space in central cities, and the subsidising of commuter rail facilities benefit disproportionately the middle classes. So a reduction in these programmes in the total set of specific transfers would promote greater equality. Moreover, some specific expenditures, like those on health care, probably at present promote greater equality than would otherwise obtain.[4] Secondly, in this chapter I shall be concerned with determining the forms of success, rather than the most appropriate instruments of success, in the pursuit of specific egalitarianism. I shall be more concerned, therefore, with the justification of this approach than with the efficacy of programmes in particular cases.

Needs and welfare

The common-sense thought about specific egalitarianism probably runs something as follows. If people are ill, then they need medical services; or if people are involved in a legal action, then they need legal assistance. These needs have a general function, in the sense that meeting them preserves the conditions for an autonomous social life, and an instrumental function, in the sense that their satisfaction is involved in maintaining the conditions within which goods wanted in themselves can be pursued. In other words, there is a set of needs that we must take into account when considering the income distribution, and for which we must standardise income receipts, otherwise we shall count as gains to consumers and citizens income expenditures that should really be counted as losses (compare pp. 33–4).

The common-sensical thought involved in this train of reasoning will turn out to have a core of truth to it, but reflection upon the argument as it stands shows it to be false. Let us consider the simple case where a government-financed service is provided to meet the need, as when public housing is provided or special arrangements are made for medical care. In the first place, even if we are able to isolate a set of commodities that in some sense are especially important in meeting needs, we shall still have to decide upon the level at which those needs are to be met. Individual needs vary and the standards of housing that are suitable for one person may not be suitable for another, or the level and type of coverage provided under medical insurance may be suitable for one person and not another. Given that individual needs vary and public provision of services is standardised, the alternative option of meeting the need by changing the income distribution, in order to make certain services affordable to persons, looks preferable. It is possible to meet this problem by means of a mixed strategy, by which citizens are given vouchers for a minimum level of service, and are then allowed to supplement the value of these vouchers out of their own income. However, the attractiveness of this strategy depends upon our placing special weight on certain forms of consumption, and this of itself is an assumption requiring justification.

In the second place, the provision of services to meet needs may look plausible when viewed at any one point in time, when some people are in need rather than others, but it looks less plausible when placed in the context of the life-cycle of needs. All of us at some time or another are likely to need the benefits of the sorts of publicly provided services that are currently allocated in kind. If there were no public provision, then as individuals and families we would make arrangements to insure against the contingency of having to buy medical care when necessary. Redistributive transfers in cash or in kind would help us buy better insurance coverage. There would of course be the problem that, with medical insurance, some persons would be worse risks than others, and they might find themselves having to pay higher premiums than others. If equal treatment of needs were an important goal, then this possibility should be avoided. But there is some empirical evidence that uncertainty creates a tendency for the equalising of premiums anyway, so this may be more a problem in theory than it is in practice.[5]

There would, of course, be special categories of people for whom cash aid would not be sufficient to meet their needs, for example the congenitally handicapped or those who found it difficult to manage otherwise adequate household budgets. But these are small and easily identifiable groups of people for whom special provision could be made. There is a problem with special provision if it involves stigma, that is the public identification of some persons as less than full and equal members of the community, but the existence of this problem is not sufficient reason for favouring the reduction of inequality by means of services rather than income transfers. It is clear that stigmatising practices can arise in systems in which there is extensive public provision in kind, for example in those cases where 'problem families' are concentrated in particularly poor council housing, whereas more 'deserving' tenants are given better housing. Moreover, although it is true that relative deprivation within modern communities involves more than a simple shortage of income, and includes access to public services and generally enjoyed standards of life, this fact does nothing to establish the superiority of in-kind transfers over cash transfers. For the policy question is: which form of transfer makes a greater marginal contribution to the reduction of relative deprivation? The argument of those who favour cash transfers is that their marginal contribution is greater, not least because they increase the purchasing power of those persons who have inadequate access to public provision and so enable them to seek other sources of supply.

Although we have so far thought of the problem as that of comparing the relative gains from income and service transfers, the difficulty is in fact rather more general than this frequently discussed dichotomy may suggest. The problem is really one of trying to justify why there should be any public concern for specific aspects of individual material welfare, rather than a concern for the general level of individual welfare. Besides the direct provision of services there are other policies within welfare states aimed at improving specific aspects of a person's well-being. For example, tax allowances given against the interest repayments of mortgages encourage persons to consume more housing than they otherwise would do. Similarly, environmental and occupational regulation is directed at protecting persons from the health hazards of industrial and manufacturing processes. These examples clearly provide instances of policy where the dichotomy between specific and general concerns does not manifest itself in terms of the distinction between provision in cash or provision in kind. Not all these specific concerns need be justifiable of course. Thus, even if the subsidy to mortgages provides an example of policy where the specific concern is unjustified, there is nevertheless a very important distinction between concern for the general material welfare of persons and a concern for their specific welfare built into the operation of the welfare state. The question of whether this distinction is a sound one clearly cannot depend on whether it happens to be justified in any particular case. For, if it cannot be justified, there could never be an occasion on which a social planner thought it better to equalise material welfare in a specific respect rather than in respect of general purchasing power.

In order to bring out the significance of the issue, let us consider a related but more general question. Why should public action to improve individual welfare be related merely to the social and economic aspects of a person's welfare? The sense of well-being that a person enjoys will depend upon many factors, including material possessions, legal status and social standing. But it will not depend solely, and not even primarily perhaps, on these social aspects of a person's life. For many people domestic life is the source of their greatest and longest-lasting satisfactions. Measured too by some of the conventional social indicators, personal circumstances have an important bearing upon one's welfare. For example, mortality figures suggest that those without a spouse are more likely to die prematurely compared with those with a spouse. Domestic satisfaction appears to be a good way of avoiding premature death. And yet no one seriously supposes that social policy ought to be concerned with matching the presently unattached in order to ensure an improvement in their welfare as measured by the conventional social indicators! Indeed, the most difficult examples produced by those, like Nozick,[6] who believe that the state should have no welfare-promoting role, are precisely ones in which he considers the social organisation of the matching of mates.

An obvious objection to government involvement in the personal aspects of people's lives is that it is likely to be misguided and heavy-handed. There are simple practical objections to the government trying to promote personal welfare as well as promote the socially related aspects of an individual's welfare. Moreover, we may suppose that the determinants of individual welfare are separable, in the sense that one can vary without that causing a variation in the other components of welfare. Yet there are difficulties with both of these solutions. We cannot simply assume separability in the determinants of welfare. Perhaps personal circumstances and social factors interact to create the conditions of a person's welfare: after all, if treating people for rat-bites without caring about the housing conditions in which rats thrive is irrational, is it not equally irrational to treat people for stress without doing anything about their personal life which gives rise to the stress? So the premiss of separability may be false, and the practicality objection does not seem to give the *intrinsic* protection to a private sphere of personal life that theorists in the liberal tradition have typically wanted to establish.

One answer to this question is to see the problem in terms of our fundamental principle of autonomy, and to say that the presumption that persons should be free to form their own projects implies that the claim that others have upon them involves the transfer of alienable resources, rather than a personal commitment. (This is not to say, of course, that certain individuals may not choose to commit themselves as well as their resources to the welfare of others.) The limitation of public concern to material and social aspects of welfare can, therefore, be interpreted as springing from an intrinsic restriction on what can be claimed from those who would be the donors to a transfer. (This is one of the reasons why blood is such an untypical case for unilateral transfers in social policy: it is intensely personal, and yet it can be alienated, without harm, from donors.) If this is so it indicates that there is no hard and fast line to be drawn in terms of those components of the welfare of beneficiaries that may be affected by public action, apart from the line that might be drawn on grounds of practicality. This being the case, it promises to be even more difficult to draw a line between that component of a person's material welfare which is general and that component which is specific. Distinctions which at first seem categorical begin to shade into one another.

In order to see whether a useful distinction can be made between a concern for the general and the specific welfare of individuals, it is useful to return to the position of the social planner who is wondering whether a greater improvement in social welfare will come about by a marginal change toward equality in the general income distribution, or by a reduction in the inequality of consumption in certain specific scarce commodities or of certain specific characteristics like health status and educational status. There are two sorts of argument available to the planner that suggest that it will always be better to prefer a general redistribution to a specific redistribution. The first argument is that a specific redistribution will always be less efficient than a general redistribution, so that social welfare must necessarily be lower with a specific than with a general redistribution. The second argument is that even if the social welfare implications were the same, the promotion of specific aspects of welfare would always be more paternalist than the promotion of general welfare, and this would violate our conception of citizens as autonomous persons. To see the basis for the criticism of in-kind transfers, let us take a simplified case. Suppose someone lacks some specific scarce commodity, for example domestic help available to persons too old or infirm to do all their own housework. In the view of social planners social welfare will be raised by a transfer of resources to this person. The planners can arrange either for the commodity to be supplied in kind, or for the cost of the commodity to be transferred as an income supplement to the beneficiary. If they supply the commodity in kind, then, it has been argued, this will be less efficient than the straight income transfer. With an income transfer the beneficiary is free to choose the level of provision that is supplied in kind; but if the beneficiary fails to consume as much, this simply means that, from the beneficiary's own point of view, he or she will be better off without that quantity of domestic help. A specific transfer, therefore, seems to raise social welfare less than an income transfer, and also appears to leave recipients with less freedom of choice.[7] From the point of view of a theory that is committed to a subjective theory of the good and a conception of persons as autonomous agents, both these results of specific egalitarianism would seem very unfortunate.

Efficiency and specific egalitarianism

However, the case for a concern with general welfare, as represented by a preference for income over in-kind transfers, is not quite so easy to establish as this example suggests. To see why, consider first the problem of whether in-kind transfers are less efficient than income transfers. If we simply focus upon the position of the recipient, then in-kind transfers will always appear as inefficient. However, social planners should surely also be sensitive to the welfare of those who are net contributors to social programmes. If we assume that contributors are selfish, then tax-based transfers will impose a net welfare loss upon them. Under this assumption we should aim at a transfer mechanism that minimised the cost of achieving any given welfare level among recipients and this in turn would indicate a preference for income transfers. On the other hand, we may regard contributors as non-selfish, and the tax-transfer system as a device by which they realise their concern for those who are poorer than they are. On this interpretation, greater equality does not involve the balancing of a welfare gain to recipients against a welfare loss to donors, but instead involves a welfare gain to both donors and recipients, because one group cares positively about the welfare of the others. In these circumstances we have an example of what has been termed Pareto-optimal redistribution.[8] The implications of this interpretation of redistribution need tracing out in some detail to assess its significance for the efficiency of specific and general egalitarianism.

Now, at first sight there may seem to be something paradoxical in construing the tax-transfer scheme as a mutually beneficial device for contributors and recipients, since taxes are levied compulsorily, that is under threat of legal penalty if they are not paid. If transfers are motivated by an unselfish concern for others, why is it necessary to have the transfers accomplished by the instrument of compulsory taxation? It would seem that voluntary transfers could meet the need as well. One answer to this question is to say that under the assumptions of this approach, the welfare of the poor becomes a pure public good for the relatively affluent, and that, in so far as there are a large number of potential donors, each has an incentive to enjoy the benefits of the transfers being made without contributing to the costs. A calculus of individual benefit on the part of each donor, therefore, suggests that it is rational not to transfer anything voluntarily. Yet the consequence of every potential donor acting rationally in this way is that all are left worse off than they would be if some transfer were made. It would, therefore, be sensible for each donor to agree to a compulsory system of transfers provided other donors did likewise. The compulsion is not the motive forcing them to give but the device which assures them that they will not be isolated in giving. The calculating concern for others which this argument presupposes is rather different from the common-or-garden variety of altruistic concern that perhaps springs more readily to mind, since it requires people to be selfish in their unselfishness by estimating the benefit they derive from seeing an improvement in welfare in the object of their concern. Yet nothing in the assumptions of the conventional critique of in-kind transfers rules out this sort of concern for others. Nothing in these assumptions requires every individual's welfare to be independent of others rather than dependent upon them.[9]

What happens to the choice between cash and in-kind transfers when we allow donors to have preferences whose satisfaction turns on an increase in welfare of others? If donor concern is simply for the general welfare of others, then the answer to this question is 'not much'. Donors just try to put themselves into the shoes of recipients, and they will transfer to them until the marginal gain the donors receive from the transfer just equals the marginal loss they incur from not being able to do other things with their income. More precisely, we may say that a social planner enforcing a compulsory scheme will set the volume of transfers at a level at which this marginal condition is satisfied. Under these assumptions about motivation, nothing upsets the argument for the superiority of cash over in-kind transfers. However, if donors value specific features of the circumstances of recipients, then the position is changed. For example, donors may prefer the elderly to be assured of heating or home-help services, but not worry about their consumption of tobacco or drink; or they may want children to be assured of clothing and education, but not be worried about toys or pets. In other words, donor concern may not extend to the general welfare of transfer beneficiaries but only to specific components of it. If these are the motives at work, then the relative advantages of cash or in-kind transfers will switch. Since the price elasticity of goods transferred under welfare programmes is greater than the income elasticity of demand, it will be more efficient to subsidise in kind rather than in cash, since, for any given volume of transfers, the in-kind mechanism will generate a higher level of consumption for the specific commodity.[10]

Even within the assumptions of consumer sovereignty, therefore, there is no *general* argument for the superiority of cash over in-kind transfers. If we allow potential donors to have a certain type of concern for recipients, then a pattern of in-kind transfers will be the best way for the government to maximise social welfare, subject to the usual resource constraints. Specific subsidies will be efficient. Moreover, such an argument suggests that social planners will not necessarily be paternalistic in preferring in-kind transfers. They may simply be being responsive to the demands of members of society at large, rather than just the demands of recipients. Paternalist assumptions, therefore, are not necessary to justify in-kind transfers. It is also worth noting that the converse also holds. Just as in-kind transfers do not imply paternalism, so paternalism does not always imply in-kind transfers. For example, a social insurance policy that forces people to redistribute their incomes across their lifetimes in a certain way may be paternalistically motivated, but it does not involve in-kind transfers.

Is there any evidence that a specific set of concerns is exhibited among potential donors or taxpayers? If we were involved in a positive exercise to explain the emergence and structure of the welfare state, then we could use the observed pattern of expenditures as constituting evidence in part at least. We should have weak confirmation of a specific set of concerns by observing the consistency between the pattern of actual expenditures and the postulated motivation. However, in a normative exercise this simple consistency argument is unavailable to us, since the evidence we should be using could not serve independently to justify current practices. Evidence for the claim that donors and taxpayers have a specific set of concerns needs to be independent of the observed pattern of government expenditures, though of course these expenditures must be consistent with such a set of concerns. One sort of evidence we can use that falls into the appropriate category is attitudinal evidence. Although not directly collected for this purpose, the voter-surveys by Butler and Stokes[11] in the 1960s reveal some significant level of support for in-kind transfers, with respondents wanting the government to spend more on housing and education as well as retirement pensions. (Family allowances by contrast received rather a low level of support, suggesting that the questions were not picking up a simple willingness to acquiesce in proposals for more government spending.) Moreover, the level of support for such expenditures declined over the period of the survey, which is at least consistent with a rational response, in terms of diminishing marginal utility, to the increased level of public expenditure and rise in the standards of items like housing and education. The surveys commissioned by the Institute of Economic Affairs also provide some evidence for the existence of external psychic benefits from social policy programmes. Among those supporting higher social policy expenditure large proportions of respondents favoured this policy because they had egalitarian sentiments.[12]

Can we rest content with this justification for the logical plausibility, at least, of specific egalitarianism? Unfortunately the answer must be in the negative, for one reason if for no others. If the specific concerns that citizens exhibited towards one another were simply manifested in the tax-transfer system, then we should have at least a potential justification for specific egalitarianism. But the contrary is the case. If we take the concern with health status, for example, we can see that a medical service that delivered treatment to those in need would be a form of specific transfer from the well to the sick. But a concern for health status is also registered in such devices as public regulation of the environment, workplace health and safety and consumer-product safety. Each of these forms of regulation may have the effect of changing citizens' behaviour in such a way that affected citizens are made to show a greater concern for their own health than they otherwise would. In these circumstances the concern for health status does not involve a transfer of resources on the part of concerned individuals, but the imposition of public standards of conduct.

The reason why regulation of this sort calls into question the external benefits argument for specific egalitarianism is the dissimilarity between income transfers and public regulation as a way of controlling the behaviour of beneficiaries. With income transfers the benefit given is essentially made conditional upon the recipient satisfying his or her demand for greater material welfare in a particular form. The transfer will be Pareto-superior to the existing state of affairs if the donor or taxpayer wishes to see the beneficiary's welfare improved in just that way. However, with regulatory measures the person who is made subject to them may have his or her perceived welfare lowered, even if other citizens thereby derive satisfaction. In other words, regulatory devices typically do not satisfy the Pareto principle in their implementation. And yet it makes perfect sense to think of regulation as one way by which specific aspects of social welfare may be improved, and of its being one policy instrument among others for the promotion of benefits. For example, the banning of smoking in public places might be thought to promote health just as much as the supply of medical facilities to cope with smoking-related diseases.

If we take into account the full range of policy instruments that might be used to promote specific egalitarianism, we can see that although some of them are consistent with the Pareto principle others may not be. Specific egalitarianism seems driven therefore to question the principle that each person is the best judge of his or her own welfare, and thence towards questioning the value of the principle of freedom of choice.

Freedom of choice and specific egalitarianism

Specific egalitarianism appears to imply a rejection of the principle that each person is the best judge of his or her own welfare because in-kind transfers constrain the consumption choices of recipients. Empirical evidence is available to show that recipients of income transfers do not always spend their income as planners intend. For example, in experiments with housing allowances it was found that a smaller proportion of a straight income transfer was spent on housing than was spent when some of the transfer took the form of a voucher tied to housing consumption. If planners want, therefore, to give priority to improving the housing conditions of potential recipients, they will typically place a higher value on this aim than will recipients themselves.

To find this an objectionable feature of specific egalitarianism is to believe that the principle that each person is the best judge of his or her own welfare has a powerful justification. But on what basis can this principle be justified? The principle cannot always be justified by reference to a general commitment to a subjective theory of the good. That theory asserts that the good comprises those projects to which persons can commit themselves upon reflection and in the light of reliable information. These projects, however, cannot be identified with the set of preferences that persons hold at any particular time. Since an individual's preferences change over time, and the later preferences contain an element of regret for earlier preferences, we cannot identify a person's long-term good with any set of individual preferences. Moreover, an individual's preferences may also change depending on the role that he or she occupies: as a pedestrian or cyclist I may want safe motor vehicles and so favour vehicle safety inspections, whereas as a motorist I may resent the trouble and spending such checks cause. An individual may even exhibit a split mind about some forms of his or her own behaviour, as is not uncommon with smoking or drinking. Even when we make persons' evaluations of their circumstances the ultimate guide to public policy, we might still want to choose the most prudent of their preference profiles as being the true guide to their welfare, and this might indicate a reason for providing services in kind, rather than transfers in cash. For example, if people are likely to misspend and undervalue their use of energy, then they may subsequently come to regret their freedom when they incur fuel debts. In one sense, metered payment is paternalist, since it implies that people cannot be trusted to save for a bill; but it is striking how popular metered payment is among persons who recognise that they may not always budget correctly. The conceptual point that is illustrated by these examples is that measures controlling behaviour or consumption are not, simply by virtue of exercising control, an infringement upon an individual's freely chosen conception of his or her own good. As with metered electricity payment, such control may well be a method for helping individuals realise one among a number of conflicting elements in their own conception of the good.

Is it possible to specify the circumstances in which persons are prone to make mistaken decisions that adversely affect their own welfare? Three circumstances in particular seem likely to give rise to this difficulty: where the consequences of a decision are remote in time; where it is difficult to apportion responsibility for those outcomes that do occur; and where there is a great deal of uncertainty about complex factual matters. These are the circumstances that are usually involved, for example, in justification of compulsory health insurance and health services generally. When taking out health insurance one is seeking to protect oneself against contingencies that are remote in time. And as the development of industrial injury and accident compensation benefits shows, the apportionment of responsibility may be so difficult that a general 'no-fault' solution is preferable. To illustrate the genuine uncertainty that exists in these matters one has only to think of the problems involved in finding a 'safe' occupation, given the complex factual problems in determining whether substances to which one may be exposed are toxic, and if so, how toxic. If the public authorities direct their welfare-maximising activity towards a specific component of individuals' welfare, like health, then they will often be in a better position than individuals to appraise standards and performance.

This is not to say, however, that the public authorities will always be in a better position than individuals. Where individual citizens have regular experience of conditions then they will often be in a better position than social planners to decide on the suitability of a certain pattern of consumption or habit of life. An example of individuals being in a better position than social planners to make decisions occurred over the policy of the 'trike' in Britain. The trike was a three-wheeled vehicle especially designed for handicapped persons and available to them under the health service. Experience of the vehicle by drivers, however, suggested certain problems of safety, and eventually the vehicle was withdrawn and a mobility allowance paid instead to help handicapped persons with transport.[13] Here it is clear that regular contact with the vehicle put individuals in a better position than social planners to know what was in their best interests.

These empirical examples are not meant to show either that social planners on balance have the advantage in estimating individuals' interests, or that individuals on balance have the advantage. All they are intended to do is show that the question of who is in a better position is often an empirical one and cannot be settled by *a priori* appeal to the principle that each person is the best judge of his or her own welfare. At this point the logic of the objection to specific egalitarianism is likely to move from a concern with the maximisation of welfare, to the principle of freedom of choice and the value of maintaining freedom of consumer and citizen choice in the face of planners' preferences. Our goal, it might be said, is not simply the maximisation of welfare but the maximisation of welfare subject to the constraint of preserving individual, and household, choice.

When we discuss the principle of freedom of choice we should distinguish between the case where freedom of choice is valued instrumentally, as a method for attaining other goals, and the case where freedom of choice is valued intrinsically. So far we have looked at the instrumental value of freedom of choice (or rather, its implied corollary in the preference for cash over in-kind transfers) in the arguments concerning the principle of efficiency. But this is not the only way in which freedom of choice might be valued instrumentally. Hayek,[14] for example, is opposed to government transfers in kind because he sees them as a route by which the powers of the state will be augmented. All such instrumental evaluations of freedom of choice may be left to one side, however, because in as much as they depend upon empirical premises about the effects of certain policies, they cannot provide an argument of principle for preserving freedom. And it is just such an argument of principle that we need if we are to provide a genuine constraint upon the goal of maximising social welfare.

One way of defending the intrinsic value of freedom of choice is to say that making up one's own mind has essential value. As John Stuart Mill[15] put it: 'He who lets the world, or his own portion of it, choose his plan of life for him, has no need of any other faculty than the ape-like one of imitation.' Yet this contention cannot in itself provide an argument for favouring cash rather than in-kind transfers. There are two reasons involved here, the one logical and the other psychological. The logical reason is that in-kind transfers do not prevent people making up their own minds, unless recipients are compelled to accept the transfer rather than have it available as a right they may choose to exercise. The psychological reason stems from the simple fact of scarce mental resources. There are only a limited number of items to which we can devote thought and attention, and there is no reason why concern about the sorts of needs that in-kind services satisfy should be important in developing the capacity for autonomous choice. Perhaps not having to worry about them frees us to concern ourselves with more intricate choices.

A second way of defending the intrinsic value of freedom is to say that the number of choices available to us is a good in itself. The more options we have open to us the better. On these grounds cash transfers would generally be preferred to in-kind transfers, since the cash mode of transfer must increase the number of choices available to us. To see why, all we have to do is note that with cash transfers the same consumption mix is available to an individual as would be available with in-kind transfers, but with cash transfers other options are available as well. The weakness with this argument is the weakness with all arguments about the good of freedom that rely merely on counting the number of options available to an agent as a measure of freedom. For the good of freedom must depend not simply on the number of options available to us but also on their quality. An increase in the number of choices available to me must strictly be regarded as an increase in freedom, but it cannot be regarded as an increase in the good of freedom unless those choices are in some sense significant for me. If I now have the choice between two brands of chewing gum rather than one, that represents an increase in my freedom but it does not represent an increase in the good of freedom to me, since neither are choices that I would want to exercise. The upshot of this distinction between an increase in freedom and an increase in the good of freedom is that it is not of itself a sufficient argument to say of cash transfers that they increase freedom. They must also increase significant freedom. If we say this, however, we are back to the sort of judgements about individual welfare that we discussed in the application of the efficiency condition to the maximisation of social welfare. The principle of freedom of choice has not provided us with a general argument against specific egalitarianism.

However, it might be objected at this point that although no direct conclusions can be drawn about the value of freedom of choice in choosing between alternative modes of economic transfer, some embodiment of freedom of choice in the social welfare system must be taken seriously by any system of social choice that claims to give priority to the idea of individual autonomy. As we have seen, this idea emerges powerfully in the requirements that we impose upon the minimum income guarantee, and there is therefore some reason why it might emerge as important in considering distribution above the minimum. One response to this problem is to say that freedom of choice is important as an ideal, but that the ideal does not always imply freedom of choice within markets, but may instead be interpreted in terms of the right to participate in social planning and collective decision-making institutions. As we shall see (in Chapter 10), the principle of autonomy does carry implications for the democratic control of social welfare institutions. Another response to the challenge is to say that there may be a clash of values involved in a respect for freedom of choice and the promotion of social welfare, and that in order to reconcile this conflict we need some criterion that makes it prima facie plausible that for some goods specific provision be made. The task of the next section is to develop such a criterion.

An alternative argument for specific egalitarianism

In order to develop a positive argument as to why certain specific scarce commodities, services or statuses should be picked out for special attention, we need first to notice a distinction that is both important and frequently made, namely the distinction between the reasons *for* an institution or social practice and the reasons that should be operative *within* that institution or social practice.[16] The most frequently cited example of this distinction arises in the institution of punishment. Here it is important to distinguish the reason for having the institution, which is for the deterrence of crime, and the reasons operative within the institution, which involve considerations of desert and responsibility. Unless we made the distinction between different types of reason we should soon run into a contradiction in the application of these two types of consideration, since in order to deter we might have to punish individuals who were not deserving of punishment and we often find it appropriate to punish individuals for whom no deterrent effect flows from the punishment.[17] Complex institutions and practices develop their own internal standards and goals which are distinct from the justification that can be advanced for having these institutions in the first place. These standards and goals provide reasons for treating persons in certain ways when they enter into the institution.

Just as with the institution of punishment, so with institutions like education, legal services and medical care, standards and goals internal to those institutions prescribe ways in which individuals are to be treated. As Bernard Williams[18] puts it: 'Leaving aside preventive medicine, the proper ground of distribution of medical care is ill-health: this is a necessary truth.' The necessity of the proposition derives from its being constitutive of the standards and goals internal to the practice of medical care. But is this a correct description of those standards? In order to see whether it is or not, we note first that the statement that ill-health is the proper ground of medical care is a claim about necessary and sufficient conditions. As a claim about necessary conditions the statement is merely asserting that those who are medically fit are not entitled to medical care by the standards internal to the practice of medicine. This is surely uncontentious: there can be no *medical* reason for giving medical treatment to the well. The obvious exception is treatment for hypochondriacs; but the equally obvious interpretation of that exception is that what is really being treated is the hypochondria, and that condition is sufficient to constitute a person as being unwell.

The claim that ill-health is a sufficient condition for medical treatment, is, however, more contentious. For the practice of medicine may be defined in such a way that ill-health alone is not a sufficient condition for treatment. This can happen in capitalist medical institutions where the ability to pay is also important, or it can happen in socialist medicine where the allocation of treatment is biased towards the working population and away from the dependent population. In such systems ill-health is not a sufficient ground for treatment. It would always be possible, of course, to meet these counter-examples with the response that it is just for these reasons that they are not properly medical institutions; but this would merely be a verbal triumph and would not help us in choosing among these different types of institution as to which was best. We have to recognise that an explicit choice of values is involved here. However, having said that, we can also recognise that, in the present context, the value choice has already been made, since the contractarian theory of choice within which we are working already implies a particular conception of the relation in which potential beneficiaries stand to entitlements. The aim of social policy above the minimum is directed towards promoting the welfare of individuals in society. This blocks any policy recommendation that resources should be allocated to individuals only in so far as its implementation will promote the contribution that those individuals can make to the welfare of others. It is precisely this latter principle that is involved in giving priority of medical care to the working population.

The conclusion to be drawn from this is, as Gutman[19] has pointed out, that Williams's internal-reasons argument presupposes a wider moral framework within which the argument is carried out, but that this moral framework is one that is in any case consistent with, and indeed implied by, contract theory. If we specify the internal standards and goals of medicine consistent with a contractarian theory of social choice, then a correct characterisation will make ill-health the sufficient, and hence proper, ground of medical treatment. Exactly similar arguments will apply to the supply of legal services and education. In these cases, one's legal status or one's ability to profit from education will be the relevant tests of allocation.

This approach does supply us with a special and positive reason for picking out certain aspects of a person's well-being and directing the attention of planners towards those specific characteristics. The reason is that unless such special attention were paid, the practice of medicine, or education or the law could not be properly realised in a society. The argument is exactly analogous to the argument for separating questions of the efficiency of punishment from the practice of legal institutions. Unless that separation is made, justice in individual cases may be blocked by the application of standards that are inconsistent with the principles that govern the practice. To introduce questions of payment into the relationship between doctor and patient would be analogous to a judge deciding whether or not an accused person deserved punishment by the size of his or her bank balance. Specific egalitarianism, therefore, involves a decision to take the standards and goals internal to certain institutions in society and to make those standards and goals part of a broader political purpose.

There are two remaining problems to be dealt with, however, when considering the force of this argument. The first problem is why we choose the particular characterisation of medical and other professional activities that we do. For there may exist a discrepancy between the internal goal of the activity and the personal goals of those practising that activity. Suppose, as Nozick[20] suggests, we substitute for the idea of doctoring the idea of 'schmoctering'. Schmoctering is the practice of curing illness *and* making money out of patients. Those for whom a discrepancy exists between their own personal goals and the internal goals of the practice might find the redescribed practice of schmoctering exactly to their taste. Why then should the characterisation of doctoring be preferred to that of schmoctering? One answer is that doctoring, rather than schmoctering, just is our conception of medicine. But even if things were not so fixed in the conceptual firmament, there would still be a liberal reason for favouring the doctoring conception. It is a long-established part of liberal theory that the avaricious designs of producers should not be allowed to interfere with consumer satisfactions. Adam Smith's famous remark to the effect that people of the same trade seldom meet together, even for merriment and diversion, but the conversation ends in a conspiracy against the public, or in some contrivance to raise prices, is a reminder of the concern that liberal theorists have had that producer groups should not define the economic game in their own way. The classic liberal prescription is, of course, the market; but since there are reasons in this case for not making ability to pay a condition of enjoying the service, this particular solution is not open to us. And so some other institutional device will have to be set up to guard against schmoctering.

The second problem, which Nozick also raises, is: why pick on medicine? Even if we add legal services and education we still have only a very limited range of services. Why not, as Nozick suggests, establish the internal goal of barbering as a social purpose to be achieved? One reply to this question again turns on our actual conception of these activities. Barbering seems closer to schmoctering than it does to doctoring. But there is another sort of answer that can be given. Suppose we take the internal standards of various institutions and allow them to define needs. What can we say about the comparative efficiency of satisfying needs defined in this way by means of cash rather than in-kind transfers? It turns out that the answer depends on the variability of the needs involved and the inequality in the distribution of income.[21] Roughly speaking, the more variable the needs among recipients and the more equally income is distributed the greater the superiority of cash transfers; whereas the more similar the needs and the more unequal the income distribution, the greater is the superiority of in-kind transfers. This technical result makes a lot of intuitive sense. What it says is that if needs are variable then standard in-kind transfers, for example the same meal to each person or the same heating allowance to each household, will be less efficient than cash transfers when incomes are reasonably equal, and individuals can choose their own distinctive patterns of consumption. On the other hand, when incomes are unequally distributed, individuals with high needs are more likely to have them unsatisfied, since they may not be able to afford the purchases. If we interpret the provision of certain services as supplying a right of access, then this result can be applied to the range of services we have been discussing; for the need for this right will be fairly standard among the population, whereas the need for a right of access to barbering services will not be standard. We have, then, in drawing attention to the crucial issue of variability of needs established a prima facie case for distinguishing some services from others.

In concluding our rationale for specific egalitarianism there are three remaining points to be made.

Firstly, because the argument turns in part upon judgements about the variability of needs, there will always be a question mark about whether some services should be classified as having high or low need variability. This residual problem of classification may explain the way in which views change about the workings of the social services. Housing at one time will seem to be an area where non-market rationing devices are more appropriate than markets, whereas with economic growth greater weight may be put on the market. An explanation for this may be that at certain stages of economic development the needs of at least a certain section of the population are fairly similar, comprising such things as running water, good sanitation and light. With economic growth, however, households have more opportunity to express their own individual preferences for more than basic features, and so a market system of allocation seems more appropriate. Similarly, the demand for medicine may become less standardised. For example, if the demand for non-standard medicine, like acupuncture, increases, there may well be a case for forms of provision that are capable of reflecting a variety of tastes about forms of treatment.

Secondly, although the first point shows that there still remain areas of judgement as to what are similar or dissimilar types of need, our rationale has at least provided an explanation as to why specific egalitarianism should take the form of regulatory devices as well as the transfer of certain specific commodities, a rationale that we noted the conventional public-good account of altruism failed to provide. There is no reason why the internal goals of the preventive health services cannot be extended into a public purpose. Whether we should choose to allocate resources to preventive or to curative practices then becomes a matter of comparative efficiency appropriately defined.

Thirdly, nothing in the above argument provides a conclusive account of the administrative form that specific services should take. For example, there are practical problems involved in establishing legal services on the model of the British national health service, since such a system would be likely to encourage frivolous litigation. Similarly, it is not possible to say solely by appeal to the above argument which forms of subsidised health care are better than others. Consider the variety that is available, including the German, Dutch and Belgium systems in which citizens are usually required to insure with private agencies against the cost of care, the French scheme in which there is a mixture of public and private insurance cover, the Canadian system in which there is prepaid public insurance against medical costs, or the British arrangements in which the majority of suppliers are nationalised.[22] Choosing between these systems will involve considerations other than the desire to achieve a redistribution of health care. These considerations will be largely administrative matters, for example the problems created by a federal rather than a unitary political system, or the problem of cost containment in an insurance system operating on a fee-for-service basis compared with the problem of emigrating medical personnel in a nationalised system in which cost control can be tight. None of these are matters of principle. The remaining matter of principle is how egalitarian one should be. There again our argument does not address that problem: for the argument has only shown that it may be proper for a social planner to prefer greater equality in the distribution of some scarce commodities and characteristics that in the general distribution of material advantage. How much equality is necessary for social welfare to be maximised is another question.

7

Social Rights

In the development of the argument so far we have worked without the concept of a right. Yet there are a number of reasons why we need to address the problems raised in the politics of social policy by the language of rights. In the first place, the language of rights is used extensively, some would say too extensively, in discussions of social policy problems. Particularly in matters of distribution, appeal is often made to the rights of the disadvantaged as a reason for rectifying inequalities in the prevailing allocation of resources. Given the prevalence of the notion of rights it would be useful if the theory that we have developed could give sense to the idea, and impose a logical structure on the use of the language of rights. Secondly, the welfare state is in part characterised by the number and scope of legal rights that citizens hold against the state, for example rights to income maintenance, to education, to housing and to employment protection. We need to be able to understand the form of these rights if we are to understand the nature of political obligation and identity in modern societies, and we need also to understand the justifications that can be offered in defence of these legal rights. Thirdly, the account of rights that I offer in this chapter is intended to form a bridge between the discussion in Chapters 3 to 6 and the discussion in Chapters 8 to 10. The earlier discussion was concerned with the justification that could be offered for certain social welfare institutions; the later discussion is concerned with the appraisal of practices within those institutions. I shall argue that the concept of a social right forms a convenient link between these two discussions, providing another way of thinking about the conclusion of the earlier discussion and also having implications for the later discussion.

Before discussing the logical form of the idea of rights, however, we shall need a preliminary distinction between legal or positive rights on the one hand and moral or human rights on the other. Legal or positive rights are those rights that persons have by virtue of some legal code or customary practice within society. For example, I have the right to vote in UK general elections, but not in the elections that take place in other countries. The legal codes of each country bestow or deny me the right as the case may be. Human rights by contrast are less tangible, being bestowed or denied by virtue of a moral code. For example, most moral codes bestow upon persons the right not to be physically assaulted by others. As a moral right, this holds typically against all other persons. The right may be forfeited in some circumstances, for example when one person assaults another and so loses his or her own right, but normally the right is possessed by all persons against all other persons. General moral rights of this sort, therefore, form one sort of moral right, along with special moral rights that arise from particular relations between persons, as when one person has the right to the performance of an action that the second has promised.

Both positive and moral rights function so as to stake out some portion of a person's interests or conduct to be given special protection. To cite a right is to cite a claim to which some special intrinsic importance is to be attached, at least in the sense of requiring some special burden of proof to be discharged for ignoring the right. The fundamental distinction between positive and human rights turns on the procedures that are involved in order to establish the existence of these rights and the manner in which the corresponding burden of proof may be discharged. With positive rights it is a question of showing that the appropriate legal or constitutional procedures have been followed in establishing the right. With human rights, by contrast, it is a question of showing that a moral or ethical argument leads to a conclusion in which the right is established. (Some assertions of human rights, of course, rest merely on the claim that such rights are 'self-evident'; this may be thought a degenerate case of the more general formula.) Just as sentences in general take their meaning from the conditions that have to be satisfied in order for them to be true, so claims to the existence of rights take their character from the procedures that must be followed in order to establish their existence.

Although positive and human rights can be distinguished in this way, the more general relationship that exists between them is not at all easy to specify. For example, some theorists have held that the function of a legal system, as an instrument of government, is to grant protection and enforcement of basic human rights. The proposition in the US Declaration of Independence that governments are instituted among men for the protection of their natural and inalienable rights and John Locke's[1] account of the origin of political society are both examples of this view. In this sort of account, the set of human rights becomes the ground for the set of legal rights. Alternatively, it may be argued that legal rules are not properly so-called unless they satisfy certain conditions embodying rights. For example, it may be argued that the rules of natural justice, for instance that no one should be judge in his or her own case or that there should be no retrospective legislation, are grounded in a right of fair and equitable treatment, and that no rule ought to be called a law unless it is consistent with these principles. Moreover, there are legal systems in which judges have gone against the letter of the law in arriving at judgements whose essential point turns on invoking a moral principle, like that of no one profiting from wrongs they have committed.[2]

These are complex and much discussed issues. In order to avoid confusion of terminology I shall simply and stipulatively state a position about them.[3] I shall assume the following. We can separate the question of when a rule is a legal rule (and consequently when a right is a legal right) from the question of whether a body of rules designated as legal rules satisfies the conditions that we should want such a body of rules to satisfy if persons are to live together in a political community governing their relationships with some minimum mutual respect for their individual interests. In other words, we can distinguish the definitional question of when is a rule a legal rule from the normative question of whether those rules that are legal rules satisfy certain standards of justice. This is not to deny the point that Hart[4] notes, namely that there are legal systems, as in the USA, in which 'the ultimate criteria of legal validity explicitly incorporate principles of justice or substantive moral values'. The practice of the law may involve judges making regular appeal not only to statutes and codes but also to widely held principles in the community; but this is quite a separate matter from the issue of whether principles so invoked entitle the resultant rules to be dubbed laws, rather than laws satisfying principles of justice.[5]

The concept of a right

Despite these differences between positive and human rights, depending on the way their existence is demonstrated, there remain significant formal similarities between the two types of right in their respective logical stuctures. This is fortunate, since legal theorists have worked on the concept of a legal right and have produced important and useful classifications of such rights. We can exploit the logical similarities between positive and human rights, using the analysis of the former to throw light on the latter.

A particularly useful classification of rights is that suggested by Hohfeld.[6] Hohfeld divides rights into four types, which he terms: liberties, claims, immunities and powers. By a 'liberty' is meant a right whose exercise does not imply that other people are under a duty to secure the ends for which the permitted action is undertaken. The usual examples of liberties in this sense are rights involving people engaged in competitive actions with one another. For example, if two groups of deep-sea divers are trying to recover some sunken treasure, then each group is at liberty to recover the treasure, but neither is under any obligation to allow the other to do so. 'Claim' rights, by contrast, do impose a correlative duty to help secure the action or condition protected by the right. For example, the right to be free from assault is a claim-right: it implies a duty upon persons to ensure that one is not subject to assault. 'Powers' and 'immunities' both concern the ability of persons or institutions to determine the rights and duties of others. Typically, for example, local authorities are given powers to make by-laws. Their rights then involve the ability to determine the rights and duties of those who fall within their jurisdiction. Immunities constitute the counterpart to powers: they are the right to be free from the exercise of someone's powers. When diplomats are granted immunity they are protected from the operation of the law as it would normally apply to them as residents.

Actual rights may be regarded as complexes of these different elements.[7] Any particular right may involve something from each of these differing conceptions. For example, the right to freedom of speech can be regarded in part as a claim-right, because other people are under an obligation to allow you to publish or to speak, and in part as an immunity, since some law-making agencies are forbidden from exercising powers which would forbid you enjoying that right. Thus, when the US Bill of Rights says that Congress shall pass no law abridging the freedom of speech or of the press, this grants an immunity to those who may wish to publish, which is in addition to the protection given them by the obligations laid upon other citizens to allow publication. As Hart[8] points out, many constitutional rights may best be understood as comprising primarily immunities of this sort.

As social change takes place, so a society's conception of its rights changes as well. Hohfeld's fourfold classification helps us understand some of the developments that have taken place in the conception of rights in the welfare state during the twentieth century. Thus, it is often said that the welfare state has seen an expansion in the positive rights, the rights of citizenship, held by individuals. In particular, it is argued that the gains in civil rights of the eighteenth century (especially rights on arrest and trial) and in political rights in the nineteenth century (especially the political emancipation of the working classes) have been complemented by gains in social rights in the twentieth century (especially the rights of social and economic security). On this account there has been an expansion in the number of rights that citizens have been able to enjoy in the twentieth century.[9]

Although this account captures the essence of the evolution of positive rights over the last three centuries, it does not seem quite correct to describe the twentieth-century developments as constituting an increase in the *number* of social and economic rights enjoyed by citizens. Rather, what has happened is that those rights have changed their *character*, and instead of being Hohfeldian liberties have now become claim-rights. For example, members of society in the nineteenth and early part of the twentieth century enjoyed the right to work, but this right was interpreted as the right to compete for work with others in the labour market. It was not construed as a right to be ensured of the conditions within which one could work, with the implication that corresponding to this claim there was a duty upon governments to ensure that those conditions were established. The changing conception of the right to work, therefore, has been to turn it from a Hohfeldian liberty into a claim-right. Moreover, the claims embodied in the right are becoming stronger, with correspondingly stronger duties imposed upon governments. As Furniss and Tilton[10] point out, the positive labour market policy of the Swedish welfare state now includes as an objective not only that citizens should be assured work, but also that they should be assured meaningful work that allows opportunities for self-development. This provides us with a good example of the way in which traditional economic and social rights are reinterpreted in the evolution of the welfare state so that their claim character comes to assume greater significance.

We can similarly use Hohfeld's classification of rights as a tool for understanding the exact nature of current political arguments about the status of welfare rights. For example, one major issue in the modern theory of welfare rights is whether such rights should be incorporated within the set of basic constitutional rights or not. From one point of view this may seem to be a non-issue. For example, even if the right to social security were made a constitutional right in those states with documentary constitutions, the government of the day would still have to decide on the form of contribution to the social security fund and the benefits the fund paid, and so the effective maintenance of social security rights would still be a matter of policy decision for the government of the day. Yet there would be some effect from making welfare rights an integral part of a documentary constitution. They would gain the status of immunities alongside other constitutional rights. In countries like Britain, where no special legislative procedure is required to make a constitutional change, this might not of itself make much difference. But arguably it could make a great deal of difference to the secure expectations that citizens could have of their welfare rights in countries that have a constitution based upon the principle of the separation of powers, where the courts have power to strike down unconstitutional legislation. Moreover, it can be argued that even in Britain the idea of rights as immunities helps make sense of those rights to welfare services supplied by local authorities. Thus the legal obligation upon local housing authorities to rehouse those whom they have evicted from their own property can be interpreted as an immunity held by council tenants against their being made completely homeless. The idea of rights, then, can function in a variety of ways in different contexts depending on which element of the liberty–claim–power–immunities complex is uppermost at the time.

Human rights and social rights

Earlier we noted that one view of the relation between positive and human rights is as follows: human rights should, where necessary, find institutional protection in positive rights. Locke's argument for political authority provides an example of this sort of argument: according to Locke, the difficulties involved in the private enforcement of natural rights provide a reason for giving such rights the institutional protection that is afforded rights in political society. Now, such a position might be taken to imply that all such rights should be given positive protection (or, perhaps, more weakly, that all such rights have a prima facie claim to be given positive protection); but it does not imply that all positive rights are grounded in human rights, or natural rights, as Locke would term them. There may be other reasons, apart from a concern with human rights, why individuals should be given positive rights in political society. Not all positive rights will correspond to human rights. The welfare state secures to persons certain social and economic rights as positive rights. So an obvious question to ask is: are these social and economic rights among that set of positive rights that correspond to natural or human rights, or are they among that set of positive rights whose justification does not presuppose that they are natural or human rights?

In earlier chapters we have relied upon the principle of autonomy to generate a claim that minimum needs be met, and also upon a contractarian argument to cover the problem of distribution above the minimum. Social and economic rights are regarded as part of that bundle of goods that enter into the determination of individual welfare. In other words, according to this conception, social and economic rights are to be regarded as goods to be distributed under appropriate principles of social choice. The idea of a right does not figure in the specification of those principles. Positive social and economic rights are justified primarily in terms of the contribution they can make towards preserving autonomy. Is there any sense in additionally invoking the notion of human rights as underlying positive welfare rights?

The idea that the social and economic rights implemented within modern welfare states correspond to an underlying set of human rights is a pervasive notion. It is, for example, incorporated into the United Nations' Declaration of Human Rights.[11] And yet the idea is not without its difficulties. Maurice Cranston[12] has suggested three criteria to help us judge whether a right is a human right. They are the criteria of universality, practicality and paramount importance. Some, at least, among the set of social and economic rights contained within the UN Declaration fail to meet all three of these tests. Some of the rights are not universal: the right to holidays with pay is restricted to the employee class, for example. Some may not be practical: poor countries may not be able to establish adequate systems of social security for their citizens or systems of higher education that are freely available to all on merit. And some may not be of paramount importance: the right to participation in the cultural life of the community and the arts seems less important than the rights to be protected from slavery, arbitrary arrest, and cruel or degrading punishment. By contrast with social rights, Cranston wants to argue that the traditional civil and political liberties do pass the three tests of universality, practicality and paramount importance.

Although Cranston's threefold test may appear to discriminate between positive rights that can be given a grounding in human rights and positive rights that cannot be so grounded, there are a number of shortcomings in his argument which mean that it fails to yield the suggested conclusion. Thus, the test of paramount importance may rule out some of the social and economic rights that have been proposed, like cultural participation, but it is not clear that it can rule them all out. Social and economic rights guarantee people the right of material subsistence, so it can be argued that they do pass the test of fundamental importance. After all, what could be more important than guaranteeing to people the material conditions in which they could come to exercise their political and civil rights? The test of practicality also fails to discriminate adequately between social and economic rights on the one hand and civil and political liberties on the other. The proposed basis for this test is the difference between rights that require positive action on the part of governments and rights that require governments merely to forbear from interfering with the lives of their citizens. To implement the right to social security, for example, requires governments to institute costly schemes of economic transfers, whereas the right to freedom of political association requires governments to forbear from imprisoning political opponents, closing down critical newspapers, and the like. Since forbearance is usually easier than activity, it seems that civil and political rights always have the edge on social and economic rights in terms of practicality. And yet there is an unjustified asymmetry here. If the threats to civil and political liberties came merely from the government the suggested contrast in terms of practicality would be justified. But governments also have the positive duty of protecting persons from breaches of their civil and political liberties intended by other citizens, and it is not at all clear that in this regard the civil and political rights are easier to implement than the social and economic ones.[13] Can it really be said that it is easier, for example, for the government of the UK to secure civil and political liberties in Northern Ireland than it is for the governments of many developing countries to secure minimally adequate standards of sanitation, water supply and education? Moreover, even if there is a problem of practicality for poor countries in implementing some of the policies that would be required to secure social and economic rights, these rights cannot be ruled out as impractical unless we beg the question as to whether rich countries do not have a part to play in supplying the resources for poor countries to implement the appropriate policies.

It is Cranston's test of universality that provides the real difficulty for the proponent of the view that social rights are natural rights, since it is possible to imagine forms of social life in which no one would have responsibility for the maintenance of social rights, although other types of rights were still respected. One way of putting this point is to construct a 'state of nature' test. This test requires that any right, to qualify as a natural or human right, must be imaginable in a Lockean state of nature, in which persons are free to appropriate the material resources for their subsistence, but within which constraints are placed on the way in which persons can affect others. Many of the traditional civil and political liberties, for example, freedom of speech, religion, association and travel, are conceivable in such a state of nature. These rights require non-interference in the right-holders' actions and the absence of government does not mean that facilities are lacking for the right-holders to undertake the appropriate actions. Moreover, even those traditional civil and political liberties which do require positive, facilitative action by governments, for example the rights to be tried by an independent tribunal or to have the vote, can be thought of as the analogues, within political society, of the right in a Lockean state of nature to enforce one's own rights against invasion by others. In other words, the traditional civil and political rights do pass the test of being imaginable in a Lockean state of nature.

One reason why social rights might seem not to pass the state-of-nature test is that they involve rights of recipience, by which holders of the correlative duty must undertake positive action, and not merely rights to freedom of action, which require only that the correlative duty-holder forbear from interference. However, this is *not* a crucial distinction between civil and political rights on the one hand and social rights on the other. Even within a state of nature there might be a right to aid from others in times of distress, and this would imply an active duty on the part of the more fortunate. The reason for postulating such a duty of aid follows Kant's[14] reasoning to the effect that, although a human society might be imagined in which persons did not care for the positive happiness of others, the persons in such a society would not be acting in accordance with the idea of treating other persons as ends, and not merely as means. Rights of mutual aid are clearly imaginable in a Lockean state of nature, even though such a state of nature would not contain any machinery for enforcing them. This is not to say that all, or perhaps most, of the rights in the UN Declaration can be thought of as the analogues to such state-of-nature rights of mutual aid, but some of them may be.

However, even if one can imagine an analogue to the case of social rights in a Lockean state of nature, the attempt to define social rights in terms of natural rights seems precarious. Some of the most important social rights presuppose economically developed social and political institutions, and they are important precisely because people do not live in a Lockean state of nature. The importance of formal education in the UN Declaration provides an example of rights that fall into this category. It is precisely because persons in the modern world grow up in an interdependent society that the provision of education is of such strategic importance. The organised use of state power to provide basic and secondary educational facilities is adapted to a world that has evolved beyond the conditions of the state of nature. Similarly, social security provision might be thought of as the contemporary analogue to the rights and duties of mutual aid in the state of nature, but it would be better to think of it as a response to the fact that Locke's condition of 'enough and as good' cannot be satisfied in the acquisition of private property in the modern world, and that individuals now need organised social protection if they are to secure for themselves the means of subsistence.

The notion of universality in the formulation of social rights has to be construed therefore as meaning something like 'applicable to all persons at a particular state of economic and social development'.

This weakens the sense of social rights as natural or human rights, since the latter are typically thought of as having very general, trans-historical application. Does this mean, then, that the language of rights is fundamentally misplaced when dealing with social and economic goals? The suggestion that the language of rights forces arguments about social policy into the wrong conceptual mould has been frequently made, and is best expressed by Brian Barry[15] in his remark that the equivalent to the right to an adequate standard of living would be the right to a moderate amount of free speech. The latter is hardly what the proponents of the natural right to free speech have had in mind, and if it is the equivalent of the former then it shows the conceptual inadequacy of harnessing the concept of rights to matters of economic distribution. More generally, we might say that political and civil rights tend to be a matter of a categorical status enjoyed by persons, whereas the provision of economic and social benefits tends to be a matter of marginal and incremental adjustments of available resources.

Despite these considerations I am inclined to think that there is some point in using the language of rights when talking about certain aspects of social policy. In the first place, the contrast between the categorical nature of the claims to civil and political liberties and the marginal nature of the claim to economic benefits can be overdrawn. The right to freedom from physical assault provides a good example of how this is so. It is clear that modern governments do not, and cannot, guarantee unconditional physical security to their citizens, just as some governments cannot guarantee social and economic security. Policies on policing and the protection of neighbourhoods typically involve marginal decisions about the allocation of resources and require, implicitly or explicitly, a judgement by the authorities about acceptable levels of crime and hence about the extent to which it is acceptable to fall short of protecting the rights of citizenship. Moreover, the language of rights is also important, not in defining the content of social rights, but in indicating the priority that is to be attached to the attainment of certain goals. In this respect, Barry's analogy between the right to free speech and the right to a minimum income seems misleading. The function of the rights assertion is not to define the content of the claim, but to indicate its force. The similarity between the two phrases does not lie in the variable term that specifies in any particular case what 'the right to X' means. The similarity lies rather in the priority and status that is being made for the two claims. Just as sentences with quite different meanings (for example, 'There is thin ice over there' and 'There is a bull in the field') can be intended as warnings, so quite different sorts of claims may be thought of as rights.[16]

Within a theory, like the one I have earlier tried to develop, in which certain basic forms of good are seen as the material and cultural prerequisites for individual autonomy, the attainment of which is taken as a political priority, it does not seem inappropriate to express these claims as rights. To do so indicates the force with which the claim is being advanced. However, as Peter Jones[17] has pointed out, to use the language of rights in this context is to presuppose a limit to the quantity of welfare goods and services that can reasonably be regarded as a right. Once the social minimum has been guaranteed, the urgency of welfare provision will decline relative to other social goals. Unless we assume that additional increments of health care, education, housing and so on should outweigh any number of increments of other goods, there must come a point where we favour other goals apart from welfare goals. As individuals we do this, and there is no reason why we should not do it as a community.

This conclusion explains why the language of social rights is so fundamental to modern social policy and yet so lacking in application in many practical areas of policy. For the bulk of modern social policy is taken up with provision above the minimum that is needed to secure the conditions of personal autonomy, and in these areas the language of social rights as human rights is inherently inapplicable, since no overriding priority can be given to any particular policy goal. Such questions as the degree of progression to be built into the tax system, the balance between hospital or community care or the merits of streamed-versus-unstreamed classes are of their nature immune to solution in terms of the language of rights. High heaven may reject the lore of nicely calculated less or more, but modern policy-makers cannot do the same.

On the present theory, then, social rights are such because they comprise goods which are preconditions for the maintenance of personal autonomy, and this is why their provision should be given priority. Recently, however, Henry Shue[18] has produced an argument that would conceptually, and not merely empirically, link economic security and political and civil liberties. If this argument were valid, then it would be impossible to conceive of a state of affairs in which civil and political rights were maintained but not the right to economic security. The thought-experiment of the Lockean state of nature, by which we established the distinction between civil and political liberties and social rights would be inappropriate. The premiss of Shue's argument is that it is logically impossible to separate the conditions under which rights are enjoyed from the enjoyment of the rights themselves. For example, being in a state of physical security is part of what it means to enjoy civil and political liberties, and similarly with economic security. From this it follows that we cannot distinguish civil and political liberties from social rights.

Can we regard the conditions of security as constitutive of civil and political rights in the way that this argument supposes? To answer this question, let us first consider the case of physical security; that is, the protection of the person from assault. A good case can be made for saying that this does constitute part of our understanding of what it is to have a civil or political right, since contained in the idea of a right is the idea of preserving some protected sphere of action within which an individual can act. However, this same argument cannot be carried over from physical to economic security, as can be seen by considering a simple counter-example. Consider a community in which everyone's rights of democratic participation are protected, but where its members are facing some natural hazard. For example, a community of farmers may have land in danger of flooding, thus destroying crops. The farmers have to decide where to build a flood barrier, but their communal efforts will not be sufficient to protect everyone's land. If everyone is able to participate in the decision then their political rights are protected, but not everyone will enjoy the condition of economic security, and the community as a whole may be too poor to compensate those whose means of livelihood is affected by the flood.

The moral of this counter-example is not that social and economic rights are unimportant to the maintenance of civil and political liberties, but that they stand as empirically required preconditions of those rights in the circumstances of the modern political community, rather than as logically constituted elements in the specification of the civil and political rights of citizens in any empirically conceivable community. Social and economic security is a condition for enjoying civil and political rights, but this is because such security provides members of the community with the material pre-conditions of the freedom with which they can participate in public affairs, discover their communal interests and exchange their opinions.

Rights and benefits

The account I have so far developed of social rights turns them into benefits distributed in accordance with a principle of social choice, in this case the principle of equal autonomy. It can be argued that this account comes close to the classical utilitarian theory of rights, according to which to have a right is to be the beneficiary of another's obligation, this obligation being specified in terms of the principle of utility.[19] In the present account the principle of utility is replaced by the principle of equal autonomy. However, the formal similarities between our account and the utilitarian theory are strik-ing enough to require comment.

There are various problems involved in formulating the utilita-rian account of rights in a consistent fashion, most notably the problem over third-party beneficiaries. However, I shall assume that a qualified beneficiary theory, of the sort offered by Lyons,[20] can take care of these difficulties of consistency. The substantive objection to the utilitarian account, and by parity of reasoning to any account that is formally similar, is that it renders the essential idea of a right nugatory. For the essential idea of a right is that it pro-vides those who hold the right with some protected sphere of deci-sion and control over a certain range of personal interests within which they can exercise choice. The intended beneficiary theory appears to lay little emphasis upon the idea of individual choice so that the rights it secures are such only in an attenuated form. Social and economic rights appear to consist merely in being entitled to receive one's portion of a communal pie, thus ruling out any idea of active control over one's income.

In order to bring out this seemingly passive feature of social and economic rights in the welfare state, consider the contrast between conventional property and the 'new property' provided through social security benefits. It seems an essential feature of private property rights that the holder of those rights can do what he or she likes with that property, consistent with the private property rights of others, despite what others might think. For example, if I choose to burn my library, nobody is entitled to interfere with my action, under a conventional scheme of private property, even though others may think that my action is wasteful and my books could be put to better use. I am given control of some portion of the world.[21] By contrast, my receipt of social security benefits does appear conditional upon the approval of others. The value of the benefit I receive and the likelihood of its continuing in the future both depend upon the decisions of social planners, even when they are merely implementing the democratic will. It seems that I am not given exclusive control over some portion of the world, and the notion of my having a right, as distinct from merely enjoying a benefit, is correspondingly weakened.

Four points are relevant in deciding on the seriousness of the charge that social and economic rights are merely passive. Firstly, the contrast, suggested by the above example, between private property rights and rights in the new property is overdrawn. The exercise of private property rights is sometimes made conditional upon more general social approval, as the example of listed buildings in Britain goes to show. Secondly, since property is a contrived institution, both private property and the new property are dependent upon the political system; to that extent the idea that private property can give some individuals complete control over some portion of the world is a fiction. Thirdly, to the extent that social welfare institutions are democratically controlled, individuals may exercise rights by active participation in democractic institutions. Fourthly, although the idea of choice is central to some rights, it is difficult to make it central to the idea of a right as such. There are rights enjoyed by persons, for example the right not to be enslaved, where there is no choice over their exercise.[22]

The notion of individual sovereign control over some portion of the world is not as central, therefore, to the concept of a right as might at first sight be imagined. However, the idea of control is important in itself and it is interesting to contrast in this respect modern social security systems with the nineteenth-century English Poor Law. Sidgwick[23] pointed out that under the Poor Law paupers had the right to relief, but they did not have the right to sue for relief. This provides a perfect example of beneficiaries lacking control within a social welfare institution. By contrast the present-day social security system, particularly since 1980, embodies a set of rules by reference to which beneficiaries can determine what is due to them. I suggest that we think of this control as deriving from a conception of social rights defined not merely as Hohfeldian claims but also as Hohfeldian powers. Conceived of in this way social rights become a means by which beneficiaries can exercise a measure of control within the institutional arrangement of the new property. The rules bestow power upon beneficiaries to determine the judgements of public officials. Thus the British Supplementary Benefit regulations now specify in detail and in the form of regulations the circumstances in which single payments can be made to beneficiaries.[24] This limits the discretion of public officials, and to that extent provides claimants with a right akin to Hohfeldian powers, since claimants can determine how a decision is to be made simply by invoking the fact that their circumstances are relevant to the decision at hand.

Administrative discretion, then, may be limited by giving claimants the power to invoke regulations to support their claims. But this does not entirely rule out administrative discretion in two crucial areas, namely in the determination of relevant circumstances and in exceptional and unforeseeable circumstances. As far as the first sort of discretion goes, public officials will still have to decide whether or not a particular case falls under the appropriate regulation that is claimed for it. Where citizen and official disagree over this question the appropriate solution is the obvious one, namely a system of impartial adjudication itself governed by rules and precedent. By maintaining the idea of rule-bound procedures at this level the idea of powers within social rights is also being maintained, since claimants can use the rules of the adjudicating body in order to establish their rights.

Exceptional and unforeseeable circumstances create a different problem. Here the argument is that because rules limit the discretion of public officials they will be unable to take positive action to aid those who need help if their circumstances had been unforeseen by the rules. Claimants may have increased legal powers, but, it is argued, they will thereby lose benefits.[25] There is, it appears, a tension between the idea of actively exercising some control within the institution of the new property and achieving the best standard of living attainable from that system.

Although there may be a conflict of values here, it is surely not as important a practical problem as it is sometimes made out to be. The vast bulk of benefits that are payable under tax-transfer schemes are routine and can easily be encoded in rules. This applies not only to regular payments, but also to one-off payments. Before the change in the Supplementary Benefits schemes, the vast majority of exceptional needs payments were for items like clothing and bedding which are perfectly foreseeable items of expenditure, the need for which is only occasioned by the inadequacy of the scale-rates for long-term claimants. Difficult cases are relatively rare, and it is compatible with having rules covering the routine items that there should be some discretion left to public officials to make payments in unusual circumstances. (The recognition that general rules cannot cover all particular cases is at least as old as Aristotle.)[26] The essential point is that one does not want the discretion spreading from the extraordinary items to the routine ones.[27]

Taking stock of the argument so far, we can see that the concept of a right acts as a convenient theoretical link between the justification of a certain set of institutions and the evaluation of the practices within those institutions. To provide citizens with social and economic rights is both to secure them a level of benefit adequate to maintain autonomy and to provide them with the standing to exercise powers of choice within the system of rules that allocates those benefits. Persons, then, are not seen as retainers of the state, but as citizens capable of determining the decisions of public officials. Our next task is to see what constraints should be imposed upon public officials so that they act in a manner consistent with the idea of rights-governed practices.

8

Procedures, Fairness and Efficiency

Let us suppose that we have a government whose institutional arrangements are in accord with the principles we have laid out. It secures the minimal autonomy for persons to pursue their projects by preventing the occurrence of poverty amonst citizens, both when they are in work and when they are not. It secures equality of educational opportunity to each member of a new generation by ensuring that each receives an education that satisfies some minimum standards of intellectual and social competence. Above the two minima of income and education the government promotes social welfare, with an appropriate degree of equality, by suitably adjusting rates in the tax-transfer system and by specific provision for some commodities, like medical care and legal advice, to ensure that they are more equally distributed than the ability to pay for them. Moreover the government provides these benefits as of right, thus giving beneficiaries the power to control administrative action. Granted that all these conditions have been fulfilled, can we say that the government is operating with a set of rules or principles that completely determine a fair allocation of resources?

The answer to this question is no. In discussing the principle of autonomy and the promotion of social welfare we have been dealing with the overall structure of the basic institutions of society and with the benefits that accrue to role positions or representative persons within those institutions. Even when discussing rights we were considering claims and powers as they might be bestowed upon a whole set of persons, and not as they might be exercised by one rightholder. It is high time, then, that we moved inside the basic institutional structure to examine the procedures and principles that ought to govern allocation within such institutions. In this chapter we shall look at three aspects of the allocative procedures internal to social welfare institutions: the purely procedural constraints that decision-makers within those institutions have to satisfy; the fairness of various rationing devices used to cope with the problem of scarce resources; and the efficiency of various rationing devices used to cope with scarce resources.

Conditions of procedural fairness

In terms of purely procedural constraints upon decision-making there are five conditions that have to be satisfied if the decision is to be a fair one: the decision-maker should be authorised to make the decision; the decision taken should be within the decision-maker's sphere of competence; the decision should be made on relevant considerations; the decision should be equitable between beneficiaries of a similar status; and the beneficiary's standing in the matter should be respected.[1]

Firstly, then, the administrator responsible for making a decision on benefits should be duly authorised to make the decision. With collectively provided benefits, the constitutional or legal system of the polity will specify who is entitled to allocate the goods to the final beneficiary. Normally, the authorised agency for a collectively provided benefit will be a public official, or an official body, but this need not always be so. For example, the Family Fund, established with the aim of providing financial assistance to families with handicapped children, had control vested in the Joseph Rowntree Memorial Trust, which is a private charitable organisation.[2] So the requirement of due authorisation must be understood as a general condition applying to the suppliers of collectively financed benefits, and not as a specific condition applicable merely to public officials.

Secondly, the decision taken should be within the administrator's competence. The idea of competence here is a normative one, meaning that it should be possible to refer to an institutional set of rules which entitle the administrator or public official to make certain decisions. For example, the study of 'gatekeepers' has shown that receptionists in the offices of social service departments can advance or retard the enquiries made by members of the public depending upon how the receptionists themselves assess the urgency of the enquiry. Such actions go beyond the brief that could be written for the relevant job description. However, it is equally clear that failure to take responsibility for decisions that are within one's sphere of competence is also a form of procedural unfairness. Thus, when social workers use receptionists to deter clients, instead of themselves explaining the situation to clients, this practice can also be regarded as involving a lack of procedural fairness.[3]

Thirdly, the decision-makers should act on relevant consideration when allocating a benefit. It has long been argued that local authorities take into account such matters as whether a beneficiary is 'decent' or 'feckless' when allocating resources. For example, these sorts of consideration are thought to enter into the judgement of local authority officials when thay allocate council houses, although the rules governing such allocations refer only to such criteria as size of family or length of time on the waiting-list.[4] In one sense the requirement that only relevant considerations be taken into account may seem to impose only a weak constraint on administrators, since the decision-making agency could always redefine its purposes, in order to make previously 'irrelevant' considerations relevant. For example, a local housing authority might have it as a purpose to avoid clustering together 'problem' families, in which case taking into consideration the fecklessness or otherwise of beneficiaries may well be relevant. However, even bearing in mind this qualification, the prohibition on irrelevant considerations can still act as a powerful constraint upon decision-makers' powers. It isolates those cases where individual administrators are acting out of accord with the defined purpose of their institution, and some institutions will be prevented from adopting certain practices, simply because they could not gain public acceptance for the purposes that would justify those practices. A local authority in Britain would find it extremely difficult to gain public acceptance for an explicit policy of concentrating problem families into certain localities.

Fourthly, administrators should act equitably, in the sense of treating like cases as like. From one point of view this condition may seem simply to be a redescription of the third condition ruling out irrelevant considerations, since one obvious way of failing to treat like cases as like is to use irrelevant considerations when dealing with otherwise identical persons. This is clearly a part of the equity condition. On the other hand, the equity condition may be thought to have broader scope than the condition of irrelevant considerations. One way in which officials may fail to treat like cases as like, for example, is not by consciously bringing in irrelevant considerations, but by being prone to unconscious bias. The equity condition therefore represents the principle that public institutions should seek to eradicate all sources of bias, including unconscious ones.[5]

Fifthly, administrators in their decisions should recognise the beneficiary's standing in the matter. In particular, potential beneficiaries should be able to acquire relevant information about the benefit being allocated, and should be made aware of their rights and obligations under the relevant procedures. It is difficult to say in general what this requirement amounts to in practice; but I have no doubt that it would rule out, for example, the practice of one local authority, by which tenants were expected to accept the keys to a council house they were offered before they had an opportunity to inspect the property in question.[6]

How are these five conditions to be justified? One way is to justify them by their results. Just as the rules of natural justice and due process embodied in legal proceeding might be justified instrumentally by their tendency to promote an accurate verdict and avoid a sense of insecurity among citizens who would otherwise fear the risk of unjustified punishment,[7] so the rules of procedural fairness embodied in allocative procedures may be thought to help secure expectations and ensure that benefits were distributed in the way that legislation and policy intended. However, there is an additional reason for the rules, namely that they are an unpacking of the idea of what it means to have a right to welfare. The notion here is not simply that citizens should have access to benefits, but that the way in which the administration of these benefits is conducted should be one in which respect for persons is displayed. Giving effect to this idea may involve more than officials and administrators acting on the above principles or even being accountable for their actions. It may also require a published and public code of conduct which sets out the range of considerations that are relevant to administrative judgements and to which reference can be made by clients who have a grievance. It is for this reason, for example, that the change in the mode of administering Supplementary Benefit exceptional payments is to be welcomed, since it involves the substitution of published regulations for a departmental rule-book.

These five conditions may be observed without complication, though not always without difficulty, by those responsible for imposing regulations or for allocating benefits where the supply is not scarce relative to the demand. For example, when a public health official enforces a hygiene regulation, there is no problem in making the regulation apply to all like-cases. Similarly, in the allocation of school places there is often no difficulty in ensuring that all eligible children are given places. So too in the allocation of benefits under social security. However, there are circumstances in which the supply of benefits is not equal to the demand, and so the official is not in a position to treat relevantly similar individuals in an identical manner. If the eligible school population expands, then places may be short until increased provision can be supplied. Frequently, the housing stock is inadequate for the demands that are made upon it, and the same is true of medical resources. How, then, is the official to behave in a fair and efficient way? Or, to put the question more generally, what rationing devices are there available to administrators that are compatible with the principles of fairness and efficiency?

I shall treat this question in two parts, first considering what rationing devices are consistent with the principles of fairness, and then considering what devices are consistent with the principles of efficiency. In both of these discussions I shall assume that the problem of scarcity is a persistent one. One response to the problem of scarcity in a particular service area is to take it as a signal that not enough public resources are being put into the service in question. Sometimes this is the right response; but it will hardly be adequate all the time. Firstly, it does not solve the problem of what to do in the short term, which may turn out to be quite long when we are considering services like the supply of housing or medical facilities. Secondly, there is the problem that an increase in the supply of some services raises demand. As housing standards improve, so people's expectations about suitable housing increase, or as medical facilities are provided so are the resources per patient increased. Shortage of supply relative to demand is always likely, therefore, to create a problem of fair and efficient allocation in the social services.

Procedural fairness and rationing devices

Social administrators have identified a number of devices that are in practice used to ration the social services.[8] They include such devices as: eligibility clauses; the dilution of the service; making the service unattractive; stigmatising procedures for receiving the service; ignorance; complexity; personal predilection of those administering the service; charges and fees; delay and queues; physical barriers to access; and deflecting potential clients to other agencies. Is it possible to use the principles of procedural fairness to ascertain the acceptability of each of these devices?

Using the five principles of procedural fairness that we have so far developed, it is clear that some of these devices are inherently unacceptable. Services should not be rationed by the personal predilections of providers, by ignorance, complexity, stigma or physical barriers to access. Each of these devices breaches one or more of the principles that have been developed. Deflecting clients to other agencies is not inherently unfair if those other agencies have similar responsibilities to those of the rationing agency and there is good reason for thinking that the other agency will provide a service that is as good or better. However, where the deflection takes place merely for the convenience of the rationing agency, then it represents a failure to act within the competence of the decision-maker and it also fails to respect the beneficiary's standing in the matter. Eligibility conditions are not in themselves procedurally unfair, although they should be laid down by those with authority to do so. They should also be laid down with a sense of natural justice, not discriminating unfairly among potential beneficiaries and making the conditions of eligibility relevant to the purposes at hand.

Thus, for the set of beneficiaries suitably designated as eligible the remaining devices are: queues, charges and the dilution of the services. There is an inherent tension involved in trying to avoid the undesirable features of these separate devices. The use of queues to avoid charges may well dilute the services, or the increase in charges may well mean that the service is made available to fewer people and in that way diluted. However, it is clear that all three devices formally meet the conditions of fairness that we wish to impose on administrative action: they may be used by those with authority and competence; they may involve no undue discrimination; and they may respect the standing of beneficiaries (provided service standards are not diluted to too low a level). Are there any other arguments of procedural fairness, not just those that apply in general to administrative action, which would enable us to choose between these devices? In other words, is there some fair procedural device that would enable us to ration resources among those who have a similar claim on those resources?

In order to understand what such a device might look like let us consider a procedural device that many regard as the paradigm of fairness in these matters, namely the lottery. The fairness of a lottery is independent of the end-state to which it gives rise, and it is also logically independent of the consent of those who are affected by its use. Yet, despite its paradigm status as a procedurally fair device, the lottery is not extensively used in social decision-making. It was used by the Greater London Council when selling part of its housing stock. A random process was also used in the Alum Rock educational voucher experiment, when excess demand for some scarce school places was regulated by the method of random selection.[9] More speculatively, lotteries have been proposed by some writers as a solution to the problem of rationing scarce life-saving medical resources, the argument being that in this case of ultimate rationing the principle of treating all alike has overriding importance.[10]

The disadvantage with using lotteries to allocate scarce resources is that it is extremely difficult by their use to cope with a changing population. Where the population is fixed, the lottery will produce an ordering of all relevant individuals. However, in an example like that of allocating scarce life-saving equipment, how does one cope with the arrival of any new individuals who may become eligible for the service? Either they are excluded from the ordering already produced by the lottery, which is unfair on them, or the ordering is rearranged to accommodate them, which is unfair on those who already have been assigned their place in the ordering. It is, of course, possible to imagine solutions to this problem. For example, a specified number of places might be allocated to the first group of those eligible, leaving some places for the next group. Alternatively, one could use the lottery to select among those who were eligible at the time the next unit of resource became available. Yet even so there are difficulties: in the first case, the more frequently eligible groups enter the lottery the more nearly the device becomes like a queue; in the second case, there is no advantage given to those who have waited, and many would regard this as unfair.

Despite these difficulties, lotteries do provide some sort of model for procedurally fair allocation devices, since their use incorporates the idea that, though not everyone can enjoy an immediate benefit, potential beneficiaries should be treated even-handedly in the process of allocation. How does the device of queueing fare in this regard? Queues, too, even out the chances of anyone obtaining the benefit in question, and where it is simply a matter of waiting, as with an application for public housing, everyone will enjoy the benefit in the end. The time at which individuals join the queue is taken to be a randomising factor, sufficient in itself for the queue to satisfy the equal-chance condition of the fair lottery, without the complications that new applicants cause to the operation of lotteries.[11] The extent to which the queue is a genuinely randomising device will depend on how much different people value time differently. If the disadvantages that attach to waiting vary greatly from individual to individual, then the claim that queues satisfy the equal opportunity condition of procedural fairness is correspondingly weakened. However the value of time is measured, either in terms of income forgone or in terms of disposition to pay for shorter waiting-time, variations in the value of time are likely to arise. Off-setting this variation, however, is the fact that persons attach intrinsic value to the passing of time. Thus, long-stay patients in hospital conceptualise their treatment in terms of a timetable, rather than in terms of medical or physiological changes, so that the length of time one has spent at a particular stage of treatment becomes a reason for passing on to another stage of treatment.[12] To the extent to which these common perceptions of the passing of time off-set individual variations in the value attached to time, the genuinely randomising aspect of queues will be preserved.

Charging is the other main device used to ration resources. Does this device treat potential beneficiaries even-handedly on the model of the lottery? Provided potential beneficiaries are capable of paying the charges there is no reason why the use of charges cannot satisfy the conditions of procedural fairness. After all, there is no intrinsic reason why the variation in the ability to pay charges should be greater than the variation in the value of time to individuals. However, there is a reason for not using charges, in preference to queues, as a rationing device between equally needy persons when the benefit being allocated is particularly important, for example when it consists of access to scarce life-saving equipment, and perhaps even for less serious matters like minor surgery. Whereas everyone can pay the price of waiting-time, not everyone will always be able to afford charges, and so the use of charging would violate the principle that like cases should be treated as like.[13] There is, however, a snag with this comparison. Queues will only preserve even-handedness among potential beneficiaries provided the allocating agency for the benefit is a monopoly supplier. By contrast, if persons can either queue for publicly provided medical care or buy the same care privately, then the use of a queue without charging may give rise to less even-handed treatment than the use of charges that cause less dilution of service provision and less incentive for persons to opt out of the public scheme. So the circumstances within which the choice between queues and charges is made will need to be carefully monitored.

Generally speaking, in these matters there is a coincidence between what is fair and what is thought to be fair. Thus, using queues, instead of charges, satisfies the widespread (in Britain at least) sense that persons should wait their turn. But we do not always find this coincidence. As Schaffer[14] points out, in allocating council housing in Northern Ireland the use of a queue with a points system for children might be seen to be unfair by the majority because it would give an unfair advantage to Catholics. What view should we take when the coincidence does not occur? If the rules that have been developed, and the devices that are used to implement them, follow from principles of fairness, then the weight given to opinions about fairness should be discounted, just as earlier (pp. 38–41) we noted the argument for not counting harmful external preferences. Principles of fairness are not to be regarded as a function of the preferences of individuals within the community, nor are procedures to be thought of as a means of attaining maximum preference satisfaction. Instead, the principles of procedural fairness are to be regarded as the constraints, or ground rules of the social game, within which individual preference satisfaction counts, and such principles may be applied to prevent a majority attaining its way about the allocation of benefits.

This brings us to the problem of dilution, including the device of making the service unattractive. The fairness of charging and queues has been judged solely in relation to those potential beneficiaries who were known to come within the scope of the service. However, there is a great deal of evidence showing that there are some persons who would be eligible for certain services if they applied, but who are either uninformed about these opportunities or do not take them up when they are informed. So, it is an open question whether the fairness of a procedure should be judged in relation to the persons who apply for the benefit, or in relation also to those persons who would be eligible for the benefit were they to apply. As standards of service provision rise, the tendency is to extend the scope of the delivery system, so that the fairness of a procedure is judged not simply in respect of the way it satisfies demand, but also in respect of how well it informs people of what they might demand. Equal opportunity is extended from the notion of an impartial ordering of a given client group to the idea that all those potentially eligible must be given the information and opportunity to see that they might be in the client group. The paradoxical result of this process is that service standards may fall in the pursuit of this extended concept of fairness: queues become longer, and professional or administrative discretion is increased as demand rises. Careful thought needs to be given, therefore, to extending procedural fairness beyond the task of ordering existing demand. In particular there should be a clearly specified point beyond which dilution should no longer be permitted.

Finally, it is worth noting that when choosing among allocational devices some account must be taken of the characteristic deficiencies to which they are subject. For example, it has been argued that queues are liable to favour those who shout longest and loudest at the expense of those who patiently wait their turn.[15] In this particular case my conjecture is that this deficiency is more plausibly put down to a combination of queues and extensive administrative and professional discretion which allows for the opportunity to reorder the queue. Nevertheless, the general point that the example illustrates is a good one. Institutions and practices do not always function as intended, and so the judgement on the merits of different procedures will depend, in part at least, on second-best considerations.

Efficiency and rationing devices

The conclusion of the previous section is that there is more than one procedure for allocating benefits within social welfare institutions, which satisfies the principles of fairness. Although the principles of procedural fairness rule out certain types of procedures, for example public officials allocating benefits by personal predilection, they still leave a range of available procedures, including lotteries, queues, charges and dilution of service. However, fairness is not the only value involved in the appraisal of the internal workings of social welfare institutions. Efficiency is another. In this context, the principle of efficiency is the counterpart at the micro level to the principle of growth at the macro level. The principle of growth directs that the overall institutional arrangements for a society should aim to maximise social welfare; the principle of efficiency is concerned with the production of welfare at the micro level. It is, therefore, worth considering whether the principle of efficiency can further narrow down our search for acceptable allocation procedures. In order to pursue this question I shall, in this section, consider the idea of efficiency, and then, in the next section, consider the extent to which the idea of efficiency can be used to appraise the argument about universality and selectivity in the social services.

In its simplest form the principle of efficiency directs social welfare institutions to do the best they can with available resources. Examples include such problems as whether district nursing services can be reorganised in order that nurses can visit more patients in the day, or whether hospital laundry services can be carried on at lower cost by replacing old capital stock with new stock, even when interest has to be paid on the money to buy the latter. The principle that policy-makers should aim for efficiency in the production of these services is fundamentally a postulate that it is preferable from the social point of view to have institutions producing a higher level of output with the same costs, or producing the same level of output at lower cost, other things being equal.[16] It has proved important in efficiency studies to look not only at the relationship between resources inputs and output but also at the relationship between what have been called 'quasi-inputs' or 'non-resource' inputs and output.[17] These latter sorts of input include such things as staff attitudes or client characteristics. Formal resource inputs, like the numbers of staff available, appear to interact with non-resource inputs in creating the level of service provided. So the search for efficiency should be broadly conceived, taking into account not only the resource inputs over which decision-makers have control, but also features of the environment or the context within which those resources are used, over which decision-makers typically have less control.

I shall assume in discussing the principle of efficiency that the relevant measure of output is always some change in the status or characteristics of beneficiaries rather than a change in the combination of service inputs, however much it may be difficult to specify and measure those statuses and characteristics. Thus, if a visit by the district nurse does not improve the health and welfare of those patients visited, then an increase in the number of visits made is not of itself an improvement in efficiency. Much of the operational literature in social policy is concerned to develop measures that are accurate indicators of the welfare, and changes in welfare, of recipients.[18] For example, measures of impairment might refer to the mobility of clients, and their ability to look after themselves. Similarly, output in education might be measured by the reading and mathematical attainments of children as measured by certain test scores. In these cases, an assessment of efficiency in the social services will depend on whether there has been a change in output following upon a service reorganisation, or whether an increase in output would be possible with such a service reorganisation. In each case, however, the relevant perspective from which to look at the matter is the effect that the service has on the recipient's state of well-being.

Two complications arise in operating with this simple notion of efficiency. The first is that some value has to be placed on the output that is achieved by the service. In order to achieve an improvement in the reading attainment of children it may be necessary to increase resources, or at least to keep resources in the educational sector, when a saving might be made by keeping reading attainments at the same level and switching the resources so saved to other services. Who is to determine the value of the relevant output? Within a liberal democracy this determination will be shared between recipients, professionals and the political process, and I shall leave to the discussion in the final chapter consideration in more detail of how this responsibility may be distributed. For this section and the next I shall assume that policy-makers are working with a consistent and authoritative set of valuations which enable them to place relative weight on alternative outcomes.

However, even if responsibility for a consistent set of evaluations has been correctly assigned, there is the second complication to be faced. The evaluations themselves will define a set of priorities between competing goals in the same service. This fact has important implications in the allocation of those goods and services, like education, health care and legal aid, which fall within the public domain. As we have seen, the rationale of bringing the allocation of these services into the public domain is so that the internal goal of the relevant practice can be turned into a public goal. And yet even in education and the health services, where the professional ethic of rendering a service to beneficiaries independently of their financial status is most entrenched, there is still a need to make judgements of priority between competing and alternative uses for the same service.

A simple model of how decisions about priorities might be made and implemented runs as follows. The policy-maker takes a consistent set of ends and then adapts the means available to the attainment of those ends in the most efficient way possible, subject to any constraints of fairness that might apply. However, such a simple model fails to do justice to the complexities of the process that may be involved in acting efficiently. In particular, there may be public preferences about the means that are to be employed in order to achieve certain end-states. If the public object to the separation of children receiving free school meals from the children paying for them, that fact in itself may make it more difficult to use a means-test in the allocation of the benefit. Similarly, if some weight is put on the idea of personal responsibility, that fact will make it more difficult to abolish charges even though there may be good administrative reasons for doing so. For example, both public and official opinion places great weight on the importance of parents whose children are taken into care paying towards the cost of the children's upkeep, and this makes it difficult to abolish the practice of levying charges even though there are good administrative reasons for doing so.[19] The interplay of ends and means becomes an important factor itself in decisions on the organisation of a service.

In order to examine this interplay of ends and means I shall discuss the question of whether benefits should be allocated universally at zero prices to those potential beneficiaries who fall within a particular demographic category, or whether there should be selective allocation, with the bulk of benefits being supplied at a charge to users but with a special reduction in the charge to those too poor to meet it. The debate between universalists and selectivists should be a good testing ground for whether the principle of efficiency suggests that some allocational devices are more acceptable than others.

Universality and selectivity

One of the problems involved in assessing the debate between universalists and selectivists is that there is not one issue involved but several.[20] In fact, it is possible to identify at least eight separate questions at issue in deciding whether or not to allocate benefits on a universal or selective basis.

Firstly, granted that some goods and services should be distributed more equally than the ability to pay for them, which goods and services from this set should be distributed free of user charges at the point of delivery and which should have a charge attached to them, even though that charge may not reflect the full economic cost of providing the goods or the service?

Secondly, among those goods and services that are provided at some charge, which are to be provided at a nominal charge so that there is little need for special administrative arrangements to remit payment to the poor, and which are to be provided at higher charges, including the special case where the charge covers the economic costs of supply, with special administrative arrangements for the remission of charges?

Thirdly, in the case where a charge is levied with the intention of covering the costs of supply, what is the correct basis on which to calculate these costs? In particular, should the estimate of costs be based upon short-run marginal costs or long-run marginal costs? This issue is important since the difference between these two estimates can be considerable, with the second, but not the first, taking into account the costs of capital renewal. To take an example: the long-run marginal costs of supplying school meals tends to be rather high, because the capital equipment is not used very extensively over the whole length of its working life, whereas the short-run marginal costs tend to be rather low, because the extra effort and expenditure involved in providing extra meals is low.[21]

Fourthly, in identifying certain goods and services as candidates for specific egalitarianism is the intention to promote horizontal redistribution within income classes, or to promote vertical redistribution between income classes? School meals may be subsidised, for example, to help families with children or to help poor families. Similarly, the cost of drug prescriptions may be kept low to subsidise the sick in all income categories or to subsidise the poor.

Fifthly, we may distinguish between vertical efficiency, the extent to which a given volume of expenditure helps a needy group, and no others, and horizontal efficiency, the proportion of a given needy group who are helped by an expenditure.[22] These two forms of efficiency do not vary together. For example, if we take the target group to be the poor, then different programmes have different levels of efficiency. Some means-tested benefits have high uptake among the target group, but little benefit elsewhere, for example food stamps in the USA; other benefits have relatively low take-up in the target group and involve a subsidy to non-target groups, for example subsidised school meals; and yet other benefits have a high take-up among the target group, along with a subsidy to others, for example, child benefits. So one question to ask is which is uppermost in the mind of the policy-maker: vertical or horizontal efficiency?

Sixthly, what problems are associated with the administrative devices that are available in order to accomplish the stated objectives? The most frequently invoked problem here is that of the stigma involved in the administration of means-tested benefits. A device that is designed to perform well on the tests of vertical and horizontal efficiency may perform less well than expected if in its operation it identifies a special group for treatment in a way that is thought to be degrading, either by members of the group itself or by society at large.[23] So one issue is whether the proponents of a scheme have taken into account these second-order, unintended effects.

Seventhly, what importance does the policy-maker as a representative of society place upon the argument that social integration and a sense of communal solidarity are promoted by every citizen undergoing a common experience in treatment? For some goods and services this consideration appears to be of overriding importance. The provision of free education in many liberal democracies, and in many developing countries, is surely intended to promote the sense of a common cultural and national identity, as well as be an efficient instrument for the transmission of some socially necessary skills.[24] The principle that public services should provide a range of common experience that all citizens undergo can be extended from the case of education and has been applied specifically to such services as health care and income maintenance.

Eighthly, is the debate between universalists and selectivists one over transitional arrangements towards competing ideals, or does it involve conflicting considerations which have to be borne in mind in any attempt to promote social welfare in a world of scarce resources? Selectivists sometimes present their case for means-tested benefits as though it were a stepping-stone on the way to a situation in which only an income floor of public support is given to persons, and no special public provision is made for the supply of certain scarce commodities. Universalists, on the other hand, sometimes present their case as though either they are supporting second-best arrangements in the absence of a more general redistribution of income, or they are establishing a bridge-head to an economic system in which more and more commodities are allocated without use of the price mechanism. Both these interpretations can be put on the provision of low-rent public housing for example.

Simply by setting down this variety of issues it should be clear that it is most unlikely that anyone can consistently take up either a universalist or a selectivist position across the whole range of social services, simply on grounds of efficiency in meeting objectives. Consider the following list: food; music lessons; cosmetic surgery; dentures; household conversions for the physically handicapped; housing; school meals; swimming pools; residential accommodation for the elderly; family allowances; compulsory child care; day care for pre-school children; renal dialysis; medically prescribed drugs; spectacles; house cleaning for those unable to do their own housework; heating insulation; training in labour market skills; rehabilitation and training after an accident; travel costs to visit an ill relative; advice on how to claim benefits; legal advice for a criminal action; or the relief from loneliness and anxiety that simply talking to a social worker can provide. All these diverse benefits are provided under social policy programmes along with many others. How can it be assumed that there is just one fair and efficient allocation device for distributing these benefits? How can it be assumed that the purposes for which housing subsidies are given are the same as the purposes for which family allowances are given, or that either set of purposes is related to the purposes in subsidising drugs purchases? Since the attainment of efficiency can only be judged in relation to a specific set of purposes, a different purpose for different areas of policy will imply different judgements about the best means to achieve those ends. There can be no general argument, then, in favour either of selectivity or universality. However, this does not mean that no general propositions can be advanced in assessing the merits of particular arguments. Perhaps the most important question to determine in relation to each of the above issues is which of them are matters of principle or political decision, where some essentially normative choice has to be made, and which are matters of empirical conjecture, where the collection of evidence may resolve the issue one way or another.

An example of an issue to which empirical evidence is clearly relevant is the problem about the disadvantages attendant upon various administrative arrangements that might be used. The claim that means-tests promote stigma is susceptible to empirical test. Such hard evidence as there is relates to the school-meals service and suggests that means-tests are stigmatising to only a minority of beneficiaries, a much smaller number than is supposed by their opponents, although many more people feel that others find means-tests stigmatising. Moreover, this evidence also suggests that it is the context within which means-tests occur that give them their unpleasant character, so that the best predictor of the divide between those who thought means-tests stigmatising and those who did not was the experience, positive or negative, that people had had with the school. This result is suggestive, since it is this sort of contextual factor that seems to be important in the fact that the means-test for a university grant is not generally thought to be stigmatising.[25]

A similar point about the role of empirical evidence can be made in connection with the supposed deterrent effect of charges. In principle this is the sort of question that can be investigated empirically, although little systematic is known about this matter. Clearly the more that is known about the level and nature of charges that do deter potential recipients, the more carefully can a charging structure be devised, and the balance of advantage between queues and charges, touched on earlier, can be drawn up.

When coming to a judgement on the normative issues, it is useful to classify the various considerations that may be involved according to the strength of claim that they may be thought to import. At least three sorts of claims can be distinguished in this way. The considerations may be regarded as constraints, goals or beneficial side-effects. To construe them as constraints is really to construe them as goals with very strong priority. For example, great importance may be attached to horizontal efficiency in some circumstances. Priority might be given to ensuring that no one who is sick be deprived of medicine on grounds of income. If this goal were taken as a priority, then other considerations, for example those of vertical efficiency, might be constrained by this prior commitment. On the other hand, the aims of a particular benefit may be difficult to prescribe in a precise way, in which case the considerations will enter into the final decision about the efficiency of administrative arrangements as competing goals. For example, the purposes of family allowances may be to relieve poverty and to accomplish a redistribution within income classes in favour of households with children. In this sort of case it may be impossible to show in general that flat-rate, non-taxable benefits for the purposes of within-income-class redistribution are inferior in efficiency to benefits tapered inversely to the income of households. The final way in which considerations may enter is as beneficial side-effects of other objectives. This case is the counterpart to the one in which certain considerations are given priority. For some selectivists the value of the social-mix argument enters as a side-effect in this way. If a pattern of service delivery can be found that produces a social mix, that is all to the good, but no sacrifices of horizontal and vertical efficiency should be incurred in order to achieve this objective. This seems to be the rationale of the frequently made selectivist point that a general form of service provision should not be determined by attention to the needs of a poor minority.

The general conclusion we can draw is about the form of the arguments that have to be used in justifying universal or selective allocational devices in particular cases. Essentially the form of these arguments is to make a clear separation between empirical and normative issues, and, within the set of normative issues, to distinguish clearly the priority that is accorded to the attainment of the specified objectives. Needless to say, because specific forms of provision grow up in an *ad hoc* and incremental way, the attempt to justify current modes of provision according to the above form will in fact lead to a judgement that existing allocational devices have to be changed. The principles of fairness and efficiency may not determine one unique procedure for allocating social welfare benefits within institutions; but reflection on the principles involved will usually lead to a search for better procedures than those we currently have.

9

Desert, Justice and Affirmative Action

The welfare state is associated in most people's minds with public expenditure, and this is indeed an important aspect of its functioning. However, there is another aspect of government intervention which has received less attention, but which nevertheless can be argued to be of equal importance. This is the aspect of the regulatory powers of the welfare state. The modern welfare state has powers to intervene in the transactions of individuals and corporations to secure outcomes and conditions that would not arise of their own accord in the course of those transactions. A most important area in which this applies is in the field of employment contracts. Governments regulate the terms and conditions of employment contracts in various ways, requiring, for example, specified health and safety conditions at the workplace, limitations on the hours and wages for which persons may work, and the attainment of certain qualifications before persons can be licensed to practise an occupation. Of course, government action in the employment field is not limited merely to these regulatory devices. Employment-creation programmes and social security payments are also important ways by which governments promote welfare by means of employment policies. Both regulation and public expenditure can support one another.

Despite these complementary functions it can be argued that there are some goals for which public expenditure is inherently unsuitable, and which regulation alone can achieve. An example is the employment of women and ethnic minorities in dynamic and expanding sectors of the economy. Public expenditure to promote economic expansion will not by itself ensure that women and minority groups are properly represented among the beneficiaries of that expansion. Only direct regulation of the conditions under which women and minority groups are employed can assure this. In this chapter, therefore, I propose to look at some of the political arguments that have surrounded programmes of affirmative action, in order to see some of the problems and difficulties to which the regulatory powers of the welfare state can give rise in this area; for policies of affirmative action, at their most politically contentious, involve the organised use of state power for regulating employment contracts.

Investigating the problems involved in programmes of affirmative action will require considering the idea of desert, since it is argued by some that affirmative action programmes are politically and ethically undesirable if they involve appointing persons to positions on grounds other than merit or desert. To consider this question is, therefore, implicitly to consider wider issues. Since the break-up of the old Poor Law with its notion of 'less eligibility', and the passing of attitudes like those of the Charity Organisation Society, with its distinction between the deserving and the undeserving poor, the idea of desert has had little currency in social policy. Yet it can be argued that the idea of desert has a powerful influence within the economy and society at large operating to justify economic and social inequalities. To show that arguments for welfare state interventions are also arguments for taming the operation of the principle of desert in the employment field refutes the claim that the principles of the welfare state are necessarily and logically subordinate to the principles of capitalist society within which the welfare state is located.

There is, moreover, one further aspect of the idea of desert that makes it relevant to the discussion of social policy. The social policy context within which the concept of desert is directly relevant is that of selection procedures for further and higher education, and appointment procedures for doctors, administrators, teachers and other personnel. In these circumstances the concept of desert functions as part of the internal standards of the relevant institution. Universities see it as part of their task to train the most intellectually able of a generation, and social welfare institutions see it as part of their task to supply competent and qualified service to those in need. These goals cannot be achieved unless those who are selected or appointed in some sense deserve what they receive. The concept of desert here functions analogously to the concept of need in determining action in accordance with the internal standards of an institution. But whereas the concept of need finds its core meaning in the idea of identifying a condition of deficiency from some end-state, the idea of desert finds its core in the idea of rewarding an accomplishment already achieved. To say more than this we must examine the way the concept of desert functions in greater detail.

The concept of desert can function in contexts where it is a question of awarding blame or punishment and in contexts where it is a question of awarding praise or reward. In what follows I shall be exclusively concerned with the second of these senses, good desert, or 'merit' as I shall sometimes call it. In such contexts the term 'desert' can and often does function as a general concept of just entitlement. Examples, from a wide range of possible uses, include: 'Technicians deserve better pay and conditions', 'The driver involved in the accident deserves compensation', 'Those patients in greatest pain deserve more attention than the others', 'The slowest learners deserve more attention from the teacher', or 'Everyone who passes the first-year examination deserves to enter the second-year'. Clearly in each of these examples the grounds of the desert claim are various – marketable skills, compensation, need, and so on – and the term 'desert' does not itself function as a special claim for treatment, but merely as the rhetorical flourish added to other claims and intended to conclude the case with vigour. Like the term 'rights' the term 'desert' has a tendency to expand its usage in common language to be used in the description of any claim that the speaker feels is justified.

However, the idea of desert has a more specific sense than this range of examples suggests. It can function as a specialised consideration in judgements about the justice of an allocation or award. In order to show the truth of this claim, it is merely necessary to show that every one of the following sentences is logically possible:

1. *A* deserves *X*, and ought, in justice, to get it.
2. *A* deserves *X*, but ought, in justice, not to get it.
3. *A* does not deserve *X*, but ought, in justice, to get it.
4. *A* does not deserve *X*, and ought, in justice, not to get it.

Clearly, sentences 1 and 4 pose little difficulty for the person who wishes to identify the idea of desert with any claim that can arise under a principle of justice. Sentences 2 and 3, by contrast, if they can be made sense of, do show that desert is only a part of justice.

The possible truth of 2 is illustrated by an example of Feinberg,[1] discussing desert in a game of skill or a race:

> Perhaps the man who truly deserved to win did not in fact win because he pulled up lame, or tore his shoe, or suffered some other unforeseeable stroke of bad luck. In a contest of skill the man who deserves to win is the man who is most skilled, but (because of luck) he is not in every case the man who does win.

Since in sports and games of skill the just winner of the prize is the person who does best on the day, Feinberg's case shows that someone can deserve an X but ought not in justice to get it. What about the obverse case, instanced in sentence 3, where someone does not deserve X but ought, in justice, to get it? An example of such a case would be that of a student who does little work thoughout the year, but manages to cram just before the examination and is lucky in the questions asked. The student ought to be given a pass for the examination, but he or she does not deserve the grade. In Feinberg's case desert did not give rise to award through ill-luck; in the examination case, lack of desert does not give rise to lack of award through good-luck.

Accepting, then, that the idea of desert can function as a special claim on benefits, how are such claims specified? The general form of desert claims is that a person, A, deserves some good, X, in virtue of some personal characteristic, C. The purpose of a desert claim is to assert that there is a fitting or appropriate relationship between the characteristic, which is the basis of desert, and the good which it is presumed to merit. Aristotle's[2] remark that we give the best flutes to the best flute-players captures this idea perfectly. We can distinguish between moral desert, which is the ascription of merit by virtue of the principles of some ethical system, and non-moral or institutional desert, which is the ascription of merit by virtue of the rules of some functioning institution. These two types of desert have both similarities and differences. I shall look first at the similarities and then at the differences.

The first similarity is that the characteristic which forms the basis of the desert will be an ability or an admired quality of the person who is deserving.[3] With moral desert the quality will be virtue. In the more mundane circumstances of social institutions the typical basis for such desert claims will be such qualities as intelligence, courage, endurance, or skills whose mastery requires effort and application. It may seem as though the relevant qualities need not always be admirable. I may be judge in a painting competition and pick the work of the artist that I think deserves the prize without thinking that the paintings in question are admirable or worthy in themselves. It is just that in the context of the competition the work I choose is the best of a bad bunch, and so deserving in that sense. However, this example only serves to show that comparative judgements of ability or quality are sufficient for desert ascriptions, not that such judgements are irrelevant.

Secondly, both moral and institutional desert are essentially matters of achievement or of realised ability. For example, when we say of someone that he or she deserves first prize in a competition, we are saying that the person concerned has displayed some skill or exercised some ability that makes that person worthy of the prize. An obvious counter-example to this characterisation of desert judgements might seem to be that claims to deserving treatment can be based upon the effort that a person has displayed rather than the achievement consequent upon that effort. However, this counter-example is more apparent than real. When effort is claimed as the basis for desert the achievement that is implicitly identified is that of having made the effort, in a situation in which others similarly placed could have made a similar effort but chose not to. If a person dives into the sea to save a drowning child, but fails, that person deserves praise by comparison with others who might also have made the attempt but failed to do so. There is nothing within the logic of merit judgements to say that successful attempts should always be judged more deserving than unsuccessful attempts, and indeed many of the disputes about particular merit claims turn on which base of desert, from a number of competing ones, ought to apply in certain cases.

Thirdly, we can extend further the idea that effort as well as attainment is an achievement that may be deserving. Basing merit on effort is an attempt to broaden the grounds for ascribing merit, so that we take into account not simply 'performance on the day' but also the preparation that went into that performance. But we can also recognise that the standards and procedures that we use to assess merit may not always be accurate or suitable to the task at hand. An examination candidate may suffer a bout of depression in the run-up to the examinations, which prevents not only a good performance but also saps the will of the candidate to prepare and work at the examined material. Despite the lack of effort and the poor showing of the candidate, we may still judge that he or she has the ability to merit a high grade. Merit then is distinct from an entitlement under the rules of an institution, as, for example, when we distinguish the person who won the race and is entitled to the prize from the person who deserved to win the race. However, we cannot ascribe merit to persons if they habitually conduct themselves in such a way as always to be undeserving by the appropriate rules. If the deserving swimmer never wins a race, then we should doubt our judgement as to the person's abilities.

Fourthly, it follows from the link between merit and attainment, that desert is essentially a backward-looking notion. Strictly speaking, the idea of desert involves reward for meritorious performance without an eye to the future. The candidate who writes good finals' papers deserves a good degree, even if he or she never opens a book again. Similarly, the person who performs an heroic act deserves praise even if he or she thenceforth leads a cowardly and shrunken existence. And yet the idea of desert can incorporate the idea that these particular performances matter in so far as they are tokens of more permanent abilities and virtues. Just as the courts have regard to the character of someone convicted of a crime when passing sentence, so the granting of qualifications or the awarding of deserved benefit to a person may be intended as a reflection upon long-standing dispositions and abilities. Because achievement can be treated as evidence of permanent features of character, the backward-looking aspect of desert can be modified by the more general notion of fitness for a particular enterprise. (As I shall later argue, this ambiguity in the nature of desert claims becomes important when examining the justice of affirmative action.)

These four features of desert claims are common both to moral desert and to the desert of particular institutions or practices. However, there are differences in the two cases, which lead to importance distinctions in the way we apportion benefits. These differences pertain to the range of qualities that can function as the basis for desert, and the range of considerations we can employ when weighing up the importance of desert in the decision as to how to allocate a benefit.

Although both moral and institutional desert rest the ground of desert upon personal qualities of the one to whom desert is ascribed, a significant difference between them is that moral desert rests upon moral qualities, whereas institutional desert typically involves non-moral qualities. Clearly one cannot be morally deserving without some virtuous characteristics. But the best swimmer deserves to win the race and the most suitable person for a job deserves to get it, and these qualities are morally neutral. There may be quasi-ethical rules that competitors for prizes or posts will have to abide by on pain of disqualification – for example, even the best swimmer should not take drugs to improve performance – but those rules are best thought of as devices for ensuring that the competition measures only relevant accomplishments, and they are not intended as tests of the moral qualities of competitors.

A second difference between the moral and institutional senses of desert is that the former can typically be overturned by a wider range of considerations than the latter. For example, moral desert may easily be overturned by considerations of need: the public welfare system does not, in theory, distinguish between the deserving and the undeserving poor. Institutional desert is not so easily overturned. Universities select their students on their merits, not, for example, on how disappointed an applicant's parents might be if he or she did not get the place. Because institutions are only interested in a limited range of non-moral qualities, the range of considerations they can employ in their decision-making is correspondingly narrowed down.[4]

An implication of this second difference between moral and institutional desert is that the rewards of desert in the second case tend to be specific and identified with the qualities on the basis of which the desert judgement is made. This specificity is most easily seen in examples like job appointments or selection for higher education, where the benefit that is being conferred involves in its description a specification of the sort of qualities that define the desert base. The same point can also be made, however, by reference to examples that seem to show little intrinsic relationship between the desert base and its reward. When cups and medals are awarded for sporting achievement or military service the intrinsic connection to the meritorious activity is made by the conventional association that exists between those objects and the activity. The same is true also for something like a pay-rise on grounds of promotion. There is no particular sum of money that is right for rewarding merit in a post, and the value of merit awards is largely determined by conventional appraisals of what their size should be.

The practice of merit

Granted that there is a distinction between moral and institutional desert, it might still be thought that the moral notion can be used as a guide in the institutional contexts. Social institutions cannot distribute benefits in such a way as to approach the distribution that would follow simply from considerations of moral merit, if only because to do so would strain their decision-making capacities, and there is no reason to think that an ability accurately to judge nonmoral qualities implies an ability accurately to judge moral qualities. Nevertheless, the principle of moral desert, that forms of treatment should be proportional to the attainment of admirable qualities, might suggest the idea that there was some intrinsic value in having a system of social organisation in which the rewards that persons received were somehow proportional to their merits. Inequalities in pay, for example, might then be justified both within skill groups, those working harder receiving more, and between skill groups, those with greater skill receiving more than those with less skill.

To take the idea of desert seriously as a distinct source of value is to drive towards some such idea as this. However, there is an alternative interpretation of the value of desert suggested by contractarian (and rule-utilitarian) theories of social choice. According to this interpretation the rationale of the merit rule is to be found in its promoting the general advantage. The reason why we expect teachers, doctors and lawyers, for example, to be appointed on merit is because this promotes social welfare more than an alternative system would do. Within the contractarian framework this general advantage may be variously conceived, depending on the weighting that we judge contracting parties would give to different positions in society. So the merit rule might be justified by saying that there was some general advantage in which all sorts of persons were likely to share, or that its adoption leads to the relatively poor securing advantages they could not otherwise obtain.

In choosing between these two interpretations of the institutional use of desert the crucial question is whether the attempt to generalise from the moral notion to the institutional notion better explains the central features of institutional practices than does the alternative contractarian account. In order to answer this crucial question it would be necessary to present examples where the instrumental features of the contractarian account failed to justify a feature of desert that was intrinsic to an institutional practice. Brian Barry[5] has attempted to offer such an example that would refute the instrumentalist interpretation. Suppose a government wished to raise the birth-rate, and paid family allowances in order to provide an incentive for couples to have children. If there was a particular religious sect in the community whose beliefs meant that they would be unaffected by material incentives to have children, then efficient, instrumentalist considerations would suggest that a rule by which the members of the religious sect were excluded from the family allowances was preferable to one in which they received them. Intrinsic desert considerations, by contrast, would suggest that all parents, including those who were members of the religious sect, should receive the allowances. The example suggests a conceptual gap between desert-based and consequentialist justifications of the same practice.

There appear to be three things wrong with using this example as an illustration of the difficulties of the instrumentalist account of desert. Firstly, it is not clear that family allowances of this sort are properly thought of as rewards to deserving conduct rather than incentives to overcome the disutility of child-rearing. If they are thought of simply as incentives, then by assumption they would not overcome disutility among members of the religious sect, and the instrumentalist approach would thereby be justified. Secondly, even if the allowances are desert-based, the example would merely show that instrumentalist accounts of desert are incompatible with a system of desert in which involuntary as well as voluntary accomplishments are rewarded. Although it is true that desert is often ascribed to persons on the basis of characteristics that involved in their acquisition no effort or decision, it is not at all clear that this practice is justifiable, and therefore ought to figure as an element in any theory of desert. Thirdly, even supposing that justified desert was allowed in the family allowance case, this would not show that all practices in which the idea of desert was used were incapable of instrumentalist justification. There may be some accomplishments in which the giving of a reward has to be interpreted as an act expressive of a principle of intrinsic desert, but it would be difficult to argue this in the case of such matters as appointments to posts or selection for higher education.

The strongest argument, however, against the notion of intrinsic desert in social practices is that the application of the concept pre-supposes a shared and unitary scale of values among members of society.[6] Such a shared and unitary scale of values about the relative worthiness of various occupations and characteristics clearly does not exist, however. Instrumental accounts of desert circumvent this problem by making the application of the merit rule depend upon empirically testable consequences. Of course, if, like Ivan Illich,[7] you dispute that benefits do flow from professionalisation, you may doubt the wisdom of the merit rule. But this sort of argument is not a clash of values about the intrinsic significance of certain occupa-tions, but rests upon a claim about the consequences that follow professionalisation, and an assertion, which is in principle empiri-cally testable, that the putative benefits that are supposed to flow from use of the merit rule do not in fact do so.

Suppose then that we interpret the practice of appointing persons on merit as justified by its general tendency to promote social welfare: what follows about the justice of claims under the merit principle? One implication is that candidates have a claim to rewards or benefits, in justice, simply by virtue of the operation of such a rule. An essential element in the idea of justice is that of not disappointing expectations that have been founded upon the existence of a public rule. According to this argument, therefore, the best-qualified candidates for a post have at least a strong prima facie claim upon that post. Those candidates have planned their lives in order to obtain those qualifications in the expectation that the merit principle will be applied, and this fact alone gives rise to a claim under justice that the rule apply.

A second implication is that those who are subject to the merit rule have a claim that the rules of procedural fairness be applied to their case. Selectors must treat like cases as like and must not depend upon irrelevant considerations in coming to a decision. These procedural considerations suggest that the concept of desert will sometimes function like the concept of need, in that between two equally deserving or needy persons no principles of general advantage can supervene to say which of the two should be given preference. When a public rule is established, then justice comes to mean being treated in accordance with that rule, independently of the considerations of general advantage which originally motivated the rule, not simply because persons have come to fix their expecta-tions upon the operation of the rule, but also because justice is seen as having an intrinsic connection with bounded and rule-like procedures.

If we accept this characterisation of the desert principle, then a difficulty arises. The practice has developed in the USA of giving preference to women and members of specific minority ethnic groups over other candidates in such matters as job appointments and university selection, particularly to some of the professional schools. To understand the nature of this practice we need to know a little of its history[8] Under the 1964 Civil Rights Act it is in fact illegal in the USA to favour a person for employment by reference to that person's race or sex. How can it be, therefore, that a policy of preference has grown up? The basic process has been that the courts and executive agencies have power to enforce remedies against previous discrimination and indirect discrimination, the latter being the use of tests of qualifications which though formally neutral in intent have the effect of discriminating against certain groups. One way of knowing whether indirect discrimination is taking place is to observe whether or not there is a racial balance in the workforce of a particular employer. So the courts and executive agencies have the power to impose timetables and goals on employers for the integration of their workforce, as a way of remedying indirect discrimination.

The process has not been taken so far in Britain, although indirect discrimination is illegal and employers are given powers by the 1976 Race Relations Act to run special training or recruitment programmes for their employees.[9] (Appointment by reference to the criterion of race remains illegal, however.) There is, of course, widespread recognition that some of the most acute social deprivation is concentrated among ethnic minority groups, particularly West Indians, in Britain. However, even as liberal and perspicacious an observer as Lord Scarman[10] baulks at the prospect of providing an advantage to members of minority groups in police employment, although accepting the need for special programmes in the allocation of public services. In what follows, therefore, I shall try to pose the question of whether a policy of preference really is incompatible with the demands of desert and social welfare. I shall consider only the most frequently discussed sort of case as far as US practice is concerned, namely appointments to professional jobs and entrance to higher education, which is of course the gateway to a professional career. I take these examples not because they are likely to be numerically the most significant for ethnic groups, or women, but because it is in these examples that the conflict between desert and affirmative action is likely to be felt most acutely. If the conflict of principle can be solved in these cases, then there are likely to be fewer problems elsewhere in the field of employment.

Policies of affirmative action

In discussing the problems associated with the practice of preferential hiring or university selection, it is important to distinguish two questions. The first of these questions is whether it could ever be compatible with, or even required by, principles of justice to practise preferential hiring. The second is whether it could ever be right to abandon the principle of appointing on merit in order to practise preferential hiring. Although these questions are sometimes treated together, or perhaps more accurately the answer to the second is thought to be the crucial issue in answering the first, I shall treat the questions separately. The problem of what practices a society ought to adopt is distinct from the problem of what practices a society ought to adopt if we follow through on the implications of just one principle.

It is easy to see why the two questions should be confused. The fundamental problem with preferential hiring is that it appears to involve not treating candidates on their personal merits, but allowing non-merited characteristics, their race or their sex, to determine the decision to select. But another, equally important, reason why preferential hiring may seem to be of doubtful worth is that it involves a breach of procedural fairness. Like candidates are not being treated as like because irrelevant considerations are being invoked by decision-makers. So arguments about desert and arguments about procedural fairness come together to cast doubt upon the rightness of the practice. Yet, as we shall see, there is still an important distinction to be made between the justification of the practice and the question of whether it is ever right to override the merit principle.

In my discussion I shall not consider the issues involved in devising the exact means by which a policy of preference is implemented. In the USA a crucial question has involved the supposed distinction between quotas and goals. This distinction was important in the US

Supreme Court *Bakke* judgement, where it was judged wrong for institutions that had not practised discrimination in the past to have a quota of places reserved for minority candidates, although it would not be wrong for such an institution to have goals for the integration of minority students into the institution. Like some others, I find this distinction more than a little puzzling, since it would seem that quotas might be one way, though only one way, of knowing whether your goals had been satisfactorily achieved.[11] However, the matter is unimportant in the discussion that follows, which is concerned with the broad issues of principle involved in the practice of preferential hiring and selection.

In order to approach a solution to the problem of when, if at all, preferential hiring or selection is compatible with justice, let us consider a number of situations in which one might think about introducing a practice of preference in order to make sure that one's practice was fair.

The first such situation would be where merit alone would be sufficient to appoint women or minority candidates, but other considerations intervene. This sort of situation can arise not because those making the selection are prejudiced against the candidates concerned, but because they bring in tie-breaking considerations, in cases where there are two candidates of equal merit, which have the unintended effect of working against minority or female candidates.[12] For example, there are two candidates of equal merit, but the man is preferred to the woman because the appointing committee takes cognisance of the fact that men generally bear the brunt of financial responsibilities for their families, whereas the woman would be a second wage-earner in the household. Another example might be one in which a minority candidate was not appointed not because of prejudice on the appointing committee's part but because they feared prejudice among those with whom the minority candidate would have to work. These would be examples of secondary sexism, or racism, cases in which discrimination is not intentionally practised against certain groups, but in which the considerations that appointing committees habitually used, and which may seem perfectly innocent in themselves, systematically worked against the interests of particular groups of candidates. In these circumstances, it would be quite compatible with justice, and may even be required by it, to operate a policy of deliberate preference to counteract the operation of secondary discrimination. Such a policy would not be required if there were other ways of achieving the same ends which were less costly than the practice of preference. On the other hand, what may seem to be only secondary sexism or racism may be a cover for the primary version, and preferential hiring is a public way of testing good faith in this regard.

A second situation in which merit considerations might imply a policy of preference would be one in which one doubted that the credentials of the candidates represented their merits. Some schools, for example, coach their students in interview technique when they apply for university places. To give preference to a candidate who interviews well may be unfairly to discriminate against a candidate who does not interview well because that candidate has simply not had the relevant training at school. This example may be generalised. Two candidates of the same ability may have different qualifications because their schools, or the general background conditions in which they had to work, advantaged one of the candidates and disadvantaged the other. If selection is on the basis of what candidates merit by their abilities, and if minority and female candidates are typically disadvantaged in obtaining those qualifications that are supposed to act as the hallmark of ability, then it may be right to introduce a policy of preferential selection. Other policies might also be indicated, of course. One might want to even out the background conditions and reform the award of qualifications so that they more accurately reflected merit, but these are often long-term and slow-moving ambitions, and meanwhile the disadvantaged members of one generation are suffering cumulative disadvantages.

There is a third situation, resembling the second in some respects, but nevertheless distinct from it, and this is one in which there may be no problem about the qualifications accurately representing the merits of the candidates in the appropriate respects, but where the merit-making characteristics for the post are broader than those the attained qualifications bear upon. Francis Cornford[13] once defined a university lecturer as a person chosen to teach on the ground that he was once able to learn. For posts like university teaching, and the other professional jobs where the practice of preference is a contentious issue, there are many qualities required apart from past academic achievement, and if the past academic achievement of two candidates is equal, then it may be proper to take into account other relevant characteristics. Female and minority members of staff may be better personal advisors to some students than male white members of staff may be. Taking their status into account in these regards may quite properly give some candidates the edge, and an explicit practice of preference may help to bring into play these broader considerations.

There is a problem of how correctly to describe this third situation. There is a tendency to describe it as one in which considerations of social welfare are allowed to supervene upon considerations of merit or justice. However, there is no necessity to describe it in this way. The only reason for doing so would be if, with Sidgwick,[14] one makes a sharp distinction between appointment to a post as a deserved reward for past achievement and appointment on grounds of fittingness for the post in question. If, like Feinberg,[15] we construe the desert basis as that of having just those qualities that fit one to do the job, then taking into account these broader considerations will be quite proper in distinguishing candidates of otherwise equal merit.

At this point there may appear to be an inconsistency in the conclusions that we have derived from the first and the third of our situations. In the first situation secondary sexism and racism involved taking into account considerations other than the strict merits of the candidates. In the third example these merits were construed as being fitness for the job, broadly conceived. But someone might now claim that this broad conception of merit allows secondary sexism or racism in by the back door. After all, ability to get along with colleagues constitutes fitness for the job, and if potential colleagues are prejudiced against women or blacks does that not mean, by the conclusion to our third example, that women and blacks are less meritorious for jobs in which their potential colleagues are prejudiced? This would seem to be an inconsistency that undermines the case for the practice of preference from the weak premises we have so far worked with.

In order to prevent the contradiction emerging, the simplest procedure is to recognise that the merit rule is being given a broadly consequentialist justification, but within the constraints of principles of justice that limit the policies that may be undertaken for the promotion of social welfare. The ability to work at a satisfying job equal to one's merits is a fundamental part of what for most people in liberal democracies constitutes their conception of the good. Because it is fundamental, it ought not to be overridden by the external preferences of others, which, if taken into account in the calculus of social welfare, would prevent the attainment of that good by some types of individual. By contrast, the reverse does not hold for those female and minority candidates who happen to be advantaged by the fact that their unmerited distinguishing characteristic is one that fits them for the post by comparison with others. The reason why it may be quite relevant for a university to ensure, for example, that minority and female students have access to advisors who share their own characteristics, is because the lack of attention to the matter in the past may have left a series of gaps that need to be filled. It is just as though a Political Science department had developed, and then realised that it did not have a specialist to teach Soviet politics. There would be nothing amiss in its favouring a Soviet specialist in its next appointment above other, equally well-qualified, candidates.

These three situations, then, would be ones in which a practice of preferential hiring or selection would be compatible with the principles of justice. As I have suggested, this practice would not necessarily be required, although if there were no other alternative it might be. Even from comparatively weak premises, then, the practice of preference might be required. In American terms this practice would be no more than is currently adopted in affirmative action programmes, and is weaker than elements in those programmes. However, in British terms such a practice would mark quite a break from that currently adopted. Finally, it is clear, in relation to these three types of situation, that rejected white, male applicants would have no grounds for complaint. They have not been treated in a fashion that is less deserving than their merits warrant.

Overriding merit?

So far we have considered the case where merits were equal, or have been judged to be equal, controlling for variations in background circumstances, and the question has been whether a practice of preference could ever be invoked to tilt the balance in favour of minority and female candidates. Now I shall consider the more difficult case, in which the merit principle may be replaced or overridden by considerations based on the sex or race of candidates. I shall consider three types of reasons why someone should think it proper that the merit principle should be overridden in this way: reasons connected with the internal standards and goals of the institution that appoints or selects; reasons connected with the aim of compensating disadvantaged individuals; and reasons connected with broader considerations of social welfare and social integration.

The first type of reason for having an explicitly preferential policy can be regarded as an extension of earlier arguments. Let us suppose that one candidate is judged better qualified than another. Someone has to do the judging. Given that institutions like universities and hospitals are usually the ones to judge these matters for themselves, they may adopt a policy of preference to guard themselves against unconscious prejudice. This is not quite the same as allowing for the fact that some persons have had greater obstacles to overcome than others. Instead it is a matter of recognising that one's judgement is fallible, and in relation to some candidates may stray in a particular direction.

This is not a powerful argument, however. Someone has to make a judgement about the relative merits of candidates. Self-policing of the impartiality of that judgement is unlikely to be effective if the impartiality is likely to be undermined by unconscious forces. Policing by government agencies is difficult to do by general regulatory measures, since there is no reason why a fair set of procedures should result in a specific ethnic balance within each institution. Italians are under-represented in American universities and Jews are over-represented[16] compared with their respective sizes in the population as a whole. One of the standard difficulties of affirmative action programmes is that of obtaining reliable estimates of the numbers of minority-group persons who are seeking work in a particular sector of the labour market.

The second type of reason that might justify affirmative action on a basis other than merit is concerned with compensation, either to individuals or to groups. Individual compensation might arise when an individual lacked merit not through his or her own efforts, but because of disadvantages suffered earlier in life in the educational system and social system more generally. These disadvantages might have been so strong as to leave the individual with no opportunity to catch up with his or her more fortunate peers. If these disadvantages were unfairly imposed upon an individual, then it might be argued that it was proper to compensate an individual by the award of a job or a university place, even though on strict meritocratic criteria the individual could not be said to have deserved those benefits. Undoubtedly many women and members of ethnic minority groups have suffered from unfair disadvantages of this sort, not only by virtue of inadequate social provision, but also through the predominance of certain cultural stereotypes which have had the effect of limiting ambitions and the autonomous development of individual plans of life. Compensation to groups involves a similar argument, except here the victims and the potential beneficiaries are identified as a set of individuals sharing a certain set of characteristics.

It might be thought that the claim about individual compensation was quite different in character from a claim about group compensation, but this is not so. In fact, the claim to individual compensation must be reducible to a claim about the compensatibility of group characteristics. To compensate an individual for a previous disadvantage is to imply that the individual would now be better placed had he or she not suffered the effects of the disadvantage. Compensation, then, implicitly involves a counterfactual judgement about what the present merits of the individual would have been in the absence of the disadvantage. A decision as to individual compensation must therefore look to the facts of a particular individual's history. A practice of preference, however, does not look to these facts. It compensates individuals on the basis of characteristics they share with other individuals. Since neither all women, nor all members of minority ethnic groups have been disadvantaged, a policy that gives them preference cannot be giving compensation to them as individuals. And this conclusion must hold even though the statistical likelihood of disadvantage is much greater among women and minorities than among white males.

Compensation, then, must essentially be a group notion.[17] It is women and ethnic minorities as such who are being compensated. However, the trouble with the practice of preference is that it seems ill-suited to serve as group compensation in this way. It is intrinsically selective among members of the compensated group, and this makes it a blunt instrument of reparation, in particular if those most disadvantaged do not receive the benefit. In any case it is not clear that all members of groups are entitled to compensation. As Goldman[18] points out, the rich American Jew is not entitled to compensation for Nazi war crimes committed on Jews. And the costs of compensation with preferential practices do not fall widely among those who have benefited from previous injustice, but are concentrated among a particular group, those white males who are not selected for university or given a job, many of whom are presumably innocent of having imposed disadvantages on others.

These difficulties with the compensation principle are perhaps not overwhelming, but they are serious enough not to lead us to rest the whole of the case for affirmative action on grounds of compensation. We may then turn to the third type of reason that may be advanced, namely that of social welfare.[19] There are many arguments from social welfare that might make one favour a programme of affirmative action. One might regard the promotion of a particular group of interests as especially important. One might believe in the value of integrating various groups together, and so the practice of preference might be justified as we now justify special quotas for handicapped workers. Or one may be so concerned by the prospect of social tensions and violence if groups are not integrated that enforcing preferential practices becomes a priority. Of course there are utilitarian arguments against such a practice. Members of the groups favoured by the practice may suffer from a lack of self-esteem if they do not know whether they have been selected on merit, or on their group characteristic; standards may fall if institutions do not select on merit; and there is the danger of a backlash from those who bear the costs of affirmative action. But I, for one, would be extremely surprised if the balance of utilitarian advantage in societies like Britain and the USA was opposed to affirmative action.[20]

Would it be unfair, however, to act on the basis of utilitarian advantage without having regard to the claims of those who would otherwise merit selection? There are really three aspects to this problem: the passing over of those with better qualifications in favour of those with less good qualifications; the disappointment of legitimate expectations; and the fact that those who suffer from programmes of affirmative action are usually those who are least responsible for the conditions that the programmes are seeking to rectify.

The first of these problems is undoubtedly serious, but it is made less serious by a consequentialist justification for the merit rule than it would be if the justification were intrinsic. If the merit rule is adopted because so doing has a tendency to promote the general advantage, then its modification to allow the less well-qualified to be appointed has more justification if that practice can be shown to be to the general advantage. It follows of course that even less well-qualified candidates should meet some minimum standards of competence, which may be quite high. Moreover, the problem of desert may be less severe if it is true, as some economists[21] suggest, that on-the-job-training is a more important component of job skills than previous qualifications. A policy of preference could then be seen as providing members of various ethnic groups with the means to acquire job skills.

The next problem is that of legitimate expectations. There is no doubt that programmes of affirmative action may breach legitimate expectations, but this fact alone cannot provide an in principle objection to such programmes, merely to the form they take. If the content of an affirmative action programme were to change rapidly the composition of certain professions or of the student body, then there would be a problem. But those currently qualified and in the bidding for jobs or university places are only a small proportion of those affected by current affirmative action programmes. The vast bulk of those affected are those who have yet to qualify. The announcement by the government of a planned programme of affirmative action, with increasingly stringent goals year by year, would not create a problem of disappointed expectations. White males intending to go to university or into the professions would have time to adjust their plans to take account of the new circumstances. Indeed, one advantage about such a programme would be that the weight of the argument about disappointed expectations would then be transferred; for under a planned programme of affirmative action it would be women and minority group members who would be entitled to complain if their expectations were disappointed.

The solution to the problem of legitimate expectations raises the third problem, however. For it would seem that those made to bear the burden of rectifying the wrong of racial discrimination are the young and those not yet in post.[22] Is it fair to expect them alone to bear this burden when racial discrimination is a social problem? There is, in fact, no obvious principle that says that specific groups of individuals, because of their own social situation, should not be asked to bear some of the burden for the solution of problems that are really those of society at large. Presumably the obligation on large employers to employ some registered disabled persons in their workforce means that other non-disabled workers either do not have jobs or have to spend longer searching for those jobs they have. Moreover, in so far as the objection is that programmes of affirmative action only apply at the level of junior appointments, and therefore disproportionately affect the young, the obvious remedy is to seek means for applying the same principles to seniority procedures.

All the above is in the hypothetical. The demand for affirmative action programmes has not been as great in Britain as in the USA, and it is striking to note, for example, the different attitudes towards busing that representatives of ethnic minorities in the two communities have evinced.[23] However, if there were a political demand for affirmative action then it could proceed by building upon the current anti-discrimination legislation. Large employers could be required, rather than merely permitted, by law to run special training and recruitment programmes,[24] and institutions of higher education and other public bodies could be requested to draw up relevant programmes of action. If the above arguments have been correct, then there need be no substantial breach of the principle that the general advantage required the operation of the test of desert, though we might have to get used to that notion in new forms.

10

Democracy and Participation

In the discussion of principles of social policy so far, we have been concerned for the most part with *what* decisions ought to be made rather than with *how* decisions ought to be made. This one-sided emphasis now needs to be rectified for a number of reasons. The contractarian theory of social choice leaves a considerable amount of indeterminacy in the specification of the social welfare objective at which the government is to aim. Although it prescribes the form that such an objective should take, namely that it should be a weighted sum of individual welfares, it does not prescribe how the weights are to be fixed. The essential indeterminacy in the attitudes towards risk of the contracting parties behind the veil-of-ignorance means that no particular level of equality can be justified by contractarian considerations alone. That task is left to the democratic process and to those persons living this side of the veil-of-ignorance. Moreover, this aspect of the contractarian theory needs to be understood in the context of our prior result about the importance of maintaining the conditions for autonomous development. A second reason why an interest in democratic control is important in our theory is that this theory presupposes that persons living in a political community are capable of choice and deliberation. A theory of democracy is therefore necessary to show how those capacities can be given effect within communities. In pursuing this subject, I shall also touch upon the elusive value of 'community'. Although one method by which people express sentiments of community and solidarity is by private gifts of time and money, another way in which the same value can be promoted is by voluntary service on public bodies that have decision-making or consultative status. The scope for decision-making on such bodies is considerable, and could be increased if desired, and so some account is needed of how such bodies might function.

In the following discussion I shall assume that the justification for democracy is well established in the general case. The use of procedures that are responsive to the popular will, and in particular to a majority vote, can be supported by appeal to a number of diverse, but mutually reinforcing, considerations. Not only does a democratic form of government respect the autonomy of persons, it provides the incentive for self-development and civic responsibility. Unless a government is accountable to the populace it is unlikely to know where the shoe is pinching. Moreover, democracy allows scope for the free competition of ideas in the solution to collective problems, and this is likely to enhance a society's problem-solving capacity. And democracy provides a set of procedures in which there is recognition of the equality of persons.[1]

The paradox of democracy

The indeterminacy at the heart of the contractarian theory of social choice helps us solve a problem that has been identified as being at the heart of democratic theory. This is the paradox of democracy.[2] The paradox of democracy is a problem that arises in the relationship between individual and collective judgement. An individual in the choice between two policies, X and Y, may think that X ought to be implemented instead of Y. However, a democratic decision may result in Y being preferred by society to X. Democrats, committed to accepting the results of the voting process, may therefore think that Y ought to be implemented instead of X. But such democrats might continue to think, in their heart of hearts so to speak, that X is a better policy than Y. However, this would seem to commit such democrats to an inconsistency; for now they are simultaneously committed to the proposition that X is better than Y and ought to be implemented, and to the proposition that Y is better than X and ought to be implemented. And this simultaneous commitment to two contradictory propositions presents a paradox.

The contractarian solution to this problem is to qualify the sense in which someone may claim that one policy is better than another, before the policies have been adjudicated by voting. In the first instance let us suppose the range of policies in question all fall within that category permitted by the principle of minimum needs. None of the policies violates the conditions for minimal autonomy. Then, a democrat, in holding that policy X is preferable to policy Y, is holding that in his or her judgement policy X is the policy that would be preferred by rational persons behind the veil-of-ignorance. In other words, the democrat is making a judgement about which policy conduces best to all-round social welfare. However, the democrat is also aware that others may perform the same contractarian thought-experiment, in order that they may come to a judgement about what is best for all-round social welfare, and that in performing the experiment they may come to a different conclusion. So, what democrats are saying when they claim that policy X is better than policy Y is that policy X is one that is eligible to be chosen by a democratic community, and that the result of their performing the contractarian thought-experiment is to judge that policy X better conduces to all-round social welfare than does policy Y. However, the judgement that X is better than Y is a conditional judgement, contingent on the results of voting. In other words, the democrat holds that because X is consistent with the results of a contractarian thought-experiment it is implementable, but that it ought not to be implemented in preference to Y if Y is also implementable and is preferred by the democratic process.

The second case to consider is that in which the person judging that X is better than Y is judging between alternatives in which Y involves a severe deprivation on some persons, and X does not. Here a person will not be committed to X in a conditional sense, for Y by definition is ineligible to be chosen by the electorate and, therefore, it is not implementable. In such cases it is the second proposition of the paradox that needs to be qualified. It will not follow from the electorate's preferring Y to X that Y ought to be implemented in preference to X unless Y is implementable. The conclusion to be drawn from this analysis is that decisions on welfare rights ought to be withdrawn from the scope of normal democratic decision-making and either incorporated in a documentary constitution, as are civil and political liberties in many political systems, or made subject to special provision for change by more than simple majority procedures.[3] If welfare rights are not protected in this way, then those who suffer severe deprivations from the operation of majority procedures have the right to engage in civil disobedience, even though the regime in which they live is a democratic one.

Types of democratic procedure

In discussing the place of democratic procedures in social policy I shall distinguish between three broad types of democratic institutions. The first type may be called competitive party representative democracy. In this system political parties compete against one another within a territorial area for the right to govern, and the party with the greatest support forms the governing team.[4] The governing party is made responsive to the electorate's wishes both by its having secured enough support to have the right to govern, and by the prospect of having to face re-election at some definite period in the future, when its conduct in office will be judged by the electorate. In the pure version of this system the governing party should not be dependent on organised interests for its ability to formulate and implement policies, although the government may consult with such interests as it chooses. The scope for widespread participation in the formulation and conduct of policies is strictly limited. The mass electorate 'participates' by its acquiescence or consent to the policies that are pursued and by the act of voting.[5] No one is formally precluded from being a candidate, however, and participation may be extended by having an extensive system of local government, which will increase the proportion of the population actively involved in the formulation and implementation of policy. Even with extensive local government, however, public participation is low. This does not mean that the government is unresponsive to the wishes of electors. Individuals may have influence through their participation in surveys, questionnaires and censuses; but their influence is as potential consumers of policies formulated by others, and not as citizens actively involved in the process. This type of democracy is the one that is characteristic of liberal democracy.

A second type of democracy is also representative in character, but the basis of representation is no longer a given territorial area, but congeries of social interests. The fundamental idea here is that a person cannot be represented in all his or her varied capacities, but only in relation to certain specific roles or interests that he or she may have. G. D. H. Cole[6] puts the principle well when he says that in this theory a person

should be called upon, not to choose someone to represent him as a man or as a citizen in all the aspects of citizenship, but only to choose someone to represent his point of view in relation to some particular purpose or group of purposes, in other words, some particular *function*. All true and democratic representation is therefore *functional* representation.

The basis of representation is left undetermined by this principle, which requires merely that significant social interests be the basis for representation without saying how they are to be selected. In Cole's theory of guild socialism the basis of representation is economic groupings, but these are not the only, and in some societies perhaps not the most obvious, basis. Cole's form of functional or social group representation was of course merely a proposal, but there are examples where functional representation of this sort can be found in social policy. Health Systems Agencies in the USA and Community Health Councils in England and Wales are supposed to be representative bodies whose bases of representation are social groups including women, ethnic groups, and various patient-interests.[7] Similarly, the Taylor Committee's proposals for the reform of school government suggested a functional basis of representation between teachers, parents, the local education authority and representatives of business and labour within the local community.[8] Finally, there are whole societies in which the representation of social groups appears to be a necessary condition for democratic stability. The Social and Economic Council in the Netherlands is a consultative body with considerable *de facto* powers, in which representatives of business and labour are selected by the main religious blocs of employers and labour associations. This last case is an example of what has become known as 'consociational' democracy, and such consociational systems provide an important and distinct type of representative arrangement from that found in simple competitive party systems based just on territorial areas.[9]

The third type of democracy I shall identify may be termed 'neighbourhood' democracy. Unlike the competitive party system and social group representation, neighbourhood democracy is direct rather than representative. In this particular form of organisation, persons within a small locality come together to decide upon a common course of action. An executive committee may be set up to carry on the day-to-day administration of policy, but the assumption is that final authority rests with the general body of citizens gathered together as a group. Examples of such neighbourhood democracies are the traditional New England town meeting, English parish meetings (and perhaps some of those parish councils effectively subject to the meeting) and tenants' associations. The common element in these different forms is that, in order to involve people directly in the discussion of business, they must be carried on on a small scale.[10]

Although these three types of democracy can be conceptually distinguished from one another, they are not in practice so separate. The most obvious arrangement in which the types can be combined is one in which competitive party democracy leaves certain sorts of decisions to be made at the neighbourhood level. The powers of parishes in English local government to provide certain social amenities and to raise a small precept on the rates is a case in point. Similarly there is no reason in principle why local authorities should not give tenants' bodies the right to make decisions on external decoration and repairs to houses. However, there are other links between the three types of democracy. Consociational democracies are systems in which competitive political parties operate and there is representation of social groups on important decision-making bodies. Moreover, neighbourhood can itself be thought of as the basis for a distinct social group, as was recognised by the Redcliffe-Maud Report[11] in its proposals for consultative district councils, and is instanced in the role that parishes play in connection with planning and transport decisions. The sense of community may exist not only between those who share certain economic interests or religious beliefs, but also between those who happen to live in the same locality.

Although these various democratic forms may be mixed together, the question naturally arises as to what is the best way to mix them. Naturally, the choice of different forms of particular circumstances will be narrowed down by practical considerations. For example, neighbourhood democracy is by definition limited in scope and these limitations are intrinsic to its nature. The attempt to develop widespread participation must inevitably founder through lack of time. As Dahl[12] has shown, some elementary calculations about the amount of time that would be needed if everyone were to discuss issues shows that neighbourhood democracy must inevitably be limited in scope, both in terms of the number of persons who can participate and in terms of the number of issues over which a neighbourhood democracy can be given control. Moreover, neighbourhood democracy cannot solve the problem of how to make allocations between areas. Many social facilities, like hospitals and schools, are geographically limited in scope, but typically involve a commitment of resources which cannot be raised locally, and so some overall decision must be taken concerning allocation between different localities. Finally, it may be difficult to secure general participation even in small-scale organisations. Studies of voluntary organisations show that key decision-makers within them tend not to reflect the social characteristics of the membership. For example, among voluntary workers in Manchester women outnumbered men three to one, whereas decision-makers were predominantly men.[13] If social characteristics are some guide to the sorts of decisions that persons are likely to take, then we cannot assume that neighbourhood democracy will, of itself, secure adequate representation of particular interests.

The most natural way to secure representation of particular interests is to recruit representatives on the basis of social groups and interests, rather than on the basis of geography. In some circumstances practical political considerations dictate that social groups be the basis of decision-making. Perhaps the most striking example in social policy is provided by education in the Netherlands. Three-quarters of Dutch children are educated in private schools run by denominational groups, but with the government covering the complete costs. This arrangement, stemming from the Pacification of 1917, was necessitated by the growing social and political tensions occasioned by the inability of the public school system to provide religious instruction of a sort thought suitable by major religious groups. It is likely that had this arrangement not been adopted the stability of the Dutch political system would have been called into question.[14]

There are other examples where the need for social group representation is less drastic, but where none the less it may be thought to be important. One such example is Community Health Councils (CHCs) in Britain, and another is Health Systems Agencies (HSAs) in the United States. The latter are intended to represent consumer interests in health-care planning. The law requires a consumer majority on each HSA governing board, with the consumers being 'broadly representative of the social, economic, linguistic and racial populations of the area'. Clearly the intention of this legislation is to establish a balance between different social interests and to provide a mechanism to act as counterpoise to producer interests unconstrained by a normally functioning price system.[15]

In circumstances in which providing a forum for social interests is a practical necessity, there is unlikely to be any difficulty about the identification of those interests, although even Dutch experience suggests that a functioning system of consociational democracy can find it difficult to cope with the rise of new social groups and new interests. However, the sort of difficulty to which group representation, when it is not required as a matter of practical necessity, can give rise is illustrated in the example of the HSAs, where there are problems about the mode of selection, defining the basis of selection, the adequacy of representation, and the conflicts that arise when the same person occupies more than one relevant role.

The mode of selection quickly became a legal issue upon the establishment of HSAs. Several suits were filed in the courts alleging inadequate means for selecting consumer representatives. In one case a New York court ruled that there were no grounds on which it could decide between competing minority representatives, even though some representatives had been selected by election. What mattered was simply the number of representatives. Nor is this simply a matter of inadequate legal drafting. As Svensson[16] has pointed out, respecting minority or ethnic interests may well involve respecting the traditional form of selection they use in choosing their representatives. Thus, traditional methods of making decisions among the Pueblo Indians involve investing the final authority in the tribal elders. To insist, as part of the law, that the mode of selection be by election may well run counter, therefore, to the conception that members of the group have of their own identity and interests.

Problems in the basis of representation occur when groups from the same minority interests compete with one another for the right to represent that interest. Morone and Marmor point out that the legal battles fought out over HSAs established that the law contained no legal principles on which the relevant basis of selection could be decided. Problems with the adequacy of selection arises because there is, in general, no reason to believe that the members of a certain social group will adequately represent the interests of that group. Just as geographical representation may mean that

certain interests are not attended to, so even social group representation may mean that those interests are not promoted. It has been
argued that, during the War on Poverty, some of the community
councils that were established were more successful when their
members did not mirror the social and cultural characteristics of
those whom they were representing.[17] Finally, there is the problem
of multiple role identifications. For example, women are typically
less represented than men on various decision-making bodies. But
this distinction begins to disappear when we consider educated
middle-class women and compare them with men. Are middle-class
women then to be identified with the middle class, whose participation rates they share, or with women, whose participation rates they
do not share? To each of these problems a theory of social group
representation must give an answer.

By comparison, how effectively does competitive party democracy based on geographical areas represent interests? Sharpe[18] has
argued convincingly that where there is public trust in officials to
carry out policies with probity and impartiality, then a competitive
party system can be functionally effective in promoting broad social
interests.[19] The nub of his argument turns on the importance of
autonomy for government units, particularly local government
units, if they are to discharge their functions. Widespread public
participation and the representation of group interests may complement functionally effective institutions, but they cannot substitute
for them. The point here may best be illustrated with the example of
air-pollution. If local authorities are to take effective action against
air-pollution then they will have to be free of day-to-day pressures
that prevent them taking such action. Such pressures may arise
either from members of the general public who might be concerned
with the extra costs of burning smokeless fuel, or from industrial
pressure groups who may be concerned at the increased cost of
curbing manufacturing waste. Only if the local authority is free of
such inhibiting pressures will it be able to pursue effective action on
air-pollution.

A further merit of the competitive party system is that it solves the
problem of multiple group membership. This is a problem to which
any theory of collective decision-making must have an answer.
Despite Cole's insistence that no one person can represent another
in all aspects of a person's interests, it remains true that decisions
have to be taken which in some roles we may approve and in other

roles we may disapprove. As a consumer of the local air I may approve of clean-air legislation, whereas as a household forced to pay for more expensive fuel I may disapprove. Collective decision-making requires that some priority be imposed on these competing points of view, and detaching political decision-makers from the pressures to which group representation gives rise is often important in ensuring that fair and efficient decisions are made.

To interpret competitive party democracy in this way may seem to turn it into the sole process for determining the content and nature of social welfare, and sometimes it has been interpreted in just this way. Rothenberg,[20] for example, sees the political process as *the* social welfare function, the means by which the objectives of public policy are determined. Support for this conception might come from Klein's[21] observation that public opinion on social policy questions follows political elite opinion, rather than guiding it. However, this interpretation of the relationship between political decision-making and social welfare is not the only one possible. Public opinion may implicitly place greater weight on the attainment of some objectives rather than others, for example improvements in education as against improvements in transport, even though these comparative evaluations may be difficult to pick up in broad movements of public-opinion sampling. One of the ways in which these evaluations are revealed is in the willingness of some parents to buy more expensive houses in order to ensure a certain type of education for their children; parents will, for example, go to some lengths to ensure that they live in a catchment area for comprehensive schooling rather than in an area where there is still a division between grammar and secondary modern schools. Exercising the 'exit' option[22] from a local authority is one way in which citizen preferences are revealed, although it is an inherently limited way because of the large number of different combinations of services that may be provided. Political authorities may also obtain information on citizen preference for particular services by conducting sample surveys of consumers' response to particular services, and sophisticated techniques have now been developed for ascertaining consumer priorities between different items of public expenditure.[23]

The conclusion so far seems to be that the model of competitive party representative government provides a means of overcoming some of the shortcomings of neighbourhood democracy and group representation, and that some of its own shortcomings may be dealt with by techniques for ascertaining consumer preferences over particular services. Does this mean that it is an adequate model by itself for democratic control of social policy? To that question we now turn.

Integrating the models of democracy

Let us suppose that we have a functioning competitive political system, in which the public authorities take trouble to ascertain citizen preferences over available service provision and in which there are no sharp social cleavages, for example blocs of religious groups who want their children educated in a particular way, leading towards a consociational form of democracy. Are there any reasons of normative theory for trying to complement that form of democratic control by other forms of control?

In posing this question I am assuming that the normative reasons will be connected to features of the democratic process and not to features of the outcomes that result from that process. It is clearly always possible to maintain, as a fall-back position, that public participation and group representation will improve the quality of decisions made. Yet this sort of instrumental argument is inadequate for present purposes. Not only does it rest on shaky foundations empirically, as we noted in the evidence from community councils in the War on Poverty, but it provides too weak a case for supplementing competitive party democracy. The sort of argument that is suitable is one in which some intrinsic value is attached to participation in the democratic process itself, so that even if increased participation or representation does not lead to improved results, it can still be justified in its own right. This does not mean that the relevant benefits of participation are not susceptible to empirical specification. But it does mean that those benefits should not be treated merely as the benefits of certain putative outcomes.

There are a number of reasons for giving a positive answer to the question of whether there is a reason for supplementing the competitive political process with other democratic forms. One such reason is to ensure the representation of certain interests in policy-making in a visible form. Morone and Marmor[24] point to groups whose special interests ought to be taken into consideration in health-care planning, including the poor, racial minorities, the elderly, women, migrant workers and workers exposed to special occupational hazards. It would be possible for planners to take note of the special interests of these groups when deciding on health-care allocations, but the presence of representatives on the board of a planning agency, even if only in a consultative capacity, provides visible evidence that the needs of these groups are recognised. Representation of this sort can of course always degenerate into one of the many symbolic uses of politics. But to be an effective symbol, representation and the powers of representatives must be genuine and not merely token, and political elites are likely to find it difficult to manipulate representatives for long. More important, perhaps, is the difference in politics between what is actually happening and what people think is happening. Health-planners may in fact be taking into account the interests of certain social groups, but they may not be thought to be doing so by members of those groups. To overcome this credibility gap, the device of incorporating group representatives into policy-making can be used. Women, members of ethnic groups, or the poor, can know that they have representatives on HSAs; they are rarely in a position to assess planning outcomes and to know whether planners have made a decision to their advantage or disadvantage, say, in sanctioning new investment in a coronary-care unit rather than in casualty facilities.[25]

Clearly one problem with incorporating group representatives lies in judging their representativeness, and this in two senses. Not all potential interests may be organised, and among those who *are* organised the individuals at the forefront of the organisation may not be representative of the general membership. The principle that 'he who says organisation says oligarchy' may not be an iron law but it is certainly a strong tendency operating in various circumstances. This second consideration will not be worrying in itself provided that the representative organisations have the confidence of their members. The problem of unorganised interests is more difficult. No government body can turn a group in itself into a group for itself, although it can make that process easier by prescribing that certain sorts of interests must be represented, even if there is no obvious organisation that stands for those interests. In the end, however, it is difficult to avoid acting on the principle that only the dogs who bark get a chance at the bone, although it is salutary to remember that one problem with the HSA legislation was that too many groups sought admittance to the councils of representation.

A particular group whose interests may need to be recognised in public decision-making is that of producers. Recent concern about the distortions of professionalism in the social services and about cost-escalation induced by producer interests means that there is now much more scepticism about recognising producer interests than once there was. Clearly the costs and benefits of occupational licensure need to be calculated before agreeing to restrictive entry, and cost over-runs are a persistent feature of much of the budgetary process. Yet acknowledgement of these points needs to be counter-balanced by an acknowledgement of the advantages of bringing producer interests into decision-making. As the Taylor Committee[26] argued in connection with the government of schools, the case for bringing teachers formally into the governing arrangements was that decisions often required technical or specialist knowledge which only teachers were in a position to provide. Moreover, teachers have experience with the day-to-day running of the school and this is often necessary in taking decisions over such matters as equipment purchase. (It is, I think, all too easy to write off the possibility of children's representatives in school government, but it would be difficult, to say the least, to build an adequate representative system in education relying exclusively on this group of consumers.) In other areas of social policy consumers may not have day-to-day experience with the running of the institution, whereas producers do. For most of us, fortunately, hospitals are an option good: we like them to be there when we need them, but we do not have regular contact with their workings. Here again the producer point of view, and in particular that of nursing and ancillary staff, can be an important source of information.

A further reason for paying attention to the producer point of view was at the centre of Cole's conception of guild socialism, and, although it may seem a little high-flown it seems to me to contain an important truth. This is the idea that one wants to tap the public-service motive of those who work in public institutions. This argument rests upon the assumption that public officials are not simply budget maximisers interested in promoting their own conditions of employment, but that they have a genuine commitment to the public service within which they are working. Empirical evidence appears not to support the budget maximising conjecture, and clearly much observed behaviour, for example pressure for more and better qualified staffing, is at least consistent with a public-service motive.[27] To provide a forum for the representation of suppliers' views is to enable supplier groups to contribute towards the improvement of public services.

A further reason why a competitive party democracy needs to be complemented by a wider range of participation is the importance of protecting that rather nebulous value, community. The idea of community is a broad and ill-defined one.[28] Communities of interest can be identified as widely dispersed across space, witness the community of interest among diaspora Jews, and as widely dispersed across time, for which the long-lasting nationalism of pre-independence Ireland can serve as an example. However, there is a sense of community as a small-scale, face-to-face collection of persons which may be especially important in social policy. The fact that people live and work in close proximity to one another induces ties of social affection among them that go beyond an instrumental concern for their well-being, and this will be reinforced if those ties are strengthened by kinship. These sentiments of community identification typically focus upon smaller areas than those of local authorities, at least in Britain. Thus the research for the Redcliffe-Maud Report found that only a small minority of persons identified themselves with a community as extensive as the local authority area. Even in towns of less than 30,000 people less than one-third of respondents identified themselves with an area that was coextensive with local authority boundaries.[29] In a competitive party democracy services are normally organised on an authority-wide basis, but this may mean that particular community interests are ignored or over-ridden.

There are two ways in which the value of community may enter into decisions on social policy. It may be a constraint upon policy-makers, preventing decision-makers doing what they would otherwise want to do, or it may be a goal of policy-making, encouraging decision-makers to do what they would otherwise not do. Either way the idea of recognising the value of community through local forms of democratic representation seems peculiarly appropriate. It is difficult for planners to take cognisance of the value of community unless community sentiment is articulated, and the easiest way to do this is through establishing and co-operating with local forms of community representation. The precise form that this recognition may take will vary from circumstance to circumstance, but may include such arrangements as community control of nurseries and schools, decision-making by local authority tenants about repairs and decorations, the right to be consulted about decisions on land-use and traffic planning, neighbourhood control of facilities for old peoples' welfare, or control of community health centres.

One important end served by extending the opportunity for participation in this way is to give scope to the voluntary-service motive in social welfare. Voluntary movements in social welfare have often been important in pioneering new forms of care and provision, and clearly the donation of money and time on a voluntary basis is still an important element of social provision. However, another form that the desire for voluntary service may take is a willingness to sit on public bodies or act in certain capacities. School governors, members of CHCs, magistrates and JPs all act in this way. The effect of extending the scope for voluntary participation is to diffuse responsibility for social welfare throughout society.

A final argument in favour of supplementing competitive party democracy with other forms rests on a contrast between the adversarial nature of the former and the consensual character of the latter. Party politics is in the nature of the case adversarial, since parties always have an incentive to show how much better their solution to a problem is than that of their opponents. By contrast, neighbourhood democracy and group representation provide a forum for discussion in which divergent interests have an incentive to move towards a common solution. The studies of consociational democracy are striking precisely because they show a willingness of groups with divergent interests to compromise and restrict their claims in the interests of an overriding goal of peaceful conflict resolution. The Dutch system of education or the resolution of their constitutional crisis in 1965 are conspicuous examples. Similarly, we can find that people of widely differing political sentiments will agree on what needs to be done at a neighbourhood level. Not too much can be made of this, of course, and the evidence from the Community Development Projects shows how local community groups could quickly become adversaries of the town hall in their battle for more social facilities.[30] Since peaceful solutions to social problems rest upon compromise and a willingness to meet people half-way, it is important to have institutions that complement the partisan processes of competitive democracy.

The difficulties in implementing neighbourhood democracy and group representation mean that they cannot be substitutes for competitive party democracy, but they may be added to it to form a valuable complement. There are broadly two ways in which this can be accomplished. Firstly, neighbourhood and social group representation may provide a useful model for consultative bodies. This is the role played by HSAs and CHCs. Although having no final formal authority in the structure of decision-making, consultative bodies can nevertheless be influential in policy-making terms. Thus, state legislatures have tended to require, as a necessary condition for approval of capital projects, that the relevant HSA agree to the proposal.[31] Consultation here clearly means more than simply rubber-stamping previously formulated decisions. A second way in which competitive party democracy can be complemented is by involving neighbourhoods or representatives of social groups at certain decision-making stages in the implementation and administration of policies. The Taylor Committee's proposal for both local representatives and representatives of business and labour on school governing bodies neatly encapsulates this formula. The scope of such a body's decision could include such matters as the choice between streaming and mixed-ability teaching in schools, the teaching of a foreign language to primary-school children, or the reorganisation of pastoral care. These are not trivial matters, and yet there is no reason why a local authority should impose a uniform policy on schools in its area rather than devolving the decision down to representative bodies.

One objection that is frequently made to extending the scope of participation is that such a policy presupposes either that people are generally anxious to exercise political responsibility, which is false, or that people ought to be made to exercise political responsibility, which is illiberal. After all, if people are happier cultivating their own gardens, why force them into political activisim? As we have already seen, a subjective conception of the good precludes us from saying that it is an integral part of virtue that persons should participate actively in public life. However, this clearly cannot work as an argument against extending the opportunity of participation, as distinct from applying a duty of participation. A subjective conception of the good precludes us from forcing people to participate in public decision-making, but the assumption of autonomy on which it rests can be interpreted as requiring that opportunities be available for participation.[32]

To illustrate what difference this distinction between opportunities and duties might make, consider a particular example.
Suppose as a planner you are faced with the decision as to whether
local authority housing should be sold to tenants or kept as a collective asset. Suppose also that the evidence was that the potential
buyers would derive more satisfaction from the houses if they
owned them, than if they continued to rent them and also had a
collective say in the way that they were managed. Then the above
distinction between opportunities and duties would preclude your
favouring the collective option simply on the grounds that the exercise of collective control was superior to the satisfactions that
individuals derived from private ownership. But the same distinction would also preclude your centralising the management in the
housing authority, and not giving a voice to the tenants, on the
grounds that only some, and not all, tenants were anxious to participate.

The point is often made that neighbourhood democracy is insufficient of itself to rectify broad inequalities in the distribution of
wealth and power in society at large, and this observation may lead
to disillusionment with the ideal of neighbourhood democracy. In
his investigation of neighbourhood experiments Douglas Yates
found some variety in the way in which democratic control func-
tioned.[33] Where the neighbourhood unit was providing a specific
service, for example a medical clinic, then rates of participation and
levels of citizen control were relatively high. By contrast,
neighbourhood control of the school system was less successful. The
span of control was too wide; routine administration swamped
attempts at basic reform; and levels of popular participation were
low. The conclusion is that experiments in neighbourhood democracy should begin with small-scale, service-focused initiatives,
rather than a devolution of power to districts of neighbourhoods
containing a number of service points.

The lesson to be learnt from this experience is that community
control cannot be a substitute for anti-poverty policies and policies
aimed at equality of educational opportunity. As I have argued,
those policies must be regarded as providing the material preconditions upon which the development of autonomy rests, which in turn
is a precondition for political participation. In order to maintain
those conditions, broad powers of intervention are required by the
political authorities. Although community groups may become
involved, for example, in the administration of a school system, the

basic structure of that system will be determined necessarily by the processes setting the basic institutional structure for society. Neighbourhood democracies cannot determine the size of the total resources devoted to education; they will have little or no influence over the processes by which teachers are trained and their overall supply determined; and they cannot have power to integrate schools across school districts as the attainment of educational equality may require.[34] However, to say that community control of schools has only an auxiliary role to play in the development of better education is not to say that it has an insignificant role. To involve parents and members of the local community in the government of schools may enable them to make important contributions in particular areas. Those who are familiar with the management of schools will know, for example, what a difference to the atmosphere and running of a school even something like an orchestra can make, and the decision of parents and community groups to supply the instruments to make this possible can often be essential.

The other limitation to which neighbourhood democracies and consultative bodies are prone is co-option by producer groups. I have already expressed some scepticism about the view that public bureaucracies are prone to over-expand the size of the services they supply at the expense of the public interest, but clearly co-option by producer groups is a danger for any organisation that has a control function. There is some evidence from studies of the Community Health Councils[35] that they tend to divide into those who are pro-provider and those who are pro-patient. The significance of this evidence is difficult to assess, however. Clearly a general orientation, either pro-doctor or pro-patient, is not virtuous in itself. What matters is whether these general attitudes preclude consultative bodies making sensible recommendations in particular cases. To assess this problem we should need a longitudinal study of particular CHCs which compared their performance to some predetermined set of criteria for making decisions. We do not have such a study, and in its absence we are thrown back onto hunches and general inclination in assessing the possibility of co-option.

Local autonomy and central relations

So far in the exposition I have concentrated upon the problems of delegating authority downwards within the political system, particularly within local authorities, or upon the problems of integrating a socially representative consultative body into the pattern of decision-making. However, there are a set of distinct problems about the relationship between democracy as it operates at the local level and democracy as it operates at the national level. Party competition at different levels is unlikely to result in governments at those different levels whose priorities are always in accord with one another. So the question arises as to what the proper relationship should be between central departments and local authorities.

This problem has multiple aspects. In part it involves purely procedural considerations of how the relationship is to be defined; who is to adjudicate in cases of disputed authority; and whether sovereignty is thought to be essentially unitary, or whether the idea can be thought to admit the separation of powers. However, in another form the problem presents itself as conflict between the desire for certain outcomes, in particular for improved standards of provision in education, housing and the social services, and for local autonomy, the right of local authorities to decide for themselves the correct mix of services between competing demands.[36]

If we look at this latter problem from the point of view of the normative theory that we have developed, then its solution falls into two parts. The first part is that central government should specify minimum standards in those services with which it is concerned, and then, in the second part, local authorities would be given complete discretion to determine service standards above that minimum.[37] The main reason for this division is the same as we noted earlier in connection with the distinction between those aspects of welfare that should be thought of as constitutional rights, and therefore protected from majoritarian procedures, and those aspects of welfare that are part of a more general aim of improving social welfare from material sources. Just as governments place limits on their own competence to reduce income support and educational provision below a certain level, so they impose obligations upon local authorities not to allow the standards of relevant services to slip below minimum standards. However, above that minimum level, the best method of promoting social welfare is a question on which the honest judgement of persons can disagree, and this is best left to the political process to decide. Since local circumstances vary and there are powerful arguments for extending the scope of participation wider than a partisan elite in central government, the case for local authority decision-making follows from these assumptions.

The overall political structure to emerge from this discussion is a complex one, therefore. Political parties compete with one another at the national level over the degree of economic and social equality they believe the government should induce, but subject the scope of their own proposals to the constraints of some constitutional or entrenched set of welfare rights that prescribe the minimum level of well-being that all citizens should enjoy. The elected government is responsible for promoting its desired degree of equality in services for which it is responsible, and also for maintaining a specified set of minimum standards in those service areas for which local authorities are responsible. Above these minimum standards local authorities may experiment as they choose, according to the majority political preference of those who live in their area. However, local authorities should also seek to develop neighbourhood and functional modes of decision-making, just as the development of functional modes of consultation for nationally provided services provides an important instrument of decision-making for those services. Within local authorities, therefore, there would be a varied and complex pattern of local community groups, tenants' associations, consumer representatives, producer representatives and volunteers serving on small-scale decision-making bodies. In other words, the political pluralism implied by a contractarian mode of social choice, subject to minimum constraints of well-being, results in a higgledy-piggledy collection of decision-making bodies. This is not tidy. But whoever said that democracy was tidy?

Epilogue: Civility and Community

The most basic principle in the theory we have been developing is an individualistic one. It requires that the material conditions for autonomy be secured for all persons. The priority of this principle rests upon the claim that the value of personal autonomy is presupposed in any attempt to govern the relations among persons by appeal to reasons embodied in a common discourse. Political relations are to be regulated by principles that all can recognise as imposing justifiable restrictions upon their liberty, in order that the conditions of liberty may be enjoyed by all. No significance, however, is attached to the goals of the political community itself. Such common goals as there are emerge from the process by which individuals form their own social identity and define their own projects and plans. No clearer example of this restricted notion of community could be found than in the place given to the notion of community within the structure of democratic control that we have defined for social policy. Within that structure community is protected only in the interstices of a rights-constrained majoritarian procedure. The concept of community did not determine our proposed structure of democratic control, except to require that some room be left for local loyalties and ties.

In order to bring out this point, let us consider a particular example. Let us suppose that a minority social group, identified linguistically, religiously or ethnically, is living in a political community. Let us also suppose that members of the group are treated justly in their dealings with the wider society. There are no political or legal restrictions upon their activities; when they come before the courts they receive impartial justice, whether or not their case involves someone who is a member of their group; their representa-

tives are effective in the legislature in protecting and promoting
their reasonable interests; unemployment and delinquency rates
are no higher in the group than in society at large; housing conditions are comparable; public amenities, like transport and utilities,
are fairly allocated to the members of the group. In short, they are
full and free members of the political community. However,
although they are neither politically servile nor economically
exploited, they remain socially separate from the wider community.
There are few marriages between members of the group and others
in the community; labour markets tend to be segregated, not
through discrimination, but because the pattern of culturally influ-
enced individual choice falls out that way; members of the group
tend to be concentrated in certain geographical areas; entertain-
ments are distinct; and school educate each new generation into the
distinctive folkways of the separate groups in society. This combination of justice and separation is difficult, particularly for Anglo-
Americans, to imagine, because we are so familiar with a pattern in
which social separateness implies injustice. But it is imaginable, and
the example of the functioning consociational democracies provides
us with an outline of what such a social and political arrangement
might look like. Yet how would we describe such an arrangement?
Our natural impulse, I think, would be to say that here is a tolerant
and just society, but not an integrated society. It is a political community in the sense of being a group of persons freely regulating
their own common affairs; but it is not a community in the fullest
sense of the term.

The eclipse of community has been a common theme of much
social thought. Indeed, writers like Robert Nisbet[1] have written the
history of sociological analysis as a response to the absence of community in the modern world. *Gesellschaft* having replaced
Gemeinschaft, the question has seemed to some to be whether the
social services can function to recreate community in the modern
state. Richard Titmuss's[2] stress upon the integrative role of the
welfare state is an example of this way of thinking. Yet, aside from
local, and essentially limited, experiments, the prospects for the
social services performing this integrative role are not encouraging.
As Tönnies[3] himself argued, *Gemeinschaft* was a historically
specific form of social organisation, and there is no reason to think
that it can be recreated in the conditions of the modern world.

Even supposing, however, that it was practical to aim at

Gemeinschaft, the question arises as to whether we should want to do so. Richard Sennett[4] has provided us with reasons as to why we should not. He contrasts the form of public life that is lived in societies based on the idea of intimacy, with societies based on the idea of the mutually acknowledged regulation of social life by public codes of conduct. In the former, politics becomes personalised and attention focuses on the personality and integrity of the individual politician, rather than the details of the programmes and policies to which he or she is committed. I think we can leave aside the accuracy or otherwise of Sennett's interpretation of his extremely rich and diverse historical examples. The overall point that he makes is an effective one. The attempt to create intimacy in the conditions of modern life, in particular the conditions of modern city life, is going to be frustrating and fruitless. We cannot relate to politicians and members of the political elite in personal terms, nor can we relate to the generality of our co-citizens in personal terms.

We can contrast the principle of community with that of civility. In civil relationships persons are related to one another politically in terms of mutually acknowledged rules. A society in which there is economic security, political freedom and a tolerance of differences can be governed by principles of civility, though it may not have much sense of community. Persons will recognise a right, even when they refuse an intimacy. They can share a country, even when they cannot share a sentiment or a way of life. Think of your closest friends. Can you say now whether, in five years' time, they will be married or single, conformist or bohemian, religious or secular, politically committed or withdrawn, fulfilled or despondent? As individuals we (should) find it impossible to answer such questions. The scope for personal development of those whom we know is too great to be confined within pre-set limits. What we shy away from predicting on the individual level, we should be wary of enforcing at the political level. A political system cannot create a network of relationships; it can only provide a framework of opportunities. The principles of civility, when drawn to their conclusions, suggest that the institutions of social policy should play a central role in promoting the autonomy and welfare of those with whom we share a political life. To do more is to do no better. To do less is worse.

Notes and References

Chapter 1

1. W. Beckerman (ed.), *The Labour Government's Economic Record, 1964–1970* (London: Duckworth, 1972); Graham Hallett, *The Social Economy of West Germany* (London: Macmillan, 1973); J. Leruez, *Economic Planning and Politics in Britain* (London: Martin Robertson, 1975).
2. For the latest state of the art in these matters see the papers by Geoffrey Stephenson, Michael O'Higgins and Chris Pond in Cedric Sandford, Chris Pond and Robert Walker, *Taxation and Social Policy* (London: Heinemann, 1980). The results reported there are in some respects depressingly similar to those in T. Barna, *Redistribution of Incomes Through Public Finance in 1937* (Oxford: Clarendon Press, 1945).
3. Compare Edgar K. Browning, *Redistribution and the Welfare System* (Washington: American Enterprise Institute, 1975) and Peter Townsend, *Poverty in the United Kingdom* (Harmondsworth: Penguin, 1980) pp. 925–6.
4. Department of Health and Social Security, *Prevention and Health: Everybody's Business* (London: HMSO, 1976); Marc Lalonde, *A New Perspective on the Health of Canadians* (Ottawa: Information Canada, 1975). In this connection it is worth noting David Reisman's acute criticism of Titmuss, to the effect that, because Titmuss saw social policy as compensating for the diswelfares of an industrialised economy, he ignored the possibility of regulating industry to prevent those diswelfares arising. See D. Reisman, *Richard Titmuss: Welfare and Society* (London: Heinemann, 1977) p. 102.
5. Compare Robert Pinker, *The Idea of Welfare* (London: Heinemann, 1979).
6. David Easton, *The Political System* (New York: Knopf, 1953) pp. 129–34.
7. Organisation for Economic Co-operation and Development, *Public Expenditure Trends* (Paris: OECD, 1978) p. 25.
8. Compare Harold L. Wilensky and Charles N. Lebeaux, *Industrial Society and Social Welfare* (New York: Free Press, 1965).

9. The best defence of functional explanation as involving more than a heuristic device is to be found in G. A. Cohen, *Karl Marx's Theory of History: A Defence* (Oxford: Clarendon Press, 1978) chs 9 and 10. Cohen's claim (pp. 261–2) is that a eufunctional effect can be cited as the explanation of its cause because it allows us to infer that society has some disposition giving rise to the effect. But this seems to ascribe no more than heuristic status to functional modes of discourse. Either the inference is validated, in which case the disposition is the true explanation of the effect, or it is invalidated, in which case it is clear that the eufunctional effect cannot be the explanation. Moreover, is it not *a priori* implausible to hold that functional discourse can be transferred from the explanation of the behaviour of numerous, relatively short-lived biological populations to the limited number of relatively long-lived societies there have been in the world? For a good introduction to problems of functional explanation, see the following: Dorothy N. Emmet, *Function, Purpose and Powers* (London: Macmillan, 1958) chs 3 and 4; Ernest Nagel, *The Structure of Science* (London: Routledge & Kegan Paul, 1961) pp. 520–35; Alan Ryan, *The Philosophy of the Social Sciences* (London: Macmillan, 1970) ch. 8.
10. Compare, Organisation for Economic Co-operation and Development, *Public Expenditure on Income Maintenance Programmes* (Paris: OECD, 1976).
11. For good examples in this mode see, Peter Flora and Arnold J. Heidenheimer, *The Development of Welfare States in Europe and America* (New Brunswick and London: Transaction Books, 1981) and Gaston V. Rimlinger, *Welfare Policy and Industrialisation in Europe, America and Russia* (Chichester: Wiley, 1971).
12. See, for example, Ted Honderich, *Punishment: The Supposed Justifications* (Harmondsworth: Penguin, 1971).
13. Compare Edmund Burke, *Reflections on the Revolution in France* (1970), ed. Conor Cruise O'Brien (Harmondsworth: Penguin, 1968), p. 152: 'very plausible schemes, with very pleasing commencements, have often shameful and lamentable conclusions . . . it is with infinite caution that any man ought to venture upon pulling down an edifice which has answered in any tolerable degree for ages the common purposes of society, or on building it up again, without having models and patterns of approved utility before his eyes'. Compare Michael Oakeshott, *Rationalism in Politics* (London: Methuen, 1962).
14. For an introduction to cost–benefit analysis, see Robert Sugden and Alan Williams, *The Principles of Practical Cost–Benefit Analysis* (Oxford University Press, 1978).
15. Jeremy Bentham, *An Introduction to the Principles of Morals and Legislation* in J. H. Burns and H. L. A. Hart, *The Collected Works of Jeremy Bentham* (London: Athlone Press, 1970) ch. 1; John Stuart Mill, *Utilitarianism* in H. B. Acton (ed.), *Utilitarianism, On Liberty and Considerations on Representative Government* (London: Dent, 1972) ch. 4; Henry Sidgwick, *The Methods of Ethics* 6th edn (London: Macmillan, 1901) book IV; J. C. C. Smart, 'An Outline of a Utilitarian System of Ethics' in J. C. C. Smart and B. A. O. Williams,

Utilitarianism: For and Against (Cambridge: Cambridge University Press, 1973); J. C. Harsanyi, 'Cardinal Welfare, Individualistic Ethics and Interpersonal Comparisons of Utility', *Journal of Political Economy*, LXIII 4 (1955) pp. 309–21.

16. As well as the literature cited in the above note, see also: D. H. Hodgson, *Consequences of Utilitarianism* (Oxford: Clarendon Press, 1967); David Lyons, *Forms and Limits of Utilitarianism* (Oxford: Clarendon Press, 1965); J. L. Mackie, *Ethics: Inventing Right and Wrong* (Harmondsworth: Penguin, 1977). The following articles are also relevant and are reprinted in Phillippa Foot (ed.), *Theories of Ethics* (Oxford University Press, 1967); J. O. Urmson, 'The Interpretation of the Moral Philosophy of J. S. Mill', *Philosophical Quarterly*, III (1953) pp. 33–9; J. D. Mabbott, 'Interpretations of Mill's "Utilitarianism" ', *Philosophical Review*, LXIV (1955) pp. 3–32; J. C. C. Smart, 'Extreme and Restricted Utilitarianism', *Philosophical Quarterly*, VI (1956) pp. 344–54.

17. For historical accounts of what follows, see: Walter Lord, *The Past That Would Not Die* (London: Hamish Hamilton, 1966); Arthur M. Schlesinger Jr, *A Thousand Days* (London: Andre Deutsch, 1965) ch. 35, *Robert Kennedy and His Times* (London: Andre Deutsch, 1978) pp. 317–27.

18. Schlesinger, *Robert Kennedy*, p. 320.

19. As the Governor himself said, 'Must it be over one little boy', quoted in Schlesinger, *Robert Kennedy*, p. 319.

20. One way of putting this point is to say that, not only does utilitarianism respond to preferences in an anonymous fashion, it also fails to give special weight to the preferences of the worst-off under alternative social arrangements. For the formal results underlying the informal presentation in the text, see R. Deschamps and L. Gevers, 'Leximin and Utilitarian Rules: A Joint Characterization', *Journal of Economic Theory*, XVII 2 (1978) pp. 143–63, and E. Maskin, 'A Theorem on Utilitarianism', *Review of Economic Studies*, XLV 1 (1978) pp. 93–6.

21. Contrast this with Meredith's own understanding of the events: 'The question always arises – was it worth the cost? . . . I believe that I echo the feeling of most Americans when I say that "no price is too high to pay for freedom of person, equality of opportunity, and human dignity".' (Schlesinger, *Robert Kennedy*, p. 325).

22. Compare T. M. Scanlon, 'Preferences and Urgency', *Journal of Philosophy*, LXXII (1975) pp. 655–69.

23. H. L. A. Hart, 'Are There Any Natural Rights?', *Philosophical Review*, LXIV (1955) pp. 175–91, reprinted in A. Quinton (ed.), *Political Philosophy* (Oxford University Press, 1967) pp. 53–66.

24. John Rawls, *A Theory of Justice* (Oxford: Clarendon Press, 1972). For other uses, see in particular: G. R. Grice, *The Grounds of Moral Judgment* (Cambridge University Press, 1967); G. Harman, *The Nature of Morality* (Oxford University Press, 1977); J. C. Harsanyi, 'Cardinal Welfare, Individualistic Ethics and Interpersonal Comparisons of Utility'.

25. Brian Barry, *Political Argument* (London: Routledge & Kegan Paul,

1965) pp. 3–8, 35–8; Brian Barry, *The Liberal Theory of Justice* (Oxford: Clarendon Press, 1973) p. 6; Isaiah Berlin, *Four Essays on Liberty* (Oxford University Press, 1969); David Miller, *Social Justice* (Oxford: Clarendon Press, 1976). See also W. D. Ross, *The Right and the Good* (Oxford: Clarendon Press, 1930).

26. Ronald Dworkin, *Taking Rights Seriously* (London: Duckworth, 1977) ch. 6.
27. H. B. Berrington, *How Nations Are Governed* (London: Pitman, 1964); Robert A. Dahl, *After The Revolution?* (New Haven: Yale University Press, 1970); Isaiah Berlin, *Four Essays on Liberty* (Oxford University Press, 1969) esp. pp. 167–72.
28. Plato, *The Republic*, trans. F. M. Cornford (Oxford: Clarendon Press, 1941).

Chapter 2

1. Compare: Derek Parfit, 'Later Selves and Moral Principles' in Alan Montefiore (ed.), *Philosophy and Personal Relations* (London: Routledge & Kegan Paul, 1973) pp. 137–69; Amélie Oksenberg Rorty (ed.), *The Identities of Persons* (Berkeley and Los Angeles: University of California Press, 1976); Susan Mendus, 'Marital Faithfulness', *Philosophy* (forthcoming).
2. I borrow the term 'projects' from Bernard Williams, *Utilitarianism: For and Against* (Cambridge University Press, 1973). I have come to think it preferable to the idea of a 'plan of life', which suggests a rational ordering of projects into an optimal combination, and therefore is too structured an idea for present purposes. For the concept of a plan of life, see: Charles Fried, *An Anatomy of Values* (Cambridge, Mass: Harvard University Press, 1970) pp. 97–101; David Miller, *Social Justice* (Oxford: Clarendon Press, 1976) pp. 133–43; and John Rawls, *A Theory of Justice* (Oxford: Clarendon Press, 1972) pp. 407–16.
3. Joseph Butler, *Fifteen Sermons*, ed. W. R. Matthews (London: Bell, 1969) passim.
4. John Stuart Mill, *On Liberty* in H. B. Acton (ed.), *J. S. Mill, Utilitarianism, On Liberty, and Considerations on Representative Government* (London: Dent, 1972) p. 74.
5. Thucydides, *The Peloponnesian War*, trans. Rex Warner (Harmondsworth: Penguin, 1972) p. 147.
6. W. G. Runciman, *Relative Deprivation and Social Justice* (London: Routledge & Kegan Paul, 1966) ch. 10.
7. Gabriel A. Almond and Sidney Verba, *The Civic Culture* (Princeton: Princeton University Press, 1963) ch. 6.
8. See A. K. Sen, *On Economic Inequality* (Oxford: Clarendon Press, 1973) pp. 43–5; 'On Weights and Measures: Informational Constraints on Collective Choice', *Econometrica*, XLV (1977) pp. 1539–72.
9. The example is adapted from J. E. Meade, *The Just Economy: Principles of Political Economy* (London: Allen & Unwin, 1976) IV, p. 59.

10. L. Robbins, *An Essay on the Nature and Significance of Economic Science* (London: Macmillan, 1932) p. 132.
11. J. Bradshaw, 'A Taxonomy of Need', *New Society*, no. 496 (30 March 1972) pp. 640–3.
12. Compare B. M. Barry, *Political Argument*, p. 48; K. Minogue, *The Liberal Mind* (London: Methuen, 1963) p. 104.
13. For the details of such examples see Mancur Olson, 'The Treatment of Externalities in National Income Statistics' in Lowdon Wingo and Alan Evans (eds), *Public Economics and the Quality of Life* (Baltimore: Johns Hopkins University Press, 1977). See also William D. Nordhaus and James Tobin, 'Is Growth Obsolete?' in Milton Moss (ed.), *The Measurement of Economic and Social Performance* (New York: National Bureau of Economic Research, 1973) pp. 509–32.
14. See, for example, Mary Douglas and Baron Isherwood, *The World of Goods* (New York: Basic Books, 1979); Peter Townsend, *Poverty in the United Kingdom* (Harmondsworth: Penguin, 1980).
15. Alfred Marshall, *Principles of Economics*, 8th edn (London: Macmillan, 1920, reset, 1949) pp. 57–8.
16. Compare James S. Fishkin, *Tyranny and Legitimacy: A Critique of Political Theories* (Baltimore: Johns Hopkins University Press, 1979) ch. 5.
17. B. Seebohm Rowntree, *Poverty: A Study of Town Life*, 2nd edn (London: Macmillan, 1902) ch. 4.
18. David Piachaud, *The Cost of a Child* (London: Child Poverty Action Group, 1979).
19. On these problems see: Barry, *Political Argument*, pp. 62–6; Ronald Dworkin, *Taking Rights Seriously* (London: Duckworth, 1977) pp. 234–9; James S. Fishkin, *Tyranny and Legitimacy*, pp. 26–32; H. L. A. Hart, 'Between Utility and Rights', *Columbia Law Review*, LXXIX 5 (1979) pp. 828–46; Alan Ware, *The Logic of Party Democracy* (London: Macmillan, 1978) pp. 19–31.
20. Compare Bruce A. Ackerman, *Social Justice in the Liberal State* (New Haven and London: Yale University Press, 1981) pp. 368–9.

Chapter 3

1. H. L. A. Hart, 'Are There Any Natural Rights?', *Philosophical Review*, LXIV (1955) pp. 175–91, reprinted in A. Quinton (ed.), *Political Philosophy* (Oxford University Press, 1967) pp. 53–66.
2. For this distinction see Henry Sidgwick, *The Elements of Politics* (London: Macmillan, 1891) pp. 40–3.
3. See John Finnis, *Natural Law and Natural Rights* (Oxford: Clarendon Press, 1980) chs 3–5; and 'Scepticism, Self-Refutation and the Good of Truth' in P. M. S. Hacker and J. Raz (eds), *Law, Morality and Society: Essays in Honour of H. L. A. Hart* (Oxford: Clarendon Press, 1977); Alan Gewirth, *Reason and Morality* (Chicago and London: University of Chicago Press, 1978); Raymond Plant, 'Needs and Welfare' in Noel

Timms (ed.), *Social Welfare: Why and How?* (London: Routledge & Kegan Paul, 1980) pp. 103–21; Raymond Plant, Harry Lesser and Peter Taylor-Gooby, *Political Philosophy and Social Welfare* (London: Routledge & Kegan Paul, 1980) ch. 3. See also Henry Shue, *Basic Rights* (Princeton: Princeton University Press, 1980). For a general discussion of the nature of transcendental arguments, see Ross Harrison, *On What There Must Be* (Oxford: Clarendon Press, 1974).

4. Jürgen Habermas, *Theory and Practice*, trans. John Viertel (London: Heinemann, 1974) ch. 1.

5. Thomas Hobbes, *Leviathan*, ed. Michael Oakeshott (Oxford: Blackwell, 1651, n.d. provided in mod. edn).

6. For the view of reasons as causes see Donald Davidson, 'Actions, Reasons and Causes', *Journal of Philosophy*, LX (1963) pp. 425–35. For the difficulties of compatibilism see Thomas Nagel, *Mortal Questions* (Cambridge University Press, 1979), in particular the essay, 'What Is It Like to Be A Bat?'.

7. Compare Derek Parfit, 'Later Selves and Moral Principles' in Alan Montefiore (ed.), *Philosophy and Personal Relations* (London: Routledge & Kegan Paul, 1973) pp. 137–8.

8. Compare Hillel Steiner, 'The Concept of Justice', *Ratio*, XV1 2 (1974) p. 221.

9. Gerald C. MacCullum Jr. 'Negative and Positive Freedom', *Philosophical Review*, LXXVI (1967) pp. 312–34, reprinted in Peter Laslett, W. G. Runciman and Quentin Skinner (eds), *Philosophy, Politics and Society*, Series 4 (Oxford: Blackwell, 1972) pp. 174–93.

10. For this conception of individual liberty, see Hillel Steiner, 'Individual Liberty', *Proceedings of the Aristotelian Society*, LXXV (1974/75) pp. 33–50.

11. Isaiah Berlin, *Four Essays on Liberty* (Oxford University Press, 1969) pp. 135–41.

12. For an elaboration of the view that standards of rational choice are presupposed in statements about freedom see John N. Gray, 'On Negative and Positive Liberty', *Political Studies*, XXV111 4 (1980) pp. 518–21.

13. Although compare Berlin, *Four Essays on Liberty*, pp. xlv–xlvi.

14. Peter Townsend, *Poverty in the United Kingdom* (Harmondsworth: Penguin, 1979) ch. 8.

15. Compare Steiner, 'Individual Liberty'.

16. Compare Charles E. Lindblom, *Politics and Markets* (New York: Basic Books, 1977) pp. 45–51.

17. Sidgwick, *The Elements of Politics*, p. 41.

18. Eduard Bernstein, *Evolutionary Socialism*, introduction by S. Hook (New York: Schocken, 1961) pp. 149–50; R. H. Tawney, *Equality*, introduction by R. M. Titmuss (London: Unwin Books, 1964) p. 164; Norman Furniss and Timothy Tilton, *The Case for the Welfare State* (Bloomington and London: Indiana University Press, 1979).

19. Thomas Jefferson, *Notes on the State of Virginia* (New York: Harper & Row, 1787, 1964 edn) Query X1X, p. 157:

It is the mark set on those, who not looking up to heaven, to their own soil and industry, as does the husbandman, for their subsistence, depend for it on the casualties and caprice of customers. Dependence begets subservience and venality, suffocates the germ of virtue, and prepares fit tools for the designs of ambition.

20. Compare G. A. Cohen, *Karl Marx's Theory of History: A Defence* (Oxford: Clarendon Press, 1978) p. 243.

Chapter 4

1. For the most recent elaboration of the institutional considerations involved here, see Bruce A. Ackerman, *Social Justice in the Liberal State* (New Haven and London: Yale University Press, 1980) ss 63.
2. See Julian Fulbrook, *Administrative Justice and the Unemployed* (London: Mansell, 1978); and Harry Street, *Justice in the Welfare State* (London: Stevens & Sons, 1968).
3. Bismark U. Mwansasu and Cranford Pratt, *Towards Socialism in Tanzania* (Dar es Salaam: Tanzania Publishing House, 1979).
4. Royal Commission on the Distribution of Income and Wealth, *Report*, no. 1 (London: HMSO, 1975). The idea of social security benefits as a form of property or wealth is also to be found in Norman Furniss and Timothy Tilton, *The Case for the Welfare State* (Bloomington and London: Indiana University Press, 1979) and Charles Reich, 'The New Property', *Yale Law Journal*, LXXIII 5 (1964) pp. 733–87.
5. G. W. F. Hegel, *Philosophy of Right*, trans. T. M. Knox (Oxford University Press, 1967), ss 41–6, pp. 40–3.
6. Compare J. E. Meade, *Planning and the Price Mechanism* (London: Allen & Unwin, 1948). These problems are brilliantly portrayed in Rudolf Bahro, *The Alternative in Eastern Europe*, trans. David Fernbach (London: Verso, 1981). I have tried to discuss some of the pressures towards authoritarian control in central planning in Albert Weale, 'William Beveridge: The Patriarch as Planner', *Political Studies*, XXVII 2 (1979) pp. 287–93.
7. Compare Edgar K. Browning, *Redistribution and the Welfare System* (Washington, DC: American Enterprise Institute, 1975); Institute of Fiscal Studies, *The Structure and Reform of Direct Taxation*, report of a committee chaired by Professor J. E. Meade (London: Allen & Unwin, 1978) p. 269; Theodore R. Marmor, 'On Comparing Income Maintenance Alternatives', *American Political Science Review*, LXV 1 (1971) pp. 83–96; and James Tobin and W. Allen Wallis, *Welfare Programs: An Economic Appraisal* (Washington, DC: American Enterprise Institute, 1968).
8. See Hugh Heclo, *Modern Social Politics in Britain and Sweden: From Relief to Income Maintenance* (New Haven and London: Yale University Press, 1974) p. 225.

9. Theodore R. Marmor, 'On Comparing Income Maintenance Alternatives'; Robert Pinker, *Social Theory and Social Policy* (London: Heinemann, 1971) ch. 4; and Bleddyn Davies, *Universality, Selectivity and Social Policy* (London: Heinemann, 1978).

10. W. Beckerman, 'The Impact of Income Maintenance Payments on Poverty in Britain, 1970', *Economic Journal*, LXXXIX (1979) pp. 261–79. Recall, however, the problem mentioned in Chapter 1 (p. 3) of defining the relevant counterfactual by reference to which we are to compare the effectiveness of income maintenance programmes.

11. For an example of how these arguments have been worked out historically, see Heclo, *Modern Social Politics in Britain and Sweden*.

12. Browning, *Redistribution and the Welfare System*.

13. J. E. Meade, 'Poverty in the Welfare State', *Oxford Economic Papers*, XXIII 3 (1972) pp. 289–326. Compare J. E. Meade, *The Intelligent Radical's Guide to Economic Policy* (London: Allen & Unwin, 1975) ch. 6. I have referred to these sources, rather than the schemes in the Institute for Fiscal Studies Report, because the statement of the principles of operation is clearer in them, being unencumbered by comparison with other schemes.

14. Compare Christopher Green, *Negative Taxes and the Poverty Problem* (Washington, DC: The Brookings Institution, 1967) ch. V.

15. James Tobin, Joseph A. Pechman and Peter M. Mieszkowski, 'Is a Negative Income Tax Practical?', *Yale Law Journal*, LXXVII 1 (1967) pp. 1–27. As far as coverage of the working poor is concerned, this proposal resembles the mixture of Back to Beveridge and Modified Social Dividend that Meade discusses.

16. For a summary of the New Jersey–Pennsylvania results see Peter H. Rossi and Katherine C. Lyall, *Reforming Public Welfare* (New York: Russell Sage Foundation, 1976) ch. 6. For other results see Glen Cain and Harold Watts, *Income Maintenance and Labour Supply: Econometric Studies* (Chicago: Rand McNally, 1973) ch. 9, and Michael C. Keeley, Philip K. Robins, Robert G. Spiegelman and Richard W. West, 'The Labour Supply Effects and Costs of Alternative Negative Income Tax Programs', *Journal of Human Resources*, XIII 1 (1978) pp. 3–36. See also Sheldon Danziger, Robert Haveman and Robert Plotnick, 'How Income Transfer Programs Affect Work, Savings and the Income Distribution: A Critical Review', *Journal of Economic Literature*, XIX 3 (1981) pp. 975–1028.

17. 'I would certainly myself allow anyone to be idle on this low income if they chose that way of life in preference to industrial activity on a higher income. I have little doubt that the community could well afford to carry any such passengers, and the increase in individual liberty and freedom from bureaucratic surveillance would in my opinion be worth the cost' (Meade, 'Poverty in the Welfare State', p. 319).

18. This is a solution suggested by the committee from the Institute for Fiscal Studies, in the proposal for a two-tier social dividend scheme.

19. H. B. Acton, *The Morals of Markets* (London: Longman, 1971) pp. 61–3, and Robert Nozick, *Anarchy, State and Utopia* (Oxford: Basil

Blackwell, 1974) pp. 149–50.

20. For a discussion of these problems see Beckerman, 'The Impact of Income Maintenance Programmes on Poverty in Britain, 1970', and A. K. Sen, 'Poverty: An Ordinal Approach to Measurement', *Econometrica*, XL1V (1976) pp. 219–31.

21. For example, J. S. Coleman *et al.*, *Equality of Educational Opportunity* (Washington, DC: US Dept of Health, Education and Welfare, 1966). See also Frederick Mosteller and Patrick Daniel Moynihan (eds), *On Equality of Educational Opportunity* (New York: Random House, 1972).

22. Raymond Boudon, *Education, Opportunity and Social Inequality: Changing Prospects in Western Society* (New York: Wiley, 1973); A. H. Halsey, A. F. Heath and J. M. Ridge, *Origins and Destinations* (Oxford: Clarendon Press, 1980); William H. Sewell, Robert M. Hauser and David L. Featherman, *Schooling and Achievement in American Society* (New York: Academic Press, 1976).

23. Michael Young, *The Rise of the Meritocracy* (London: Thames & Hudson, 1958).

24. Bernard Williams, 'The Idea of Equality' in Peter Laslett and W. G. Runciman (eds), *Philosophy, Politics and Society*, Series 2 (Oxford: Blackwell, 1962) p. 128.

25. Compare M. F. D. Young (ed.), *Knowledge and Control: New Directions for the Sociology of Education* (London: Collier-Macmillan, 1971), where this 'incommensurability thesis' is not explicitly stated, but would seem to be implied. For some good examples of cultural exploitation, see the empirical evidence quoted by Nell Keddie in her paper, 'Classroom Knowledge'.

26. I have tried to set out some of the relevant issues in Albert Weale, *Equality and Social Policy* (London: Routledge & Kegan Paul, 1978) ch. 6. For an excellent discussion favouring parental choice, see John E. Coons and Stephen D. Sugarman, *Education by Choice: The Case for Family Control* (Berkeley: University of California Press, 1978).

Chapter 5

1. Norman Furniss and Timothy Tilton, *The Case for the Welfare State* (Bloomington and London: Indiana University Press, 1979) pp. 16–18.

2. Furniss and Tilton, *The Case for the Welfare State*, pp. 18–20.

3. For a theory in which the Pareto principle functions as a necessary condition, see J. M. Buchanan and G. Tullock, *The Calculus of Consent* (Ann Arbor, Michigan: University of Michigan Press, 1965). For a criticism of the Pareto principle as exceptionally conservative when thought of as a necessary condition of social choice, see Brian Barry, *Political Argument* (London: Routledge & Kegan Paul, 1965) pp. 313–14; Douglas W. Rae, 'The Limits of Consensual Decision', *American Political Science Review*, LXIX 4 (1975) pp. 1270–94; and Amartya K. Sen, *Collective Choice and Social Welfare* (San Francisco: Holden-Day Inc., 1970) p. 25.

4. This is the 'general conception' of John Rawls, *A Theory of Justice* (Oxford: Clarendon Press, 1972) p. 62, and a similar principle is formulated by J. Raz, 'Principles of Equality', *Mind*, LXXXVII 347 (1978) pp. 321–42.
5. For fuller and more formal treatments of these ideas, consult Sen, *Collective Choice and Social Welfare*, chs 1 and 1*, and Dennis C. Mueller, *Public Choice* (Cambridge University Press, 1979) ch. 10. For a fuller presentation of the conflict between the equality and the Pareto principles, see Albert Weale, 'The Impossibility of Liberal Egalitarianism', *Analysis*, XL 1 (1980) pp. 13–19, and Iain McLean, 'Liberty, Equality and the Pareto Principle: A Comment on Weale', *Analysis*, XL 4 (1980) pp. 212–13. When I wrote 'The Impossibility of Liberal Egalitarianism' I did not realise that attention had been drawn to some aspects of the implicit conflict between these two principles in Douglas Rae's 'Maximin Justice and an Alternative Principle of General Advantage', *American Political Science Review*, LXIX 2 (1975) pp. 646–7.
6. Robert Sugden and Albert Weale, 'A Contractual Reformulation of Certain Aspects of Welfare Economics', *Economica*, XLVI (1979) pp. 111–23.
7. The terms are, of course, Rawls's.
8. The argument here parallels Dworkin's argument that the theory of the social contract presupposes a theory of rights. See Ronald Dworkin, *Taking Rights Seriously* (London: Duckworth, 1977) ch. 6.
9. See Sugden and Weale, 'A Contractual Reformulation of Certain Aspects of Welfare Economics'.
10. The sure-thing or dominance principle may seem so intuitively obvious that it may be worth remembering that it has its own problems. These are well brought out in Newcomb's Problem, for a good discussion of which see Robert Nozick, 'Newcomb's Problem and Two Principles of Rational Choice' in N. Rescher (ed.), *Essays in Honour of Carl G. Hempel* (Dordrecht-Holland: Reidel, 1969) pp. 114–46. Nozick provides a number of reasons for retaining the dominance principle, despite difficulties.
11. For these results, see Sugden and Weale, 'A Contractual Reformulation of Certain Aspects of Welfare Economics'.
12. A. M. Okun, *Equality and Efficiency: The Big Trade-Off* (Washington DC: Brookings Institution, 1975) pp. 91–106.
13. See, for this metaphor, Cotton M. Lindsay, 'Medical Care and the Economics of Sharing', *Economica*, XXXVII (1969) pp. 351–62, reprinted in M. H. Cooper and A. J. Culyer (eds), *Health Economics* (Harmondsworth: Penguin, 1973) pp. 75–89.
14. Peter Lambert and Albert Weale, 'Equality, Risk-Aversion and Contractarian Social Choice', *Theory and Decision*, XIII (1981) pp. 109–27.
15. See J. R. Hicks, 'The Foundations of Welfare Economics', *Economic Journal*, XLIX (1939) pp. 696–712; J. R. Hicks, 'The Rehabilitation of Consumers' Surplus', *Review of Economic Studies*, VIII (1941)

pp. 108–16; N. Kaldor, 'Welfare Propositions of Economics and Inter-Personal Comparisons of Utility', *Economic Journal*, XLIX (1939) pp. 549–52.

16. This contradiction was first noted by T. Scitovsky, 'A Note on Welfare Propositions in Economics', *Review of Economic Studies*, IX (1941) pp. 77–88. The nature of this contradiction is well discussed in W. J. Baumol, *Welfare Economics and the Theory of the State*, 2nd edn (London: Bell, 1965); I. M. D. Little, *A Critique of Welfare Economics*, 2nd edn (Oxford University Press, 1957) ch. VI; and Robert Sugden, *The Political Economy of Public Choice* (Oxford: Martin Robertson, 1981) pp. 111–19.

17. This difficulty is well discussed by Little, *A Critique of Welfare Economics*. See also James S. Fishkin, *Tyranny and Legitimacy* (Baltimore and London: Johns Hopkins University Press, 1979) ch. 11.

18. Rawls, *A Theory of Justice*, pp. 48–51.

19. R. H. Tawney, *The Acquisitive Society* (London: Bell, 1921) in a typical passage:

> It is foolish, for example, to maintain property rights for which no service is performed, for payment without service is waste; and if it is true, as statisticians affirm, that, even were income equally divided, income per head would be small, then it is all the more foolish. Sailors in a boat have no room for first-class passengers, and, the smaller the total national income, the more important it is that none of it should be misapplied.

20. J. Feinberg, 'Rawls and Intuitionism' in Norman Daniels, *Reading Rawls* (Oxford: Basil Blackwell, 1975) pp. 108–24.

Chapter 6

1. See A. J. Culyer, *The Political Economy of Social Policy* (Oxford: Martin Robertson, 1980) pp. 64–9.

2. James Tobin, 'On Limiting the Domain of Inequality', *Journal of Law and Economics*, XIII 2 (1970) pp. 263–77, reprinted in Edmund S. Phelps (ed.), *Economic Justice* (Harmondsworth: Penguin, 1973) pp. 447–63.

3. Julian Le Grand, *The Strategy of Equality* (London: Allen & Unwin, 1982).

4. Compare Le Grand, *The Strategy of Equality*, p. 133.

5. K. J. Arrow, 'Uncertainty and the Welfare Economics of Medical Care', *American Economic Review*, LIII 5 (1963) pp. 941–73, reprinted in M. H. Cooper and A. J. Culyer (eds), *Health Economics* (Harmondsworth: Penguin, 1973).

6. Robert Nozick, *Anarchy, State and Utopia* (Oxford: Basil Blackwell, 1974) p. 269.

7. For these claims, compare Edgar K. Browning, 'The Externality Argument for In-Kind Transfers: Some Critical Remarks', *Kyklos*, XXVIII

(1975) pp. 526–44, and David Heald, 'The Rehabilitation of the Market in Social Policy' in Noel Timms (ed.), *Social Welfare: Why and How?* (London: Routledge & Kegan Paul, 1980) esp. pp. 58–64.

8. H. M. Hochman and J. D. Rogers, 'Pareto-Optimal Redistribution', *American Economic Review*, LIX 2 (1969) pp. 542–57.

9. For a review of the literature on the collective good/free rider problem on which this paragraph rests, see Dennis C. Mueller, *Public Choice* (Cambridge University Press, 1979). The argument that the British National Health Service can be justified by this sort of argument is clearly expounded in A. J. Culyer, *Need and the National Health Service* (London: Martin Robertson, 1976) ch. 7. This argument is criticised in Robert Sugden, 'Altruism, Duty and the Welfare State' in Noel Timms (ed.), *Social Welfare: Why and How?*, pp. 165–77.

10. See Lester C. Thurow, 'Government Expenditures: Cash or In-Kind Aid?', *Philosophy and Public Affairs*, V 4 (1976) pp. 361–81.

11. David E. Butler and Donald Stokes, *Political Change in Britain*, 2nd edn (London: Macmillan, 1974) ch. 14.

12. Ralph Harris and Arthur Seldon, *Choice in Welfare 1965* (London: Institute for Economic Affairs, 1965) tables XXIII and XXVI. The 1970 survey supports the interpretation of the trend in Butler and Stokes – see Ralph Harris and Arthur Seldon, *Choice in Welfare 1970* (London: Institute of Economic Affairs, 1971) table XI. For a different, but suggestive, sort of evidence about the extent of specific egalitarian sentiments, see Samuel Brittain, *Is There An Economic Consensus? An Attitude Survey* (London: Macmillan, 1973).

13. K. R. Cooke and F. M. Staden, *The Impact of the Mobility Allowance: An Evaluative Study* (London: HMSO, 1981). For details on the policy background, see also Kenneth Cooke, *A Study of Child Beneficiaries of the Mobility Allowance* (University of York, Social Policy Research Unit, Working Papers, March 1979) ch. 2.

14. F. A. Hayek, *The Constitution of Liberty* (London: Routledge & Kegan Paul, 1960).

15. John Stuart Mill, *On Liberty* in H. B. Acton (ed.), *John Stuart Mill, Utilitarianism, On Liberty and Considerations on Representative Government* (London: Dent, 1972) p. 117.

16. The distinction has a long literature going back in the modern discussion to Ludwig Wittgenstein, *Philosophical Investigations*, trans. G. E. M. Anscombe, 3rd edn (Oxford: Basil Blackwell, 1967), in which meaning is thought to be internal to some social activities. For a clear introduction, see John Rawls, 'Two Concepts of Rules', *Philosophical Review*, LXIV (1955) pp. 3–32, reprinted in Philippa Foot (ed.), *Theories of Ethics* (Oxford University Press, 1967) pp. 144–70. Compare also J. R. Searle, *Speech Acts* (Cambridge University Press, 1969) pp. 50–3.

17. See H. L. A. Hart, 'Prolegomenon to the Principles of Punishment' in *Punishment and Responsibility* (London: Oxford University Press, 1973 reprint) pp. 1–27.

18. Bernard Williams, 'The Idea of Equality' in P. Laslett and W. G. Runciman, *Philosophy, Politics and Society*, series 2 (Oxford: Basil

Blackwell, 1962) p. 121.
19. Amy Gutman, *Liberal Equality* (Cambridge University Press, 1980) pp. 104–5.
20. Robert Nozick, *Anarchy, State and Utopia*, pp. 232–5.
21. Martin L. Weitzman, 'Is the Price System or Rationing More Effective in Getting a Commodity to Those who Need It Most?', *Bell Journal of Economics*, VIII 2 (1977) pp. 517–24.
22. For these systems see Alan Maynard, *Health Care In The European Community* (London: Croom Helm, 1975), and Malcolm G. Taylor, *Health Insurance and Canadian Public Policy* (Montreal: McGill–Queen's University Press, 1978).

Chapter 7

1. John Locke, *The Second Treatise of Government*, in John Locke, *Two Treatises of Government*, ed. Peter Laslett (Cambridge University Press, 1963) ch. 9.
2. See Ronald Dworkin, *Taking Rights Seriously* (London: Duckworth, 1977) ch. 2.
3. Here I follow John Mackie, 'The Third Theory of Law', *Philosophy and Public Affairs*, VII 1 (1977) pp. 3–16 in his criticism of Dworkin's arguments. See also H. L. A. Hart, *The Concept of Law* (Oxford: Clarendon Press, 1961) ch. 9.
4. Hart, *The Concept of Law*, p. 199.
5. Compare John Finnis, *Natural Law and Natural Rights* (Oxford: Clarendon Press, 1980) p. 351, who argues that the proposition 'unjust laws are not law' is a 'subordinate theorem' of the natural law tradition. But compare J. M. Cameron, *Images of Authority* (London: Burns & Oates, 1966) p. 30.
6. W. N. Hohfeld, *Fundamental Legal Conceptions* (New Haven: Yale University Press, 1923).
7. T. M. Scanlon, 'Preferences and Urgency', *Journal of Philosophy*, LXXII 19 (1975) pp. 655–69.
8. H. L. A. Hart, 'Bentham on Legal Rights' in A. W. B. Simpson (ed.), *Oxford Essays in Jurisprudence* (Oxford: Clarendon Press, 1973) pp. 171–201.
9. Compare T. H. Marshall, *Citizenship and Social Class* (Cambridge University Press, 1950).
10. Norman Furniss and Timothy Tilton, *The Case for the Welfare State* (Bloomington and London: Indiana University Press, 1979) p. 136.
11. For the text of the United Nations Declaration of Human Rights see Ian Brownlie, *Basic Documents on Human Rights* (Oxford: Clarendon Press, 1971).
12. Maurice Cranston, *What Are Human Rights?* (London: Bodley Head, 1973). I follow in my criticisms of Cranston some of the lines of argument developed in David Watson, 'Welfare Rights and Human Rights', *Journal of Social Policy*, VI 1 (1977) pp. 31–46.

13. Henry Shue, *Basic Rights* (Princeton: Princeton University Press, 1980) pp. 37–8.
14. Immanuel Kant, *Groundwork of the Metaphysic of Morals* in H. J. Paton, *The Moral Law* (London: Hutchinson, 1969) pp. 92–3.
15. Brian Barry, *Political Argument* (London: Routledge & Kegan Paul, 1965) p. 150.
16. Compare Searle's distinction between illocutionary force indicators and the propositional content of an illocutionary act: J. R. Searle, *Speech Acts* (Cambridge University Press, 1969) ch. 2.4.
17. Peter Jones, 'Rights, Welfare and Stigma' in Noel Timms (ed.), *Social Welfare: Why and How?* (London: Routledge & Kegan Paul, 1980) p. 133.
18. Henry Shue, *Basic Rights*, ch. 1.
19. Henry Sidgwick, *The Elements of Politics* (London: Macmillan, 1891) pp. 26–8.
20. David Lyons, 'Rights, Claimants and Beneficiaries', *American Philosophical Quarterly*, VI 3 (1969) pp. 173–85. On the essential feature of control in rights, see Hart, 'Bentham on Legal Rights'.
21. The importance of this idea of control in the historical development of the theory of rights is well brought out by Richard Tuck, *Natural Rights Theories* (Cambridge University Press, 1979) ch. 1.
22. See D. N. MacCormick, 'Rights in Legislation' in P. M. S. Hacker and J. Raz (eds), *Law, Morality and Society* (Oxford: Clarendon Press, 1977) pp. 189–209.
23. Sidgwick, *The Elements of Politics*, p. 28.
24. For a discussion of this sort of change, see Supplementary Benefits Commission, *Annual Report* 1979 (London: HMSO, 1980) Cmnd 8033.
25. Compare R. M. Titmuss, 'Welfare "Rights", Law and Discretion', *Political Quarterly*, XLII 2 (1971) pp. 113–32. See also Richard Wilding, 'Discretionary Benefits' in Michael Adler and Anthony Bradley (eds), *Justice, Discretion and Poverty* (London: Professional Books, 1975) pp. 55–63.
26. See Aristotle, *Nicomachean Ethics*, bk 5, ch. 10, in J. A. K. Thomson, *The Ethics of Aristotle* (Harmondsworth: Penguin, 1955 edn):

    Equity essentially is just this rectification of the law, where the law has to be amplified because of the general terms in which it has to be couched. This is in fact the reason why everything is not regulated by law; it is because there are cases which no law can be framed to cover and which can only be met by a special regulation.

27. Compare Kenneth Culp Davis, *Discretionary Justice* (Baton Rouge: Louisiana State University Press, 1969) pp. 78–80, who provides an example in housing allocation of how practices can be tightened into regulations. See also Julian Fulbrook, *Administrative Justice and the Unemployed* (London: Mansell, 1978) esp. pp. 201–5.

Chapter 8

1. This section and the next draw upon, and modify, Albert Weale, 'Procedural Fairness and Rationing the Social Services' in Noel Timms (ed.), *Social Welfare: Why and How?* (London: Routledge & Kegan Paul, 1980) pp. 233–57. The model of the sort of social welfare agency presupposed in the text is of the bureaucratic sort, described for example in Harold L. Wilensky and Charles N. Lebeaux, *Industrial Society and Social Welfare* (New York: Free Press, 1965) ch. 10.
2. See Jonathan Bradshaw, *The Family Fund* (London: Routledge & Kegan Paul, 1980). A similar arrangement, with a government body allocating funds to a charitable body, was initiated in Saskatchewan in 1920, when municipalities allocated monies to the Anti-TB League for the care of those suffering from tuberculosis. See Malcolm G. Taylor, *Health Insurance and Canadian Public Policy* (Montreal: McGill–Queen's University Press, 1978) p. 73.
3. For a description of these practices see Anthony S. Hall, *The Point of Entry* (London: Allen & Unwin, 1974).
4. E. James and N. Timms, 'Charging for Local Social Services', *Public Administration*, XL (1962) pp. 407–18.
5. For a further discussion of this equity condition, see Albert Weale, *Equality and Social Policy* (London: Routledge & Kegan Paul, 1978) pp. 19–29 and the references there cited.
6. N. Lewis, 'Council House Allocation: Problems of Discretion and Control', *Public Administration*, LIV (1976) pp. 147–60.
7. Compare Brian Barry, *Political Argument* (London: Routledge & Kegan Paul, 1965) pp. 102–3, and J. R. Lucas, *The Principles of Politics* (Oxford: Clarendon Press, 1966) pp. 106–12, 132.
8. See Hall, *The Point of Entry*, pp. 17–19; R. A. Parker, 'Social Administration and Scarcity: The Problem of Rationing', *Social Work*, XXIV 2 (1967) pp. 9–14, reprinted in Eric Butterworth and Robert Holman, *Social Welfare in Modern Britain* (Glasgow: Fontana, 1975) pp. 204–12; A. M. Rees, 'Access to the Personal Health and Welfare Services', *Social and Economic Administration*, VI 1 (1972) pp. 34–43.
9. Alan Maynard, *Experiment With Choice in Education* (London: IEA, 1975) p. 28.
10. J. F. Childress, 'Who Shall Live When Not All Can Live?' in R. M. Veatch and R. Branson, *Ethics and Health Policy* (Cambridge, Mass.: Ballinger, 1976) pp. 205–10.
11. Compare B. Schaffer, *The Administrative Factor* (London: Frank Cass, 1973) p. 287.
12. See J. A. Roth, *Timetables* (New York: Bobbs-Merrill, 1963).
13. It is easy, however, to overestimate the deterrent effects of charges. For a discussion see Ken Judge and James Matthews, *Charging for Social Care* (London: Allen & Unwin, 1980).

14. Schaffer, *The Administrative Factor*, p. 294.
15. H. B. Acton, *The Morals of Markets* (London: Longman, 1971) pp. 70–1.
16. See Alan Williams and Robert Anderson, *Efficiency in the Social Services* (Oxford: Blackwell, 1975).
17. Bleddyn Davies and Martin Knapp, *Old People's Home and the Production of Welfare* (London: Routledge & Kegan Paul, 1981) pp. 7, 181.
18. For a good example see Lowden Wingo and Alan Evans, *Public Economics and the Quality of Life* (Baltimore: Johns Hopkins University Press, 1977).
19. Compare Judge and Matthews, *Charging for Social Care*, pp. 52–63.
20. Compare Mike Reddin, 'Universality Versus Selectivity', *Political Quarterly*, XL 1 (1969) pp. 12–22. See also his useful report to the National Economic and Social Council of the Irish government, published in National Economic and Social Council, *Universality and Selectivity: Strategies in Social Policy*, Report No. 36 (Dublin: Stationary Office, n.d. probably 1977).
21. See Bleddyn Davies, *Universality, Selectivity and Effectiveness in Social Policy* (London: Heinemann, 1978) pp. 218–21.
22. Burton Weisbrod, 'Collective Action and the Distribution of Income: A Conceptual Approach' in 'The Analysis and Evaluation of Public Expenditures: The PPB System', a compendium of papers submitted to the Joint Economic Committee, Washington, DC: Congress of the United States, vol. 1, reprinted in Reprint Series, 34, Institute for Research on Poverty, University of Wisconsin, pp. 177–97, from which references are taken.
23. Compare Weisbrod, 'Collective Action and the Distribution of Income'.
24. As I note in the final chapter, it is a striking feature of some 'consociational' democracies that there is no national system of education.
25. Davies, *Universality, Selectivity and Effectiveness in Social Policy*, chs 4 and 5. See also the evidence discussed in Joel F. Handler and Ellen J. Hollingsworth, *The 'Deserving Poor': A Study of Welfare Administration* (Chicago: Markham, 1971) ch. 7.

Chapter 9

1. Joel Feinberg, *Doing and Deserving* (Princeton: Princeton University Press, 1970) p. 64.
2. Aristotle, *The Politics*, trans. T. A. Sinclair (Harmondsworth: Penguin, 1962) bk 3.
3. See David Miller, *Social Justice* (Oxford: Clarendon Press, 1976) p. 89. As will be clear, my own discussion owes much in general to Miller's.
4. Contrast Feinberg, *Doing and Deserving*, p. 59.
5. Brian Barry, *Political Argument* (London: Routledge & Kegan Paul, 1965) p. 166. Miller, *Social Justice*, pp. 93–4, appeals to the same example.

6. Compare F. A. Hayek, *The Constitution of Liberty* (London: Routledge & Kegan Paul, 1960) pp. 97–9.
7. See, for example, Ivan Illich, *Limits to Medicine* (Harmondsworth: Penguin, 1977).
8. For a clear account, though one with a critical appraisal, see Nathan Glazer, *Affirmative Discrimination: Ethnic Inequality and Public Policy* (New York: Basic Books, 1975). For a well-written discussion of the first relevant case to be taken to the Supreme Court, see Robert M. O'Neil, *Discriminating Against Discrimination* (Bloomington: Indiana University Press, 1975).
9. Laurence Lustgarten, *Legal Control of Racial Discrimination* (London: Macmillan, 1980).
10. *The Brixton Disorders 10–12 April 1981*, Report of An Inquiry By the Rt Hon. The Lord Scarman, OBE (London: HMSO, 1981) Cmnd 8427, ss 5.7, ss 6.32.
11. I follow Alan H. Goldman, *Justice and Reverse Discrimination* (Princeton: Princeton University Press, 1979) p. 5, in holding that there cannot be any moral significance in this distinction, and certainly none of the sort used in the *Bakke* judgement.
12. Compare Mary Anne Warren, 'Secondary Sexism and Quota Hiring', *Philosophy and Public Affairs*, VI 3 (1977) pp. 240–61, who gives a long list of secondary sexist practices.
13. Francis Cornford, *Microcosmographia Academica* (Cambridge: Bowes & Bowes, 1908) p. 11.
14. H. Sidgwick, *The Methods of Ethics*, 6th edn (London: Macmillan, 1901) p. 283.
15. Feinberg, *Doing and Deserving*, pp. 77–8.
16. A point well made by Goldman, *Justice and Reverse Discrimination*, p. 81.
17. For a full discussion of the idea of group compensation, see Owen M. Fiss, 'Groups and the Equal Protection Clause', *Philosophy and Public Affairs*, V 2 (1976) pp. 107–77.
18. Alan H. Goldman, 'Affirmative Action', *Philosophy and Public Affairs*, V 2 (1976) p. 192.
19. Compare Thomas Nagel, 'The Policy of Preference' in *Mortal Questions* (London: Cambridge University Press, 1979) pp. 91–105.
20. I confess though that I appear to be in a minority of one on this issue, at least as far as Britain is concerned. Even the Thunderer has clear convictions in quite the opposite direction: *The Times*, Tuesday, 30 March 1982.
21. See Lester C. Thurow, *Generating Inequality* (London: Macmillan, 1976), which traces out the striking implications of this suggestion.
22. An objection forcibly raised by Lustgarten, *Legal Control of Racial Discrimination*, p. 19.
23. Lewis M. Killian, 'School Busing in Britain: Policies and Perceptions', *Harvard Educational Review*, XLIX 2 (1979) pp. 185–206.
24. As suggested by Lustgarten, *Legal Control of Racial Discrimination*, pp. 36-7.

Chapter 10

1. For a review of these, and a number of other arguments, see J. Roland Pennock, *Democratic Political Theory* (Princeton: Princeton University Press, 1979) ch. 4.

2. R. Wollheim, 'A Paradox in the Theory of Democracy' in P. Laslett and W. G. Runciman (eds), *Philosophy, Politics and Society*, series 2 (Oxford: Basil Blackwell, 1962) pp. 71–87.

3. Compare Amy Gutman, *Liberal Equality* (Cambridge University Press, 1980) p. 177.

4. The best account of this form of democracy is still to be found in Joseph Schumpeter, *Capitalism, Socialism and Democracy* (London: Allen & Unwin, 1942, 4th edn 1954), who defines this form of democracy as 'that institutional arrangement for arriving at political decisions in which individuals acquire the power to decide by means of a competitive struggle for the people's vote' (p. 269).

5. Compare Schumpeter, *Capitalism, Socialism and Democracy*, pp. 294–5.

6. G. D. H. Cole, *Guild Socialism Re-Stated* (London: Leonard Parsons, 1920) pp. 32–3.

7. On Health Systems Agencies see A. A. Atkinson and R. M. Grimes, 'Health Planning in the United States: An Old Idea with New Significance', *Journal of Health Politics, Policy and Law*, I 3 (1976) pp. 295–318, and James A. Morone and Theodore R. Marmor, 'Representing Consumer Interests: The Case of American Health Planning', *Ethics*, LXL1 3 (1981) pp. 431–50. On Community Health Councils, see Rudolf Klein and Janet Lewis, *The Politics of Consumer Representation: A Study of Community Health Councils* (London: Centre for Studies in Social Policy, 1976).

8. Department of Education and Science and Welsh Office, *A New Partnership for Our Schools*. Report of the Committee of Enquiry under The Chairmanship of Mr Tom Taylor, CBE (London: HMSO, 1977).

9. For the Social and Economic Council, see Arend Lijphart, *The Politics of Accommodation – Pluralism and Democracy in the Netherlands* (Berkeley and Los Angeles: University of California Press, 1968) pp. 112–15. For an account of consociational democracies in general, see Arend Lijphart, *Democracy in Plural Societies* (New Haven and London: Yale University Press, 1977). See also Hans Daalder, 'The Netherlands: Opposition in a Segmented Society' in Robert A. Dahl (ed.), *Political Opposition in Western Democracies* (New Haven and London: Yale University Press, 1966), and 'The Consociational Democracy Theme', *World Politics*, XXV1 4 (1974) pp. 604–21.

10. See Robert A. Dahl and Edward R. Tufte, *Size and Democracy* (Stanford: Stanford University Press, 1973) ch. 2.

11. *Report of the Royal Commission on Local Government in England and Wales* (London: HMSO, 1969).

12. Robert A. Dahl, *After the Revolution?* (New Haven: Yale University Press, 1970).
13. *Report of the Royal Commission on Local Government in England and Wales*, vol. 3, pp. 132–6.
14. Lijphart, *The Politics of Accommodation*, pp. 109–12, and Daalder, 'The Netherlands: Opposition in a Segmented Society', p. 214.
15. Here, and in the account of HSAs, I follow Morone and Marmor, 'Representing Consumer Interests: The Case of American Health Planning'.
16. Frances Svensson, 'Liberal Democracy and Group Rights: The Legacy of Individualism and Its Impact on American Indian Tribes', *Political Studies*, XXV11 3 (1979) pp. 421–39.
17. Paul E. Peterson, 'Forms of Representation: Participation of the Poor in the Community Action Program', *American Political Science Review*, LX1V 2 (1970) pp. 491–507.
18. L. J. Sharpe, 'American Democracy Reconsidered. Part II', *British Journal of Political Science*, 111 2 (1973) pp. 129–68.
19. The assumption of trust is a large one to grant, however. One study of citizen attitudes towards public services in ten cities in the United States showed a majority thinking that there was at least some illegal activity among local officials, and a majority in some cities thought there was an even higher level of illegal activity. See F. J. Fowler Jr, *Citizen Attitudes Towards Local Government Services and Taxes* (Cambridge, Mass.: Ballinger, 1974) pp. 185–9.
20. J. Rothenberg, *The Measurement of Social Welfare* (Englewood Cliffs: Prentice-Hall, 1961) pp. 316–23.
21. Rudolf Klein, 'The Case for Elitism: Public Opinion and Public Policy', *Political Quarterly*, XLV 4 (1974) pp. 406–17.
22. Albert O. Hirschman, *Exit, Voice and Loyalty* (Cambridge, Mass.: Harvard University Press, 1970). Tiebout presents the standard account of how people can vote with their feet to obtain the level of public services they want: C. M. Tiebout, 'A Pure Theory of Local Expenditures', *Journal of Political Economy*, LX1V (1956) pp. 416–24. I follow Mueller in his criticism of this model: D. C. Mueller, *Public Choice* (Cambridge University Press, 1979) ch. 7.
23. See Gerald Hoinville and Gillian Courtenay, *Measuring Consumer Priorities*, Methodological Working Paper No. 15 (London: Social and Community Planning Research, 1978).
24. Morone and Marmor, 'Representing Consumer Interests: The Case of American Health Planning', pp. 443–4.
25. Here and in the next paragraph I drew on material in Albert Weale, 'Representation, Individualism and Collectivism', *Ethics*, LXL1 3 (1981) pp. 457–65.
26. Department of Education and Science, *A New Partnership for Our Schools*.
27. T. G. Maguire, 'Budget-Maximizing Governmental Agencies: An Empirical Test', *Public Choice*, XXXV1 2 (1981) pp. 313–22.

28. For a clear discussion of its various senses, see Raymond Plant, *Community and Ideology* (London: Routledge & Kegan Paul, 1974).
29. *Report of the Royal Commission on Local Government in England and Wales*, vol. 3, p. 161.
30. See Hugh Butcher, Patricia Collis, Andrew Glen and Patrick Sills, *Community Groups in Action* (London: Routledge & Kegan Paul, 1980).
31. Brian Abel-Smith, *Value for Money in Health Services* (London: Heinemann, 1976) p. 161.
32. Compare Geraint Parry, 'The Idea of Political Participation' in Geraint Parry (ed.), *Participation in Politics* (Manchester University Press, 1972).
33. Douglas Yates, *Neighbourhood Democracy* (Lexington, Mass.: D. C. Heath, 1973).
34. See Owen M. Fiss, 'School Desegregation: The Uncertain Path of the Law', *Philosophy and Public Affairs*, 1V 1 (1974) pp. 3–39.
35. Klein and Lewis, *The Politics of Consumer Representation*.
36. Compare Bleddyn Davies, *Social Needs and Resources in Local Services* (London: Joseph, 1968).
37. Compare Alan Day's Note of Reservation in *Local Government Finance, Report of the Committee of Inquiry* (Layfield Committee) (London: HMSO, 1976) Cmnd 6453, pp. 302–14.

Epilogue

1. Robert Nisbet, *The Sociological Tradition* (London: Heinemann, 1967) ch. 3.
2. Richard M. Titmuss, *Commitment to Welfare* (London: Allen & Unwin, 1968).
3. Ferdinand Tönnies, *Community and Association*, trans. Charles P. Loomis (London: Routledge & Kegan Paul, 1955) esp. pp. 270–3. On the historical problem of how accurate this supposed contrast is, see Alan Macfarlane, *The Origins of English Individualism* (Cambridge University Press, 1979).
4. See Richard Sennett, *The Fall of Public Man* (Cambridge University Press, 1974) pp. 287–93, on the connection between politics and the arts.

Index